Escaping the Dark, Gray City

Escaping the Dark, Gray City

Fear and Hope in
Progressive-Era Conservation

BENJAMIN HEBER JOHNSON

Yale UNIVERSITY PRESS/NEW HAVEN & LONDON

Published with assistance from the income of the
Frederick John Kingsbury Memorial Fund, and from the
foundation established in memory of Amasa Stone Mather of
the Class of 1907, Yale College.

Yale University Press books may be purchased in quantity for
educational, business, or promotional use. For information,
please e-mail sales.press@yale.edu (U.S. office) or
sales@yaleup.co.uk (U.K. office).

Set in Minion type by Integrated Publishing Solutions,
Grand Rapids, Michigan.
Printed in the United States of America.

ISBN 978-0-300-11550-5
Library of Congress Control Number: 2016949701

A catalogue record for this book is available from the British
Library.

This paper meets the requirements of ANSI/NISO Z39.48–1992
(Permanence of Paper).

10 9 8 7 6 5 4 3 2 1

For Michelle and Tobias

Contents

Introduction

The extraordinary intelligence of human beings can seduce us into thinking that we are the sole architects of our history, with the rest of the world—plants, animals, weather, geography—simply the props and stage on which we enact our dramas. The premise of environmental history is that this larger world is also an actor in human stories. Most of the time, the dialogue between humans and the world in which they live is a hushed murmur, a conversation whose echoes we can make out only much later: farmers chose to plant the seeds from a grass with the largest heads, and a thousand years later developed corn. Or Europeans bring with them to the Americas diseases that allow for their multiplication and expansion, the unexpected product of past animal domestications and the easy spread of plants and pathogens across the Eurasian land mass.

At other moments, however, the background hum reaches a crescendo that itself becomes the subject of thought, comment, and perhaps action: the last passenger pigeon dies, a scientist discovers that the chemicals propelling hair spray and other conveniences are also destroying the ozone layer, or a hurricane brings exceptional flooding that strikes many as a harbinger of a warmer planet.

One such extended moment occurred at the beginning of the twentieth century in the United States. Influential scientists, writers, political leaders, and a large portion of the general population became convinced that humanity had lost its proper place in the larger world. Americans, they believed, were destroying species, overconsuming natural resources, and moving to homes and cities that isolated them from natural beauty and wildness. These women and men sought to restore a spiritually renewing and materially sustainable relationship with a nature made vulnerable by the unprecedented power of industrial humanity. Eventually adopting the term "conservation" to describe their efforts, they tried to do this by passing laws regulating such things as hunting and logging, turning over larger portions of the country to the management of foresters and other scientists, creating cities and buildings that evoked rather than denied nature, and replacing obliviousness and profligacy with understanding and responsibility. They sought to create both a culture that fostered appreciation, awareness, and restraint when it came to the natural world, and a vigorous state to enforce the dictates of that culture.

The prominence of conservation in the early-twentieth-century United States is widely known: elected officials such as President Theodore Roosevelt and environmental writers and activists such as John Muir appear in history textbooks and have spawned numerous studies by professional historians, journalists, and environmental enthusiasts. Those wishing to expand their knowledge of conservation can consult numerous biographies of its leading lights as well as studies of particular agencies and protected areas, of the concept of wilderness, and of the impact of conservation on rural people. So why write another book on the subject?

Escaping the Dark, Gray City grew from two mounting frustrations: with the ways that environmental historians write about conservation, and with how little other historians of the period write about it. Before the late 1990s, scholars and journalists examining conservation and conservationists generally wrote with the assumption that their subjects were virtuous, and that their task was to trace the emergence and accomplishments of environmental enlightenment and the grave ecological crises that this enlightenment sought to combat. This approach colored accounts of wilderness thought, of the careers of such figures as Gifford Pinchot and John Muir, of the establishment of national parks and other protected areas, and of organizations such as the Sierra Club and the Save-the-Redwoods League. This kind of environmental history was not merely academic and was not read exclusively by professional historians, for it endowed histories of environmental thought and politics with moral power and political urgency, much as had the politics of older and better established histories of labor, women, emancipation, and civil rights. These writings drew me to become a professional historian. I began devouring these books, even taking them with me on backpacking trips. How there came to be national parks and forests, I thought, was just as riveting as the mountains and wildness that they encompassed. I went to graduate school to learn how to tell just such stories.[1]

My plans were derailed, for the study of conservation went through a dramatic transformation. In the 1990s, a growing number of scholars asked skeptical questions about conservation and environmentalism. What did it mean to call a place a wilderness when it had been home so long to human beings whose hunting, fires, and crops had shaped the landscape now valued for its supposed isolation from the social world? Could appreciation of the wild lead people to ignore or even denigrate the more quotidian nature of their backyard, neighborhood, and city? What happened to the hunting, fishing, and gathering of people living in and around the new national parks and forests? Why did establishing a park or forest so often result in the removal of Indian people and the criminalization of their ways of living off the land? Given the sometimes disastrous consequences of the fire suppression and predator extermination that conservationists pursued with such vigor, were the purported saviors not sometimes as destructive as those whose environmental profligacy they so roundly condemned?[2]

I embraced this turn to a more critical history and contributed modestly to it with an article about how conservation restrictions in Minnesota had subordinated Indians and immigrant miners by depriving them of access to natural resources. My enthusiasm for the study of conservation had not waned, I told myself, but rather matured. To regulate nature was to regulate society, I now saw, and this had often been done unjustly. Conservation's importance lay in its failures and blindness as well as its accomplishments. These kinds of histories were not so inspiring to read on a backpacking or canoe trip, but they spoke powerfully to the sense of disfranchisement palpable in the old mining-turned-tourist towns that I had come to know and love. These revisionist stories angered some environmentalists and environmental historians, but I saw in my own classes how they did a valuable service by forcing environmentally minded people to think about what had been done in the name of protecting nature, to leaven their environmentalism with a concern for social justice.

But after a few years, I became increasingly uncomfortable with the consequences of narrating the history of conservation by focusing on its sins. A comment from one of my less environmentally minded students brought this home: at the end of a class session in which we discussed the dispossession of Indians and rural whites by conservation bureaucracies, he shrugged his shoulders and said, "This just sounds like the kind of bullshit that goes down when the government does any-thing." I shuddered: was this my lesson to my students, to bolster their already robust cynicism about the wisdom of the American public using the powers of its government to limit environmental damage? Would we be better off without the game laws, the protected areas, and the myriad ways that conservationists had pushed Americans to think about na-ture? I had helped my students see the limits, oversights, and even crimes of conservation. I wanted them to see its accomplishments, too, so that the critical histories would inform a contemporary politics that melded environmental protection with social justice. Indeed, in a time when humanity faces the extraordinary challenge of global climate change, I thought that this synthesis was one of the duties of environmental history.

So this book began as an effort to offer a more comprehensive and balanced portrayal of conservation. I wanted both to explore how con-servation perpetuated race and class hierarchies (a subject that some historians continue to ignore or dismiss) and to show how the move-ment laid the basis for real and lasting environmental improvements.[3] Early research into the history of Los Angeles seemed promising. In the decades around 1900, the metropolitan area fostered something of a renaissance of conservation. Scientists and landowners looked to the chaparral-covered mountains hemming in the city as a key source of water for their prosperous orchards and growing city, but one they thought endangered by fires and rapid timber cutting. They helped make these forests among the first brought under permanent federal control and management. Some of these figures aspired to bring the principles of plant breeding and conservation to the management of human reproduction, writing of "conserving" what they considered the better sort of human beings. The mountains drew many thousands of Angelenos, including those of more modest means, to their wild and harsh beauty. Outing and hunting clubs built lodges to welcome travelers, and were joined by private entrepreneurs offering hiking and pack trips to nature enthusiasts. Writers extolled the ruggedness of the mountains and the vast, austere desert to the east in newspaper columns, simple but eloquent letters to newspaper editors, and in popular books. In the metropolis itself, homeowners and orchardists planted their grounds, and architects designed homes to evoke the region's natural beauty, practicing what some considered a kind of suburban or domestic conservation. Progressive reformers proposed ambitious public parks, warned of the dangers of cutting off urbanites from regular contact with the nonhuman world, and advocated modeling large city parks after the region's wilder expanses. Neighborhood residents sought more and better parks, wrote eloquently of threats to their favorite trees, and debated the merits of camping in their municipal parks. The participants in these conversations included women and men, scientists and laypeople, conservative business owners and socialist labor leaders, and those of affluence and modest means. They all seemed to share some sense that something about modern life—wage labor, industry, urbanization, and materialism—had poisoned the relationship between humans and the larger natural world.

Exploring these conservation circles seemed like a promising way to push beyond the limits of both the hagiographic and revisionist accounts of conservation. Such a work also promised to uncover the continuities between some strains of conservation and more recent environmental movements. The time that I spent in Los Angeles in the early 2000s exposed me to a dynamic urban environmentalism, one concerned less with a nature far away and supposedly pure, and more with the places close at hand, like the Los Angeles River, which had been despoiled, neglected, and often forgotten. These activists often understood their actions as a break from past environmental politics. Yet some of their proposals, as in the case of calls to transform the paved and sewer-like Los Angeles River into a public green space lined with parks, bore a striking resemblance to plans made but never implemented in the decade after 1910. Moreover, some of the Angelenos who called themselves conservationists were deeply, even centrally concerned with ethnic pluralism and questions of labor and capitalism. At least some conservationists had seen more connection between questions of environmental and social justice than scholars had thought; what is generally assumed to be a new conversation about the interconnectedness of the social and environmental, I came to see, was actually an old one.

These deep ties between conservation and other Progressive-era reforms led me to embrace another goal: to prompt historians of the period in general to take conservation more seriously. Like most U.S. environmental historians, I found the debates over the study of this period to be compelling and fruitful. Ours was surely a field rising in prominence. Yet the flowering of environmental history in the past three decades has conspicuously failed to put important environmental chapters such as conservation into the larger stories told by American historians. Recent treatments of Progressivism as a whole have paid slight attention to conservation, portraying it as a minor character that walks on stage, remains briefly, and exits a central drama whose main themes concern political reform, monopoly, ethnic diversity, labor, and gender.[4]

At least some observers realized that conservation had a lot to do with Progressivism. In 2010, after the conservative pundit and television show host Glenn Beck launched a diatribe against Progressivism as a form of closet communism, Jon Stewart, host of the left-leaning satirical news program *The Daily Show*, fired back. In addition to lampooning Beck's hypocrisy for researching Progressivism at a public library (exactly the sort of contribution to the common good that Progressives thought state institutions offered that the private sector could not), Stewart took his viewers to "an alternate universe where America was saved from the scourge of Progressivism." The *Daily Show* reporter Samantha Bee appeared live from the "Yellowstone National Tire Fire," sporting a beard caused by the dumping of hormone disruptors by pharmaceutical companies unencumbered by the regulation of such agencies as the Food and Drug Administration. Stewart and Bee discussed the dubious glories of life in a country where there had been no Theodore Roosevelt or Woodrow Wilson presidencies, no income tax, no national parks, no antitrust laws, no women's suffrage, and no regulation of polluters or the chemical industry.[5]

The Daily Show seemed a step ahead of professional historians in its satirical argument that environmental measures were among the most important legacies of the Progressive era. Why had we environmental historians not been able to persuade more of our colleagues of this? Perhaps part of the problem was that focused case studies continued to dominate environmental history as a field. No professional historian had written a wide-ranging synthetic treatment of conservation, one that would systematically trace the ways in which conservation was part and parcel of Progressivism as a whole. I came to hope that a book that took a national rather than regional approach to the subject would stand a better chance of restoring conservation to its central place within Progressivism, much as Samuel P. Hays's study of conservation and ideas of efficiency made a mark on the field after its publication in 1959.[6]

So by the time I sat down to write this book, three goals came to the fore. First, I want to offer a new and more expansive synthesis of conservationist thinking and doing, one that stresses the movement's complexity, heterogeneity, ambition, and breadth. Second, I hope to show how deeply tied this movement was to the larger course of Progressivism, particularly in the way that its advocates invested their hopes in both expanded state power and widespread cultural change. Not all conservationists were Progressives, and not all Progressives were conservationists, but (as many observers at the time noted) conservation was a central part of the Progressive quest to humanize industrial capitalism. Third, and as much implicitly as explicitly, I want to argue for the relevance of conservation for contemporary environmental reform. As we confront environmental challenges today, we can learn not only from the mistakes and blind spots of previous reformers, but also from the ways that they delegitimized markets, validated state action in the defense of the common good, and fostered a culture of appreciation for nature both distant and close at hand.

Organizationally, what follows is a straightforward narrative of mounting concerns about environmental crises in the later nineteenth century, the emergence of an ideologically diverse intellectual and grassroots movement to address these problems, the debates within this movement about its proper scope and meaning, and its bureaucratization and consequent narrowing. I trace important conservationist policy victories such as the creation of metropolitan parks, national game legislation, and the creation and expansion of such agencies as the Forest Service and National Park Service. Yet the book's center of gravity lies with ideas rather than policies. Conservation was a set of ideas and hopes as much as it was policies and agencies. As is common in social movements, its reach exceeded its grasp; a focus on policy rather than ideas risks obscuring the most interesting and compelling aspects of Progressive-era environmental reform. Breadth and unity are the dominant themes of the book's first half, whereas faction and discord characterize its second half. This is a story of the congealing of a movement, its rise to prominence, the swelling ambitions of its proponents, and the dashing of its greatest hopes despite substantial accomplishments. In the epilogue, I assess conservation's legacies for subsequent environmental politics, arguing that many later developments were adaptations of diverse traditions of conservation thinking rather than breaks with prior practice, as most scholarship has emphasized.

Any narrative, especially of a subject as large and sprawling as this one, necessarily imposes an order on a messy and fractious reality. One of the most difficult choices that I had to make while crafting this book was who to count as a conservationist. One of my primary arguments is that conservation was ideologically much broader than it is usually conceived, with the publisher Horace McFarland as a key figure and with a family tree that includes the radical American economist Henry George and the English socialist John Ruskin as well as more familiar environmental figures such as the scientist and legislator George Perkins Marsh. Some of these people did not call themselves conservationists. Indeed, some could not have: the word "conservation," as I explain at length, did not take on its specifically environmental connotations until 1907, well after many of the figures now included in the conservationist pantheon—George Perkins Marsh, John Muir, and Gifford Pinchot, to name three—had published some of their most influential works (or, in the case of Marsh, were long dead).

Just as applying the term "conservation" only to those who used it to describe themselves would exclude too much, broadening it to encompass all environmental thinkers and reformers of the late nineteenth and early twentieth centuries would be similarly problematic. It would risk making my argument about the ideological breadth of conservation tautological: conservation would look robustly diverse simply because I retroactively placed a wider cast of characters into the category "conservationist." This approach risks becoming the wholesale imposition of a particular brand of contemporary environmentalism on the past, with no consideration for how historical actors defined themselves or for important changes in environmental politics in the past century.

The way out of this dilemma was for me to distill the essence of conservation from the words and actions of those who used the term, and then to explain where their movement came from and what its consequences were. At the heart of conservation lay two ideas: that industrial life had badly skewed humanity's relationship with the nonhuman world, and that this relationship had to be carefully and self-consciously remedied for the mutual benefit of society and nature. Cities took central stage in both of these beliefs. Burgeoning urban areas epitomized the artificiality, ugliness, and alienation that so many conservationists believed characterized modern life. This book's title, which includes a phrase taken from an essay by the suburban nature writer Dallas Lore Sharp, is meant to evoke the effort to escape industrial cities, sometimes in the literal sense of finding refuge in wild nature, but also metaphorically, by reforming urban landscapes. Recognizing the importance of cities to conservation helps us see the movement's complexity and its democratic side, and it points to some of the ways in which American conservation was produced by a dialogue with European reformers similarly preoccupied with the environmental and social harms of industrialism.

Using this definition of conservation allows me to make an argument that is in some ways revisionist. This definition makes room for the commonalities among the ideologically diverse environmental reformers that I first encountered in my study of Los Angeles, including those more likely to label themselves suffragists, reformers, or Progressives than conservationists. Some of these people focused on the material side of conservation, in such concerns as the destruction of other species or the threat to or monopolization of valuable natural resources such as timber and soil. Others found themselves preoccupied with the spiritual costs of alienation from nature, fearing for those who had no access to natural beauty or wildness. Regardless of their emphasis on the spiritual or material, conservationists focused on a range of landscapes: most prioritized the countryside, but more conservationists than we have realized were deeply invested in the design of cities and suburbs, where more than half of Americans lived by 1920. The human body was for some also a landscape in need of conservation, whether through general notions of health and vigor or a eugenic focus on heredity and the environment. The objects of conservation reformers were broader than we have realized, and so too were their methods. Some conservationists emphasized laws, regulations, and bureaucracies to enforce them, and others placed their faith in civic organizing and cultural change. Vanishing wildlife, for example, could be protected by laws forbidding their transport across state lines, but also by stigmatizing the use of plumage in women's hats or the killing of does. A forest might be valued for its timber and watershed, or for the sublime majesty of its trees, or both; and it might be protected by forest rangers as well as by a heightened vigilance among campers about fires. A neighborhood might be made more "natural" by the city government planting trees or constructing a park, but also by private homeowners carefully landscaping their properties.

So there were many different kinds of conservation, beyond the now old distinction between conservationist (the materialistic approach epitomized by Gifford Pinchot) and preservationist (the spiritual and Romantic approach epitomized by John Muir). I also show a bit more diversity among conservationists, particularly regarding class and gender. There was little racial or ethnic diversity: like most Progressive reform efforts rooted in the Protestant middle class, conservation was largely a native-born white affair, though some African Americans, such as those in the National Association of Colored Women and a *Chicago Defender* columnist, articulated visions of conservation adapted to black experiences.

Even as this definition of conservation allows me to present a more heterogeneous and fractious conservation, it leads me down some traditionalist paths. Radical and urban-centered voices loom large in early chapters, but figures such as George Perkins Marsh, Gifford Pinchot, and John Muir receive even more attention. I resisted this at first, wanting to tell a more original story of the roots of conservation, one with a truly diverse cast of characters. Unable to come up with a plausible and compelling version of this story, I left the first two chapters for last. Eventually I embraced elements of the traditional account, and so many of the subjects of the early portions of this book are familiar figures in the conservation pantheon. Their arguments that industrial humanity imperiled nature (and thus, ultimately, the prosperity and health of people) laid the intellectual foundation for conservation a century ago and environmental sanity today.

The conservation movement described in this book created lasting legacies in politics, the structure of the American state, the landscapes of cities, and environmental thought. Later environmental activists and leaders drew on these legacies, both in trying to revive what they thought conservation was about, and in distancing themselves from what they understood to be its mistakes. My own assessment of these legacies is not celebratory. The expanded state power that conservationists advocated could be antidemocratic and even authoritarian, as it was with other aspects of Progressivism. Conservation succeeded in subjecting much of rural America to the authority of public lands bureaucracies, which often crushed local opposition, expelled Native peoples from their homelands, and forced people out of subsistence economies and into markets on very unequal terms. Conservation policies of fire suppression, timber harvesting, and predator control had disastrous environmental consequences in many places, suggesting the potential hubris of scientific knowledge. But just as important, conservation embodied the great promise of Progressive democracy: that an awakened people could check the dangers of industrial life and concentrated economic power by organizing themselves and using the powers of their government. This democratic version of conservation was a legacy that environmentally conscious people today can still turn to and build upon. Like the rest of Progressivism, conservation, more than a century after its inception, still speaks to the present.

Frontier, Market, and Environmental Crisis

T he United States of the late nineteenth century straddled the continent. Its bustling factories and newly acquired overseas empire suggested a nation clearly emerging as one of the earth's great powers. In the cities whose factories produced perhaps a third of the world's manufactured goods, streetlights drowned out the stars and buildings reached to the sky. The warm glow of electricity replaced the smoky flicker of candles or kerosene lanterns in many a house. The railroad network, the world's largest, made possible the sure and speedy delivery of goods ordered from such national retailers as Montgomery Ward and Sears, Roebuck, and Company. The telegraph allowed news that once took weeks to spread to be transmitted nearly instantaneously, across the continent or to the other side of the Atlantic and back. Not even time itself was beyond the reach of the new industrial order. Railroads introduced the four time zones that Americans in the lower forty-eight states still use today. Watches and clocks replaced the sun, moon, and stars as ways by which Americans measured out their lives.

Why, then, were so many members of the reading public, including educated white elites, so haunted by visions of the abrupt destruction of modern civilization? In the stories they read, volcanoes blotted out the sun with ash, tidal waves swept away cities, and a polyglot industrial workforce fought climactic battles with its plutocratic overlords in confrontations that often destroyed the country itself. Sometimes extraterrestrial (or simply "dark-skinned") archaeologists from the future came to inspect the ruins of New York City, with much the same curiosity that contemporary Americans brought to the question of what had happened to the lost civilization of Atlantis. In these scenarios, the United States and other advanced, industrialized nations were not so much perched at the summit of human achievement as they were poised on the abyss of destruction.[1]

A society's vision of apocalypse—of how it, or even the earth itself, might perish entirely—reflects its fundamental fears and values. Puritans envisioned their fiery destruction at the hands of an angry God, slaveholders the carnage of a race war, Cold War societies the holocaust of nuclear annihilation or even Godzilla and other monstrosities of the atomic age. In the late nineteenth century, visions of wholesale environmental destruction began to seize the American imagination. The prevalence and the content of these visions suggest a number of important aspects of American environmental thought and reform. In the most obvious sense, these visions reflected a growing preoccupation with questions of nature and the fragility of civilization. Even when their worries did not reach the level of the apocalyptic, Americans noted and talked about environmental changes—the cutting of forests, the fall of the passenger pigeon and bison toward oblivion, the fouling of urban waterways. Humanity was often at the mercy of nature in these stories, but at other times seemed to cause its own demise.

Moreover, these visions were warnings of social conflict as much as they were of purely environmental problems. Indeed, the most common scenario in the apocalyptic imagination centered on a violent revolution by the dispossessed or its equally violent suppression. Social antagonism frequently accompanied environmental destruction. Finally, cities featured centrally in these scenarios and in the growing environmental consciousness that colored them. Cities embodied the power and achievements of industrial civilization, but also the artificiality, alienation, and social divisions that seemed the most threatening.

Not all of the people who laid the foundation for conservation feared apocalypse. Nevertheless, these writers, reformers, and government bureaucrats shared the belief that they lived in an era of environmental crisis, a crisis in some way part of larger challenges faced by American society as it entered a period of new prosperity and might. By arguing that the United States and other economically dynamic societies had brought about severe environmental crises, and by seeking to explain why, these men would develop many of the ideas necessary for the flowering of a robust movement to protect nature and people alike from this damage. Conservation was born and lived as an idea before it grew up to become a social and political movement. But conservation led a complicated childhood and adolescence. Those who built its intellectual foundations were not of a single mind about how to define the most pressing environmental problems. Some focused on forests and agrarian landscapes, others on species extinctions, yet others on industry and cities. Those most concerned with cities directed their energies in several directions: providing escape from urban conditions; "naturalizing" cities by park systems, boulevards, and private plantings; or envisioning the eclipse of cities by decentralized forms of economic development that would fuse the virtues of rural and urban life. These thinkers shared a sense that all these crises were deeply tied to the size and dynamism of the economy, but differed in their evaluations of American economic change. While some heralded industrialization as a boon to wealth, national power, and economic security, one whose attendant gains more than compensated for the problems it caused, others could not make their peace with wage labor, the rise of cities, or the political power that industry brought to elites.

In short, the exponents of the ideas that shaped the later conservation movement could be found across the political spectrum, from those who comfortably socialized and sympathized with the country's economic elites to those who railed against them. Some, such as George Perkins Marsh, are remembered as environmental thinkers; others, including Henry George, are remembered for their arguments about economics and class. Marsh, George, and countless others convinced many Americans that there was in fact an environmental crisis, and the differing ways in which they understood this crisis marked the later conservation movement. There was no single form of conservation, no single landscape upon which it was enacted, and no way to separate efforts to redress an environmental crisis from reforms aimed at wider social issues.

The Environmental Crises of the Nineteenth Century

Warnings of environmental damage predated the industrial cities that were the key sites of the imagined apocalypses. "Every middle-aged man, who revisits his birth-place after a few years of absence," George Perkins Marsh told a crowd of farmers at a small county fair in Rutland, Vermont, in 1847, "looks upon another landscape than that which formed the theatre of his youthful toils and pleasures." Marsh was prosperous and powerful, a college graduate in an era when very few were formally educated, a sitting congressman, and a key backer of the young Smithsonian Institution. He began his story with a learned and impassioned ode to American progress and greatness. Their history, he told his listeners, was the story of how "the full energies of advanced European civilization . . . guided by its accumulated intelligence, were brought to bear at once on a desert continent." The United States had just dramatically demonstrated its power: two weeks before his talk, its army crushed Mexico's, occupied its capital, and secured the victory that made Mexico's north the United States' far west. So from his perspective, the young nation's history had a triumphal arc: "It has been but the work of a day to win empires from the wilderness, and to establish relations of government and commerce between points as distant as the rising and the setting sun." The rise to greatness could be seen on the agricultural landscape of the republic, where "unproductive wastes" had been made into "fertile fields" and where the "silent recesses of our aboriginal forests and mountains" were now "filled with light and life."[2]

Midway through Marsh's oration, his tone shifted from triumphalism to warning. It was not a conflict with a foreign power such as France or England that gave him pause, or even the tensions over slavery and sectionalism that, exacerbated by the conquest of Mexico, would soon plunge the country into a cataclysmic civil war. Instead, the warning signs appeared in the very landscape that marked national greatness. A middle-aged man returning to the landscape of his childhood might well find the signs of progress outweighed by destruction: "The signs of artificial improvement are mingled with the tokens of improvident waste, and the bald and barren hills, the dry beds of the smaller streams, the ravines furrowed out by the torrents of spring, and the diminished thread of interval that skirts the widened channel of the rivers, seem sad substitutes for the pleasant groves and brooks and broad meadows of his ancient paternal domain." Americans had made this landscape too. By cutting down too much of their forests in "the rage for improvement," American farmers, the source of the nation's prosperity and democracy, were wrecking their own homes and threatening to deprive their descendants of the blessings of their achievements.[3]

Marsh later achieved fame in intellectual if not popular circles with the publication of his book *Man and Nature; or, Physical Geography as Modified by Human Action* (1864). In this sweeping treatise that drew upon his education in the classics of Western civilization, and his travels and years of living as a U.S. diplomat in the Ottoman Empire and Italy, Marsh argued that humans could radically and unfavorably alter the fabric of nature. Much of the Mediterranean world, heavily forested in antiquity, was now a desert incapable of supporting the farms and vineyards that provisioned its once mighty empires. Nor was environmental destruction confined to a more primitive and less enlightened past; as he had warned years before in Rutland, the rapidity of American ascension brought with it equally rapid damage. Marsh was conventional, though eloquent and learned, in believing that people could "improve" nature. He was radically and powerfully new in his insistence that they could also wreck it.

Marsh is remembered today as an environmental thinker in large part because subsequent advocates of active state interventions into environmental issues were explicit in acknowledging their intellectual debt to him. Gifford Pinchot, the first head of the U.S. Forest Service, called *Man and Nature* "epoch-making," and later writers tagged him with such monikers as the "fountainhead of the conservation movement" and the "prophet of conservation." Yet framing him as an environmental thinker can obscure the ways in which Marsh and others like him bound up their environmental arguments in larger considerations of social and economic values and institutions. There was no tradition of purely "environmental" thought that analyzed "nature"; there were, instead, numerous writers and thinkers who explicitly addressed the connections between the social and natural worlds. Marsh, for example, was a philologist, natural historian, collector and translator of Icelandic and Scandinavian literature, and diplomat. In his talk at Rutland, he presented deforestation as a troubling chapter in a larger tale of the triumph of private property and growing scientific enlightenment. Environment, society, politics, and philosophy all bled into one another, first in conservation as an idea and later in conservation as a practice.[4]

Some of the landscape changes that Marsh pointed to in his Rutland talk and in *Man and Nature* were rapid when considered in the timescale of decades, generations, or centuries, yet gradual from the vantage of daily life. Other environmental problems presented themselves much more dramatically.

The citizens of Peshtigo, Wisconsin, found this out in the fall of 1871. A small village of some twelve hundred on the western shore of Green Bay in northeastern Wisconsin, Peshtigo owed its prosperity to the harvest of the surrounding pine forests. Bordered on the south by cleared farmlands, the town boasted several sawmills; substantial factories that produced pails, tubs, churns, sashes, doors, and other wood products; and boardinghouses and hotels that lodged its numerous workers. This year, however, the forest seemed to turn against the people who made their living from it. Virtually no rain had fallen since early July, and in late September numerous fires broke out across the region. They occasionally consumed outbuildings, worried mill owners enough to have their workers dig protective ditches and clear brush, and, in the words of a local journalist, "permeated the atmosphere" with smoke "sometimes so dense as to prevent seeing objects a few rods distant, seriously affecting the eyes and the lungs." Even in the larger towns of Green Bay and Appleton, "buildings at the distance of a square were invisible." On Green Bay and the main body of Lake Michigan, "the smoke assumed the dimensions of an immense fog, obscuring the shores and rendering navigation difficult." Travel by land was compromised, too, since "trees, fallen and burning, obstructed the highways, and bridges in every direction were burned."[5]

These conditions were unpleasant and threatening, but the full dimensions of the danger did not become apparent until October 8. As the few surviving eyewitnesses told the journalist C. D. Robinson, they heard an "unusual and strangely ominous sound, a gradual roaring and rumbling." Some likened it to "the approach of a railroad train" or "the roar of a waterfall," others to "the sound of a battle, with artillery going on at a distance." Horrified residents saw flames sweeping toward them, "not along the ground, as they had been accustomed to meet them, but consuming the tree tops and filling the air with a whirlwind of flame." Hundreds saved themselves by fleeing into the river, but where "there was no stream deep enough for such a refuge," no such escape awaited: "Men, women, and children, horses, oxen, cows, dogs, swine—everything that had life was seized with pain and ran without method to escape the impending destruction. The smoke was suffocating and blinding, the roar of the tempest deafening, the atmosphere scorching, children were separated from their parents and were trampled upon by the crazed beasts; husbands and wives were calling wildly for each other and rushing in wild dismay, they knew not where. While others, believing that the day of judgment was surely come, fell upon the ground and abandoned themselves to its terrors."[6]

Contemporaries estimated that fifteen hundred people lost their lives to this blaze. "Of the village of Peshtigo," Robinson recounted, "there was not a vestige left standing except one unfinished house which stood apart from the others and escaped." The next morning, "the sad remnant of the Peshtigo people, tired and maimed," made its gloomy exodus to the relative safety of Marinette, better protected by the meeting of the Menominee River and Green Bay.[7]

The citizens of Peshtigo were hardly the only Americans threatened by fire. On that very day, a blaze fanned by strong winds laid waste to the heart of Chicago, leveling nearly four square miles, killing perhaps three hundred, and leaving around a third of the city's residents homeless. Such smoking ruins had long been a hazard of urban life, since dense conglomerations of timber construction provided an ideal environment for the rapid spread of fires. Chicago's breathtaking rise from a small village on a marsh to the home of vast rail yards, steel blast furnaces, and packing plants underscored the point: for all of their modern sheen, American cities were just as vulnerable as their European predecessors.[8]

The catastrophic forest fires of 1871 consumed entire towns, as in this depiction of the flight of survivors from Peshtigo, Wisconsin. (Harper's Weekly, *December 2, 1871, 1133; courtesy Newberry Library)*

The rapid growth of industrial cities such as Chicago embodied the rise of national power and wealth. But cities were vulnerable to disaster, as shown in an illustration of the Great Chicago Fire of 1871. (Harper's Weekly, *October 28, 1871, 1012; courtesy Newberry Library*)

The devastation of such a rising metropolis kept the incineration of Peshtigo from attracting widespread media attention, but residents of the Great Lakes states and careful readers of newspapers all over the country knew that the fires of that single day had singed a million and a half acres in Wisconsin, taking with them not only Peshtigo but also a dozen other hamlets. Unlike the Great Chicago Fire, these sorts of woodland blazes claimed few historical precedents. The winds of that day fed blazes on the other side of Lake Michigan, too, burning the towns of Holland and Manistee on the lake's eastern shore, and pushing flames into Port Huron in southeastern Michigan. The range of midwestern fires over the course of the year encompassed Illinois, Indiana, Wisconsin, Michigan, and North Dakota. And 1871, though bad enough to earn the moniker the "Black Year" from the *Chicago Tribune,* was just one of many marked by holocausts that devoured towns, killed hundreds, burned millions of acres, and sometimes produced enough smoke to close the Great Lakes to navigation. For six decades, from 1870 to the early 1930s, variations on the theme occurred: in the Midwest, the years

1881, 1894, 1908, 1910, 1911, and 1918 were especially bad. The Great
Lakes conflagrations were particularly important for their severity and
timing. As the historian Stephen Pyne observes: "The fires coincided
exactly with the great debate over conservation: they began in the 1870s
and concluded with the end of the Progressive Era. The entire controversy over forest conservation and wildland fire protection took place
against the violent backdrop of the worst fire disasters in the national
experience." Devastating fires destroyed towns and claimed countless
lives also in New England, on the West Coast, and in the Rocky Mountain States in 1903, 1908, and 1910.[9]

It did not take much debate or reflection to determine why fires
were disastrous: they destroyed valuable property and killed people. The
consequences of other environmental changes were less clear-cut: was it
such a problem if once common animals became hard to find or vanished from the earth altogether? Some might see such changes as the
replacement of buffalo by cattle as a marker of national progress and
economic "improvement." Indeed, Hugh Strickland, the British naturalist who made the case that the disappearance of the dodo proved that
humans could drive species to extinction, acknowledged in 1848 that
"we cannot see without regret the extinction of the last individual of any
race of organic beings," yet added that this regret could be balanced by
a larger consideration: "Man is destined by his Creator to be 'fruitful and
multiply and replenish the Earth and subdue it.' The progress of man in
civilization, no less than his numerical increase, continually extends the
geographical domain of Art by trenching on the territories of Nature."[10]
Others were not so sure about that. In the latter half of the nineteenth century, many Americans became increasingly concerned that the scarcity
and eventual disappearance of such animals as salmon, moose, and deer
meant that people were destroying the larger natural world upon which
they still depended. By making nature less abundant, and thus making
people less prosperous, such damage imperiled progress as much as it
marked its passage.

The extinction of the passenger pigeon and the near extinction of
the American bison provoked extensive media coverage and public discussion of these issues. "Millions and millions, reduced to one and now
naught but history, is the sad story of the passenger pigeon," reported

Forest and Stream in 1914, when the last known of her kind, Martha, died in a Cincinnati zoo. Perhaps Martha's story resonated widely not just because of the pathos of a solitary member of a highly social species pining away in captivity, but also because many Americans had first-hand knowledge of the pigeons and their spectacular abundance. As an Indiana newspaper noted in 1898, after a Smithsonian expedition had failed to encounter a single wild passenger pigeon, "persons yet in middle life can remember the vast flights of pigeons that could be seen any day in the fall." Writers old enough to recall the enormous flocks almost invariably invoked their own memories of them. Hunting the pigeons, whether by shotgun or net, was so common for boys that the sportswriter W. B. Mershon began his book *The Passenger Pigeon* in 1907 with a chapter titled "My Boyhood Among the Pigeons." Mershon's descriptions of the flocks of his childhood were typical of the enormous body of such publications, evoking not so much the character of individual birds as their collective presence. The pigeons "swept like a cloud," "passed in waves over the tree tops," and "poured." "Sometimes even now," he wrote, "forty years after the last of the great passenger pigeon flights, I fall to day-dreaming" about hunting them.[11]

The unbelievable, exuberant abundance of the pigeons was one of the leading tropes of reminiscences such as Mershon's. Countless newspaper and magazine articles quoted the naturalist John James Audubon's description of his encounters with the birds in the 1810s. A flock in Kentucky took more than five hours to pass, leading Audubon to estimate that it consisted of at least 500 million birds. The noise it made, even at a distance, reminded him of "a hard gale at sea" passing through a ship's rigging; when they flapped their wings to alight, together the pigeons made "a noise like the roar of distant thunder." Men and boys firing into the massed birds killed enough that "for a week or more, the population fed on no other flesh than that of pigeons, talked of nothing but pigeons." The *Indianapolis News* described the flocks that Audubon called to mind as "an immense army patrolling the blue field of heaven." When Audubon originally published this account, in 1832, he found his own depiction of abundance so extravagant that he wrote: "After having viewed them so often and under so many circumstances, I even now feel inclined to pause, and assure myself that what I am going to relate is fact.

Hunting passenger pigeons, depicted in a drawing from 1875 that illustrates the birds' abundance. This very abundance made the pigeon's later extinction convey the idea that humans could effect dramatic and adverse environmental change over a comparatively brief period. (*Harpers Weekly Journal of Civilization and Frank Leslie's Illustrated Newspaper, February 20, 1875; courtesy Archives and Manuscripts Department, John B. Cade Library, Southern University*)

Yet I have seen it all, and that too in the company of persons who, like myself, were struck with amazement."[12]

The slow-moving disappearance of such exuberant abundance led popular and scientific publications to discuss the causes of the pigeon's decline, along with numerous proposals for its protection. Spanning decades, this discussion helped cement the idea that humans could effect dramatic and adverse environmental change over a comparatively brief period. By the 1880s, as sightings of the once mighty flocks became more and more sporadic, scientists began to contemplate the real possibility that the passenger pigeon was bound for annihilation. The Bird Protection Committee of the American Ornithologists' Union issued just such a warning in 1886. Writing in *Science,* the group, headed by the Harvard zoologist Joel Allen, issued a sharp warning about, in the words of its title, "The Present Wholesale Destruction of Bird-Life in the United States." Continued hunting and collecting of birds, and the destruction of their habitat, would result not only in local scarcity, but also in the "extermination over vast areas" of "numerous forms of animal life." Extinction "will sooner or later prove the fate of all of our larger game-mammals and not a few of our game-birds," and it threatened to "overtake scores of our song birds." This disappearance could be checked only if "the friends of the birds—the public"—became fully aware of "the magnitude of the evil and enlightened as to its causes and the means for its retrenchment."[13]

A more concrete and focused proposal came later during the pigeon's slide to extinction. In 1909, the American Ornithologists' Union offered a reward of three hundred dollars (the equivalent of about eight thousand dollars in 2017) for the discovery of a nesting pair of the pigeons. A reporter who covered this offer opined that if a breeding pair were found, "we ought to quickly effect the organization of a passenger pigeon restoration club" that could "obtain adequate legislation and warden service, so that for a term of years the birds may be permitted to feed and breed in absolute safety and be accorded the freedom of the continent."[14]

Such efforts failed to save the pigeon. They did, however, ensure that its crash from omnipresence to extinction became a parable of wider environmental profligacy. The Bird Protection Committee opened its *Science* article with the declaration that "it is only when man comes upon the scene that nature's balance is seriously disturbed," and condemned "Man's destructive influence" as being "in far greater part selfish and wanton."[15] Such judgments became more common after Martha the pigeon died, in 1914. The Cornell University biologist Albert Hazen Wright used her death to point to the birds' collective behavior—"they all acted in common, and eat in common; no avarice or private interest appearing among them, but each laboring as much for the rest as for himself"— as a model for people. "If only the human species would emulate this communal spirit," he concluded, and "act in unison for bird-protection," then "some of our threatened birds would re-establish their slender hold and escape their impending extinction." Martha's death was a clear sign that ignoring the environmental damage that came with progress was no longer responsible or sensible: "In the early settlements, Pigeons, Turkeys, Paroquets and Heath Hens were plentiful; civilization and culture came; the hills and valleys were deforested; the lowlands were cultivated; in short, the balance of nature was excessively disturbed. Yet where have we collectively provided these original occupants refuge, or how have we restrained ourselves, to promote their greater increase, when they were most rapidly lessening? The conscience balm has always been, 'They will ever be common.'"[16]

The American bison's brush with extinction prompted similar hand-wringing about wanton destructiveness. Like the pigeon flocks, the enormous numbers of buffalo stunned observers. Americans traveling on the Great Plains in the nineteenth century strained to gauge their numbers. Observers on the Santa Fe Trail guessed that single herds they encountered numbered at least one hundred thousand. One saw bison congregated to the horizon for three days of his journey, leading him to conclude that the herd covered more than thirteen hundred square miles. A member of a federal expedition in 1820 typified such accounts in his report of "immense herds of bisons, grazing in undisturbed possession and obscuring with the density of their numbers the verdant plain; to the right and left as far as the eye was permitted to rove, the crowd seemed hardly to diminish, and it would be no exaggeration to say that at least ten thousand here burst on our sight in the instant."[17] General Philip Sheridan offered what he considered to be a conservative estimate of 100 million as the population of the Plains bison. Although recent scholarship has suggested much lower initial population numbers, by the late nineteenth century the bison had become a kind of terrestrial counterpart of the passenger pigeon as an icon of the endless abundance of North American nature.[18]

And as with the passenger pigeon, the decline of the bison prompted calls for action in the form of self-restraint, hunting regulation, and captive breeding. Bison populations collapsed more rapidly than did those of the passenger pigeon—or rather they seemed to. While Indian market hunting and cyclical drought may have reduced bison numbers substantially by the 1830s, and Indian peoples dependent on the bison encountered local shortages starting in the 1840s, it was the actions of white hunters with large-gauge rifles in the 1870s that first prompted the realization that Americans might well exterminate this iconic animal. Such hunters could kill thousands of buffalo every month, shipping them on the new rail lines that crossed the plains.[19]

As sightings of the once mighty herds grew ever scarcer, some observers argued that in fact these hunters were not just killing many individual animals, but also threatening the bison as a whole. Concluding that fewer than three hundred of the animals remained, in 1886 the taxidermist and naturalist William Temple Hornaday issued a dire warning: "The wild buffalo is practically gone forever, and in a few more years . . . nothing will remain of him save his old, well worn trails along the water-courses, a few museum specimens, and regret for his fate. If his untimely end fails even to point to a moral that shall benefit the surviving species of mammals which are now being slaughtered in a like manner, it will be sad indeed." A few years later, working under the auspices of the Smithsonian, Hornaday managed to bring six of the surviving bison to Washington, D.C. They soon became a public attraction in their paddock on the National Mall. In the 1890s, working with the New York Zoological Park, he managed to purchase enough of the remaining bison from western ranchers to establish a small herd capable of reproducing itself.[20]

The imperiled bison became a slightly different cultural symbol from the passenger pigeon. Calling to mind the thundering herds that once covered the Plains evoked a time of untroubled abundance, much as did the sky-darkening pigeon flocks. But the bison, at least for its most prominent defenders, also strongly evoked a distinctively American set of historical experiences. As the founders of the American Bison Society wrote shortly after the group was organized in 1905, "This picturesque wild creature . . . has played so conspicuous a part in the history of America." Calling the bison "our national animal," the society acknowledged the animal's economic value, but argued that it had a "far better and stronger hold on the American people than can be estimated in dollars and cents." To let the noble beast vanish would be not simply an environmental mistake, but also a "disgrace to our country." Letting the bison go extinct, another early society publication warned, would be another reflection of the ways that Americans were losing their "respect and love for the animal life of field and forest."[21]

These chords struck by the American Bison Society deliberately echoed a larger theme in Anglo-American culture at the time: the nostalgia for a supposedly vanishing frontier. This theme was perhaps most strongly identified with the historian Frederick Jackson Turner, whose "frontier thesis," first articulated in the 1890s, held that the United States had grown to be a more egalitarian and democratic country than European nations because of access to "free land" and the perpetual return to "primitive conditions" afforded by the frontier. "To the frontier," he insisted, "the American intellect owes its striking characteristics": "That coarseness and strength combined with acuteness and inquisitiveness; that practical, inventive turn of mind, quick to find expedients; that masterful grasp of material things, lacking in the artistic but powerful to effect great ends; that restless, nervous energy; that dominant individualism, working for good and for evil, and withal that buoyancy and exuberance which comes with freedom—these are traits of the frontier, or traits called out elsewhere because of the existence of the frontier." Unfortunately, according to Turner, by the definition of the frontier used by the Census Bureau—which used population density as a proxy for the availability of land—the frontier had vanished as a distinctive place by 1890. If the frontier had fostered democracy and egalitarianism, then what would happen to these distinctively American qualities in its absence? Far from being an academic question, this conundrum struck political and literary figures as diverse as Theodore Roosevelt, the artist Frederic Remington, the naturalist Ernest Thompson Seton (all members of the American Bison Society), the political economist Henry George, and the novelist Owen Wister as one of the leading questions facing the country at century's end.[22]

Thought of in this context, then, the vanishing buffalo represented not so much the death of the species as the death of the culture of the frontier; its preservation, in turn, ensured not just the survival of the animal but the survival of something of the culture of the frontier as well. As an early publication of the American Bison Society warned, "We may so lose ourselves in the artificial maze and swirl of city life as to have no longer the stars to guide our course, the sturdy oak and the tall tapering pine to give us strength and aspiration, the flowers of the field to teach us beauty and humility. By saving and returning bison to the wild, the society was, in a sense, "bringing man back to nature" and ensuring a "future wholesome and higher development of man."[23]

"Bringing man back to nature" seemed all the more pressing, because more and more people lived in cities. The rise of American cities outpaced even the general growth of the nation. From 1800 to 1890, the urban population multiplied eighty-seven times, while the total U.S. population increased by a factor of twelve. Whereas less than 4 percent of Americans lived in cities at the start of the nineteenth century, nearly 33 percent did by 1890. Industrialization drove this process. Writing at the end of the nineteenth century, the scholar Adna Ferrin Weber concluded that "the Industrial Revolution and the era of railways, both of which opened earliest in England and in the United States, have been the transforming agent in the re-distribution of the population," pulling people to industrial cities from abroad and from the rural districts of their own countries.[24]

Such urbanization could be unsettling, especially for those Americans indebted to the long tradition of thought and letters that rooted the nation's identity and practice of liberty in an agrarian tradition of family farms. Thomas Jefferson, writing near the end of the eighteenth century, famously declared that "those who labour in the earth are the chosen people of God, if ever he had a chosen people, whose breasts he has made his peculiar deposit for substantial and genuine virtue." His confidence that "corruption of morals in the mass of cultivators is a phaenomenon of which no age nor nation has furnished an example" allowed Americans to imagine themselves as an agrarian republic superior to the more commercial and aristocratic nations of Europe. A century later, it gave them just as much of a reason to fear for their future. The ethnic gulf between rural and urban America—by the 1910s, the nation's industrial cities were heavily Catholic and Jewish islands surrounded by a Protestant ocean—sometimes leavened this fear with smug ethnocentrism. The Reverend Josiah Strong, for example, a prominent advocate of the Social Gospel, warned that "the problem of the twentieth century will be the city." He identified "wealth, socialism, intemperance, . . . Romanism, and immigration" as challenges to republican self-government. All were con-centrated most heavily in cities, whose rapid growth, he repeatedly warned, undermined American virtues and the primacy of Anglo-Saxons.[25]

Yet it is unwise to reduce widespread concern, which sometimes approached revulsion, about the living conditions of modern cities to a simple backlash from those who clung to a nostalgic and reactionary vision of what the country had once been. Critiques of urban life offered by authors and political leaders in the nineteenth century singled out environmental conditions too as one of the major problems facing cit-ies and their residents. Some were reflexively and implacably antiurban, while others envisioned better cities whose design and operation would benefit their humblest inhabitants. As a whole, these critiques ensured that alleviating urban environmental conditions would constitute a major part of the subsequent conservation movement.

City life deprived its residents of direct contact with the larger rhythms of nature. This type of environmental crisis differed from the problem of scarce deer, vanishing bison, incinerated forests, or cutover wastelands, but it was an environmental crisis all the same. The Chicago civic leader Henry Foreman spoke for many with his flat assertion about the noxiousness of urban living: "The movement from the country to the city is a cause for alarm. While the well-to-do, recognizing the need of pure air and change of scene for their health and contentment, are seeking country life, vastly greater numbers are leaving a natural exis-tence to take up one that is artificial and baneful." An investigation of tenement houses in Foreman's city at the turn of the century extensively documented the conditions to which he referred, conditions in which much of the urban working class lived across the nation. The continued construction of tightly packed tenement homes, it warned, would fully separate the urban working class from nature: "The city man will soon have new conditions to confront. The factory by day, the tenement by night, will be his environment. By living in the city, man has divorced himself from the soil. He must now live in rooms where the sun never enters. The air he breathes must reach him through dark passages and foul courts. He must be content with about two yards square of earth's space for himself, for each one of his children, for each one of his thou-sand close neighbors, and for each one of their children." What in other contexts might have been seen as a triumph—the migration of European peasants to American cities in search of opportunity—could also be a tragedy. "These restrictions of the crowded tenements," the report noted, "become all the more oppressive when they are viewed in the light of the past lives of most of the inhabitants of these crowded districts." Perhaps immigration had not resulted in an a better or healthier life: "Comparing the life of the dweller in the city to that of the olive-grower of Southern Italy, or the plowman of Roumania—the ancestors of many tenement-house dwellers—the hardships of the present are more serious than those of the past; for whatever difficulties life offered, the people still had air to breathe and expanse of earth." Here the conclusions of the tenement study turned stories of American triumphalism on their head. Instead of freedom and prosperity, immigration brought suffering, illness, and artificiality.[26]

The sanitary and environmental hazards faced by the most impoverished urbanites went well beyond the lack of pleasant sunlight and flower-scented breezes. By concentrating so many thousands of people in small areas, cities exacerbated long-standing health threats and created new ones. Horse manure, a source of fertility on a diversified farm, became in cities a source of massive pollution. The hundreds of tons of droppings produced each day in larger cities bred flies and disease, and turned into noxious dust when dried and trampled. High population density and the constant circulation of people ensured the rapid spread of epidemic diseases such as smallpox and tuberculosis; in such outbreaks, the most popular and effective remedy for those who were able was to flee the city. Cholera, a disease originally from South Asia that spread through human feces and quickly drained its victims of their bodily fluids and could leave them dead within hours, arrived in the nineteenth century. The fouling of water supplies in cities—a virtual inevitability—made them the sites of the cholera epidemics that wracked almost all major American cities from the 1830s to the 1890s. So dangerous were the combined threats of urban life that city dwellers almost everywhere lived shorter and less healthy lives than did rural folk. Indeed, it was not until 1900 that the mortality rates in cities in the industrialized world declined to below the rates of their population growth; until then, urban growth depended on attracting migrants more quickly than cities could kill them off. In the United States of 1900, the best public health data indicated that the life expectancy at birth for the rural white population was 54.7 years, compared with only 46 years for white city dwellers. Put another way, living in the countryside meant living 16 percent longer. Cities were indeed unhealthy places.[27]

The very industries that drew migrants to cities made them all the more dangerous. Tanneries, meatpacking plants, dye and chemical manufactories, and steel forges all dumped their waste directly into the closest and most easily accessible waterways as a matter of course. In larger industrial cities, this ensured that rivers and creeks became open sewers, highways of stench and disease. By the 1860s, for example, many Chicago residents had moved well beyond exasperation with the state of the Chicago River. After the spread in river districts of erysipelas, a potentially disfiguring bacterial skin infection, one prominent lawyer expressed his "profound astonishment" that "a city of nearly two hundred thousand inhabitants . . . should quietly permit a river running through its entire limits to be converted into a giant sewer, . . . here red with blood, there slimy with grease, and black with filth and putrid matter, turning what is in itself a noble and beautiful object into a sight so foul and loathsome as to excite only thoughts of a 'River of Death.'"[28]

In 1900, the city ameliorated some of these problems by reversing the flow of the river so that it carried wastes away from Lake Michigan rather than draining them into the lake, the source of the city's water supply. This massive engineering job, however, failed to rectify smaller-scale environmental hazards in many of the city's poorest neighborhoods. An investigation of living conditions in these places found ongoing problems that characterized many industrial cities. In one predominantly Polish neighborhood, the researchers pointed out that "water stands upon the ground almost the entire year, which makes it dangerous for people to live in basements. . . . The entire district lies in a swamp. . . . There is no sewerage, unless that name is given to a system of gutters by which a certain amount of sewage is carried off." Because "the land is undrained and in some cases the water stands for months under the houses and upon vacants [sic] lots," in many places "there was a green scum upon the water which showed that it had been standing stagnant for some time." The conditions were not created by the intentional ne-

The pollution and ugliness captured in a photograph of Bubbly Creek in Chicago from 1911 helped catalyze urban environmental reform. *(Chicago Historical Society negative DN-0056899)*

glect, sloth, or filth of the residents, but rather by the lack of basic sanitary infrastructure: "There are no water-closets and the outlawed privy vault is in general use. The yards, streets, and alleys are indiscriminately used for the disposal of all sorts of garbage and rubbish. Almost no garbage boxes were found. None of the streets are paved, and the whole district is filthy beyond description." Ugliness and ill health were the result; as the commission concluded, "The atmosphere of the neighborhood is clouded with smoke and the district is extremely dreary, ugly, and unhealthful."[29]

The stark conclusion about environmental hazards in the Chicago commission's report was part of an increasing focus on the conditions

of urban life by reformers and civic leaders from the 1880s onward. Cities, the historian Daniel Rodgers observes in his seminal work *Atlantic
Crossings*, "stood at the vital center of transatlantic progressive imagina-
tions." The burgeoning metropolises of the greater Atlantic world embodied both the enormous capacity of industrial capitalism to create
new wealth and the suffering, squalor, and social division engendered
by the production of that wealth. "The city," proclaimed Josiah Strong,
"is the great center of influence, both good and bad. It contains that
which is fairest and foulest in our civilization. It is the mighty heart of
the body politic, which sends its streams of life pulsating to the very
finger-tips of the whole land; and when the blood becomes poisoned, it
poisons every fiber of the whole body."[30]

To walk or ride through such a city in the late nineteenth century was to see, in Rodgers's words, "distended collections of contrasting subcities: a financial district here, mansion district there, tenderloin
sections, factory towns, a concentration of warehouses and department
stores, middle-class suburbs, and vast working-class regions." Yet despite
the radically different prospects of those who resided and worked in
this fragmented landscape, the urban landscape revealed the inescapa-
ble connections that bound them together: diseases bred in the ponds
of household garbage and human waste easily spread from their neighborhoods of origin; the miserly wages of the workers who slaughtered
the livestock whose offal fouled the water fueled the prosperity of their
employers. For some, these connections both demanded reform and
marked some of the courses that it might take: if a city could reverse the
flow of a waterway, could it not also pave its streets, require its landlords
to install toilets, or even build parks and plant trees?[31]

One of the most important figures demonstrating the connections between urban growth, social inequality, and nature was Henry
George. Largely forgotten today, he achieved widespread prominence in
his own time for his explanation of economic inequality and insecurity.
Long after his death, George's writings exercised a great influence on
urban-oriented environmental reformers. Born in Philadelphia in 1839,
he moved west with the country as a whole, settling in California in
the early 1860s and soon making a name for himself in the newspaper
business. A return to the East Coast presented him with the puzzle that

the poor of older and more developed cities like New York had a harder lot than those of San Francisco and the other young cities of the West. His most influential work, *Progress and Poverty* (1879), explained this by linking inequality more to the control of land than to the exploitation of labor (as Marxists posited). "In spite of the increase of productive power," George concluded, "wages constantly tend to a minimum which will give but a bare living," because "with increase in productive power, rent tends to even greater increase, thus producing a constant tendency to the forcing down of wages." His solution was to tax land rather than the labor, machines, and capital that generated new wealth, since it was the unequal possession of real estate and the unearned wealth funneled to its owners that lay at the root of inequality. *Progress and Poverty* quickly sold more than three million copies. George even ran for mayor of New York City as the nominee of the United Labor Party, a contest he narrowly lost in 1886. His death in 1897 found him still a major figure in political and economic thought in the Western world, opposed by Marxists and conservative advocates of laissez-faire alike.[32]

Social inequality was George's great preoccupation. As he declared in *Progress and Poverty*, "So long as all the increased wealth which modern progress brings goes but to build up great fortunes, to increase luxury and make sharper the contrast between the House of Have and the House of Want, progress is not real and cannot be permanent." And for George as for so many others, it was the landscape of cities that embodied such inequality: "These vast aggregations of humanity, where he who seeks isolation may find it more truly than in the desert; where wealth and poverty touch and jostle; where one revels and another starves within a few feet of each other, yet separated by as great a gulf as that fixed between Dives in Hell and Lazarus in Abraham's bosom— they are centres and types of our civilization." Although his apparent lack of concern with the exhaustion of resources set him apart from early conservationists, George's insistence that nature was a key part of the story of inequality marked subsequent environmental thought. Even in a nation where a smaller and smaller portion of the population made its living from agriculture, the ownership of the key natural resource of land caused enormous disparities of wealth and opportunity. And he

The journalist and economic theorist Henry George, whose *Progress and Poverty* (1879) catapulted him to fame across the English-speaking world, pointing to the connections between urbanization, social inequality, and environmental destruction. *(Print Collection, Miriam and Ira D. Wallach Division of Art, Prints, and Photographs, New York Public Library, Astor, Lenox, and Tilden Foundations)*

meant to be capacious in his use of the word "land," which for him included "not merely the surface of the earth as distinguished from the water and the air, but the whole material outside of man himself . . . in short, all natural materials, forces, and opportunities."[33]

But nature was not just a storehouse of resources. Alienation from nature bore a cost, spiritual as well as material. "The vast populations of these great cities are utterly divorced from all the genial influences of nature," he wrote in 1883. "The great mass of them never, from year's end to year's end, press foot upon mother earth or pluck a wild flower, or hear the tinkle of brooks, the rustle of grain, or the murmur of leaves as the light breeze comes through the woods." The "House of Want" that economic development built "shut out" its inmates from the "sweet and joyous influences of nature." In cities, this meant that the wilder sounds "are drowned by the roar of the streets and the clatter of the people in the next room, or the next tenement, her sights shut out by tall buildings." It was all too easy for cities to leave their dwellers alienated from nature's majesty:

> Sun and moon rise and set, and in solemn procession the constellations move across the sky, but these imprisoned multitudes behold them only as might a man in a deep quarry. The white snow falls in winter, only to become dirty slush on the pavements, and as the sun sinks in summer, a worse than noonday heat is refracted from masses of brick and stone. Wisely have the authorities of Philadelphia labeled with its name every tree in their squares, for how else shall the children growing up in such cities know one tree from another, how shall they even know grass from clover?[34]

Those who could tell trees from one another and grass from clover faced their own environmental crises. George's environmental and social critique applied to the countryside as well. While he relied on the long-standing rhetorical contrast between an artificial, modern city and a more natural, potentially wholesome countryside, rural America was no timeless refuge from modernity: "Just as the wen or tumour drawing the wholesome juices of the body into its poisonous vortex impoverishes all other parts of the frame, so does the crowding of human beings into great cities impoverish human life in the country." There was both a material and spiritual dimension to this. Noting the thousands of cattle slaughtered every year in Chicago and New York, George urged his readers to "consider what this single item in the food supply of a great city suggests as to the elements of fertility, which, instead of being returned to the soil from which they come are swept out through the sewers of our great cities. The reverse of this is the destructive character of our agriculture, which is year by year decreasing the productiveness of our soil, and virtually lessening the area of land available for the support of our increasing millions." Moreover, just as in the city, modern economies caused spiritual as well as material problems for rural Americans. "Man is a gregarious animal," George reasoned. "He cannot live by bread alone." The social conditions of rural America brought with them the inverse of the problem of the cities: "If he suffers in body, mind, and soul from being crowded into too close contact with his fellows, so also does he suffer from being separated too far from them. The beauty and the grandeur of nature pall upon man where other men are not to be met; her infinite diversity becomes monotonous where there is not human companionship; his physical comforts are poor, and scant, his nobler powers languish; all that makes him higher than the animal suffers for want of the stimulus that comes from the contact of man with man." Just as in cities, helter-skelter urbanization unsettled the balance between a vibrant society and a productive and beautiful nature.[35]

Apocalypse Soon?

The diverse ways in which authors like George described a range of environmental problems also marked the doomsday scenarios that appeared in novels, the mass press, and more scholarly accounts.

George Perkins Marsh once again articulated what became a much more widespread preoccupation two generations later. *Man and Nature* (1864) included the sober verdict that the "earth is fast becoming an unfit home for its noblest inhabitant." Continued profligacy, he warned, "would reduce it to such a condition of impoverished productiveness, of shattered surface, of climatic excess, as to threaten the depravation, barbarism, and perhaps even extinction of the species." Later observers followed his line of argument in extrapolating from past and current localized environmental problems to a more generalized environmental destruction. For Marsh, this grim possible future could be seen in the past of "parts of Asia Minor, of Northern Africa, of Greece, and even of Alpine Europe, where the operation of causes set in action by man has brought the face of the earth to a desolation almost as complete as that of the moon." Similarly reasoning from a smaller area, the Southern California real estate developer and forestry advocate Abbot Kinney warned his readers in 1900 about the encroaching wasteland: "The desert is at our door today. It is pushing up against the mountain barrier that divides us. It is creeping up on the passes, north and east and conquering a corner how here, now there and even has footing on and inside our mountain wall." Reflecting on incidents of severe erosion and destructive flooding that he had witnessed since moving to Los Angeles two decades earlier,

Kinney found present glimpses of future catastrophe: "The deserts even now come into our lovely valleys for a few days, with their fire and furnace breath, to look at the rich booty they may some day hold." Still he held out hope, looking to the region's embattled forests as the "armies . . . steadfast and true to their posts," guarding "the rampart between our orchards, fields, flowers and cities and the frost and fire of the glittering wastes of the deserts of death."[36]

Marsh and Kinney notwithstanding, apocalyptic visions of the future rarely centered on environmental destruction alone. Just like the better remembered utopian tracts epitomized by Edward Bellamy's *Looking Backward: 2000–1887* (1888), prospective accounts of the destruction of the United States (or of civilization more broadly) dealt most often and most centrally with class divisions. Bellamy's portrayal of Boston more than a century in the future powerfully showed how suffering, class conflict, and competition could give way to universal prosperity delivered by cooperation and technological efficiency. Countless authors demonstrated how they might also lead to some form of Armageddon. Just as present-day Americans willingly spend hours of their lives watching and reading stories of how epidemic diseases, vampires, zombies, and aliens remake all that is, so too were Americans of the later nineteenth century transfixed by the prospect of annihilation.[37]

Some of these accounts were so successful in rendering anxieties associated with industrial civilization that they are still read today. H. G. Wells's *The Time Machine* (1895) captured both the power of technology and the depth of alienation in its story of time travel to a future Earth where social classes had evolved into two distinct branches of humanity, with the apelike descendants of the proletariat laboring underground and the listless progeny of the upper classes living in primitive communism amid the ruins of great cities. Jack London's *The Iron Heel* (1907) combined dream and nightmare in its account of a capitalist oligarchy—as seen from the twenty-ninth century, when it had finally been supplanted by a socialist state—that represented the culmination of the most coercive aspects of the Gilded Age's business class. The monopolies of the author's adult life had congealed into "The Oligarchy"; the Pinkerton detectives frequently employed to break strikes into "Mercenaries of the Oligarchy"; and the most menial laborers into "people of the abyss."

In one of the novel's central passages, the plutocratic dictatorship destroys the Commune of Chicago, slaughtering innumerable revolutionaries and civilians and razing much of the city in the process.[38]

London's depiction of a brutal capitalist dictatorship drew more explicit parallels between contemporary reality and a possible future than did many accounts. In general, however, the power of these dystopias originated in their depictions of a world their readers already knew. Many of the dark futures prophesied in these novels embodied the warnings of nonfiction writers and political movements about their own times and the future alike. The scenes of mobs of dispossessed workers locked into savage combat with the shock troops of the wealthy in *The Iron Heel* were extrapolations not only of clashes at Haymarket Square and the Pullman company, but also of the warnings of Henry George and others. Writing of the social conditions in London, Chicago, and their counterparts, George issued a stark warning about "these vast aggregations of humanity where he who seeks isolation may find it more truly than in the desert; where wealth and poverty touch and jostle; where one revels and another starves within a few feet of each other." Their enormous scope and sometimes-terrifying vigor masked a fragility: "Let jar or shock dislocate the complex and delicate organization, let the policeman's truncheon be thrown down or wrested from him, and the fountains of the great deep are opened and quicker than ever before chaos comes again. Strong as it may seem, our civilization is evolving destructive forces. Not desert and forest, but city slums and country roadsides are nursing the barbarians who may be to the new what Hun and Vandal were to the old."[39]

Other doomsday stories were still more directly connected with contemporary politics. The 1892 platform of the People's Party baldly declared that "we meet in the midst of a nation brought to the verge of moral, political, and material ruin." Warning darkly that "urban workmen are denied the right to organize for self-protection, [that] imported pauperized labor beats down their wages," and that "a hireling standing army, unrecognized by our laws, is established to shoot them down," the Populists contemplated the prospect of "terrible social convulsions, the destruction of civilization, or the establishment of an absolute despotism." Ignatius Donnelly, the Minnesota lawyer instrumental in crafting the Populist declaration, contemporaneously offered a fictional account of just such despotism and destruction. In his widely read novel *Caesar's Column* (1890), he presented a New York City of 1988 as a seeming high-tech utopia complete with an extensive subway system, universal lighting powered by the aurora borealis, abundant menus drawing from across the earth, and centralized heat and air. But the facade of abundance rested on brutal labor exploitation. A workers' revolt culminates in a worldwide battle with the forces of capital, leading to the destruction of New York and other cities. The protagonists look down from an airship upon a world burning in the fires of the class animosity and social anarchy of which the Populists warned.[40]

The terror in such accounts derived from the horrific nature of what some people or classes might do to others. In many of these stories, however, civilization met its end for environmental as well as social reasons. These presented environmental destruction as part of a wider social crisis, underscoring the sense of alarm that later justified conservation's political program and linking conservation closely with other Progressive reforms.

It is thus revealing that Ignatius Donnelly penned one of the most evocative depictions of environmental paradise lost in *Atlantis: The Antediluvian World* (1882). The book, which had sold out nearly fifty editions by 1890, made the case that Atlantis had been a real civilization whose glories and later destruction by flood inspired the biblical story of the deluge and other accounts of large-scale inundations across the world; in addition, surviving Atlanteans established colonies that grew into distinct civilizations. In his rendering, Atlantis epitomized a happy marriage of commercial prosperity and agrarian abundance. The products of sophisticated agriculture and horticulture were carried across the land on an elaborate canal system, providing a lush diet to the residents of towns and cities planted with "all manner of trees of wonderful height and beauty." Indeed, Donnelly maintained that "tree worship" had been practiced widely across the Americas and Europe. His account of a lost world of environmental and social harmony was "powerfully compelling for many Americans," writes the historian Aaron Sachs, "because a significant number of those millions who accepted the new industrial order nevertheless experienced a keen sense of loss." Donnelly sought to combat this sense not only through his writings, but also in politics by sponsoring tree-planting legislation and investigating sloppy and illegal harvesting by lumber companies, measures that would be taken up again decades later by conservationists.[41]

What caused the destruction of Atlantis? Donnelley attributed it to a cataclysmic flood—in his rendering, the very same event depicted in Genesis, Platonic dialogues, and Mesoamerican traditions. In this sense, despite Donnelly's deep ties to Populism and the connections that he drew between environmental and social harmony, his work partook of an earlier, pre-conservation sensibility in which humanity was more at the mercy of nature than vice versa. His depiction of a lost Eden carried with it no explicit Marshian sense that people were destroying their own future by way of environmental profligacy. Other seers of possible futures and glorious pasts, however, made the source of environmental apocalypse more central to their stories. The numerous Atlantean novels spawned by Donnelley's runaway success, for example, "tended to invoke the possibility of a new Armageddon, triggered by society's denial of nature." Thus the earthquakes and tidal waves that inundated Elizabeth Birkmaier's Atlantis novel, *Poseidon's Paradise: The Romance of Atlantis* (1892), came as punishment for the island civilization's hubris in seeking an "elixir of life," a quest that required draining the lifeblood of scores of women. Jules Verne's *Paris in the Twentieth Century* offered a more naturalistic portrayal of social-environmental disaster. Verne's Paris, like Donnelley's New York, epitomized the achievements of technological society, including what would now be called electric calculators, computers, automobiles, subways, and fax machines. This new civilization, however, was soulless, venerating banking and engineering. And all of its technical powers were not enough to save it from dramatic climate change: in 1961, winter brings temperatures so cold that agriculture is compromised, food supplies quickly dwindle, and mass starvation ensues. The novel ends with its protagonist, a frustrated poet, wandering through a Paris encased in ice, slowly freezing to death. As in Atlantis, or Henry George's America, the hubris of power and progress ultimately delivered impoverishment and environmental apocalypse.[42]

Although written in 1863, Verne's novel was not published until the 1990s, when its depiction of abrupt climate change bore an uncanny resemblance to climatologists' predictions that rising carbon dioxide levels would produce unexpected results, such as the cessation of the Gulf Stream. (Such scenarios spawned a new set of films and novels that centered on wholesale environmental destruction, including the 2004 movie *The Day After Tomorrow,* which portrayed the burial of New York under rapidly moving ice sheets and the flight of millions of American climate refugees to Mexico.) Other publications evoked sights that were familiar to millions of nineteenth-century readers. Writing in the radical reform journal *Arena* in 1890, Joseph Rodes Buchanan pointed to the connections between political disputes, labor conflicts, and natural disasters in his article "The Coming Cataclysm of America and Europe." Pointing to populist discontent and recent earthquakes and storms, he argued that "the crisis is much nearer" than it was represented in Donnelley's *Caesar's Column*. In his fantastical rendering, massive typhoons, earthquakes, tidal waves, and "a labor and capital war intermingled with a religious element of discord and with a mixture of the race question from the presence of a powerful negro element confronting the Caucasian negro-phobia" were sure to destroy much of Europe and the United States. The emergence of a "more thorough democracy," with the full emancipation of women and the alleviation of race and class oppression, would be some recompense for the misery and suffering produced by the cataclysm that Buchanan envisioned.[43]

Instructing his readers to "not ask me . . . how I have reached so positive a conclusion" about such matters as future earthquakes and tornados surely failed to inspire confidence in many of them. Yet Buchanan also pointed to real and immediate environmental problems, of the sort described and explained by George Perkins Marsh and his intellectual heirs. As in the writings of Henry George and Ignatius Donnelly, social crisis and environmental crisis went hand in hand, not metaphorically but directly. "As the destruction of forests goes on," Buchanan wrote, "our floods increase in power, and large regions are threatened with barrenness, as in the old world. . . . The American statesman had not yet learned that the woodman's axe is a far greater menace to our future than foreign cannon." Evidence for this proposition could be found in the "huge Mississippi," which "has already converted its shores into a vast inland sea . . . which may continually grow more and more disastrous as it has in China and Italy," argued Buchanan: "The Yangtse has become the scourge of China, overwhelming in its last flood three hundred and fifty thousand square miles, and near a million lives. The Mississippi is becoming our scourge." Just as he hoped that class confrontation would yield to a more just and harmonious society, so too did Buchanan claim to perceive, through the looming chaos of erosion, flood, earthquake, and storm, an era when "exhausted nature and exhausted humanity will then end their struggles." If social and environmental discord came together, so might social and environmental harmony.[44]

Causes

Convincing much of the public that the modern era faced grave environmental problems was one of the ways in which scientists and other intellectuals paved the way for the conservation movement. Trying to explain those problems was another. Of course, there was no single or straightforward "cause" of such diverse environmental events as catastrophic fires, depleted resources, razed forests, eroded fields, fouled water supplies, blighted cities, and the isolation of poor urbanites from anything resembling wild nature. But three central themes emerged in the discussion of these developments: the expansion of humans, with their increasingly powerful technologies and complicated institutions, into all corners of the continent and, indeed, the world; the profligate attitudes of Americans toward natural abundance; and the scope and power of the economy. These themes, present in a broad range of writings in the second half of the nineteenth century, shaped the measures that conservationists advocated to address environmental crises. The commitments to creating parks set aside from normal patterns of human use, to inculcating knowledge of and respect for wildness, and to regulating markets emerged not only from a widely shared sense of environmental crisis but also from explanations of this crisis.

To read accounts of forest fires or warnings of the depletion of game and timber in the later nineteenth century was to be presented with images of a voracious, buzzing horde of humanity, replete with draft animals, guns, steel tools, increasingly powerful engines, and an almost devilish ability to transform nature. This accidental yet well-equipped army of destruction spilled out across the continent. A Catholic priest stationed in northern Wisconsin described its advance into a boreal forest that once stretched as far as the eye could see. Farmers took advantage of dry spells to "enlarge their clearings, cutting down and burning the wood that stood in their way." Meanwhile, "hundreds of laborers employed the construction of a railroad had acted in like manner, availing themselves of both axe and fire to advance their work." In addition, the forest was transformed by those who exploited it with tools other than axes: "Hunters and Indians scour these forests continually, especially in the autumn season, at which time they ascend the streams for trout-fishing or disperse through the woods deer-stalking. At night they kindle a large fire wherever they may chance halt, prepare their suppers, then wrapping themselves their blankets, sleep peacefully, extended on the earth, knowing that the fire will keep at a distance any wild animals that may happen to range through the vicinity during the night." "In this way," he concluded, "the woods particularly in the fall, are gleaming everywhere with fires lighted by man."[45]

This description made it difficult to blame any single person or institution for the fires: when the wind blew across a landscape filled with such people and the fires they set, the woods would surely burn. Indeed, a systematic federal investigation into forest fires conducted after the conflagrations of 1871 offered a lengthy list of sources rather than the more focused sort of explanation that might have provided the basis for an effective fire-fighting policy. Almost all the fires reported by state officials within their jurisdictions were caused by humans rather than lightning. Only about a quarter were intentional, produced by farmers firing their pasture or woodlots, or (in less than a tenth of the total) "incendiary and malicious firing." The leading causes of the fires categorized as accidental in origin were agricultural practices (escaped brush fires), the "careless neglect of camp fires" by hunters, and the carelessness of "travelers, emigrants, explorers, pleasure parties &c. who thoughtlessly leave burning fires," as well as locomotive sparks, and charcoal burning.[46]

It seemed easier to explain the dwindling numbers of game fish, birds, and animals by blaming those who fired the guns and dragged the nets. Yet even here, numerous human activities contributed to adverse environmental change. Joel Allen's explanation of "wholesale" wildlife destruction pointed not so much to hunting as to the transformation of the landscape by agrarian settlement: "The removal of forests, the drainage of swamps and marshes, the conversion of wild lands into farms, and the countless changes incident to the settlement of a country, destroy the haunts and the means of subsistence of numerous forms of animal life, and practically result in their extermination over vast areas." New technologies exacerbated this: "Electric-light towers, light-houses and light-ships are also a fruitful and modern source of disaster to birds, particularly during their migrations, when, in thick weather, thousands upon thousands kill themselves by dashing against these alluring obstructions. Telegraph wires contribute also largely the destruction of bird life." Allen's observations on the destructive side of agricultural settlement reflected the abiding influence of George Perkins Marsh, whose warnings about the destruction sometimes brought by progress were regularly quoted in New England and agrarian newspapers throughout the late nineteenth century.[47]

The collective impression conveyed by these sorts of accounts was of a continent rapidly filling up with people and their inventions. Consistent with the Turnerian idea of a closing frontier, this sensibility resonated beyond the United States and North America. The historian Rosalind Williams points to moments when "even slow changes may quite suddenly crystallize into events of consciousness, when individuals recognize the extent and significance of human domination of the planet." For her, the late nineteenth century was one such moment for European writers such as Jules Verne, William Morris, and Robert Louis Stevenson, who wrote in the shadow of "the realization that soon the entire globe would be mapped." While not entirely repudiating the values that had enabled Western nations to extend the grasp of their societies across the globe, these writers searched for an escape from human dominion, whether in the realm of the genres of what would now be called science fiction and fantasy, in a re-creation of the medieval world, and sometimes (as with Morris's socialism) in politics. Conservation was similarly marked by a deep sense of living through a new historical moment in which the negative consequences and inescapability of human dominion had become undeniable.[48]

The number of people occupying almost all the continent and the powerful technologies that they brought with them explained some of the numerous environmental problems, but so too did the attitudes toward nature that they carried with them. Thus reasoned the pioneering forest scientist Franklin Hough and many other writers. Trying to explain the wave of forest fires of the 1870s, Hough pointed to the vices of the "unstable and transient class" that lived in the recently settled districts of the West. These pioneers were "accustomed to regard the world around them as open for their use," he wrote, "and in matters of pasturage for their stock, as well as forest products for their own supply . . . they often appropriate wherever it is most convenient." The celebration of the frontier's role in shaping American democracy, which was a dominant motif in the writings of Frederick Jackson Turner and others, did not necessarily lead to an appreciation of settlers themselves: the frontier, after all, was supposed to give way to a more settled, cultivated, and modern society. The ethos of backwoods residents, Hough argued, meant that "it is from this class of our population that we have the most to fear in the way of forest fires." Particularly because of their apparent belief in the rights of possession and use rather than of ownership, they routinely set blazes: "Habitually careless and improvident, they do not hesitate, where there is a motive and an opportunity, to apply fires to lands not their own, for the purpose of improving and extending the range for their cattle, or to clear lauds for cultivation, and sometimes to destroy the evidences of their own trespass and depredations." Writing a decade before Turner, Hough portrayed the frontier in nearly opposite terms: it produced anarchy rather than social democracy. The frontier was more curse than blessing. Hough's argument implied that individual settlers could not be entrusted with nature, that laissez-faire resulted in environmental degradation.[49]

Yet it was not only the supposedly ignorant residents of the backcountry who carried with them destructive attitudes. Joel Allen was just as irate as Hough, but focused his disapproval on the habits of the respectable classes and their children, declaring:

> Many song birds are killed "for sport" by the "small boy" and idler whose highest ambition in life is to possess a gun, and whose "game" may be any wild animal that can run or fly,

and wears fur or feathers. Some slight depredation on the small fruits of garden or on field crops is ample pretext for war of extermination on robins, catbirds, and thrashers, jays, and chewinks, as well as blackbirds and crows, and the birds so unfortunate as to fall into the category of hawks and owls, notwithstanding the fact that every one of these species is in reality a friend.

Particularly irritating to him was the "bad small boy" who resided in "both town and country": "Bird-nest robbing is one of the besetting sins—one of the marks of 'natural depravity'—of the average small boy, who fails to appreciate the cruelty of systematically robbing every nest within reach, and of stoning those are otherwise inaccessible." Here, environmental profligacy joined original sin in a kind of theology of conservation.[50]

Many writers pointed to the general expansion of the human realm and its inhabitants' profligate attitudes as underlying causes of multiple environmental problems. Some offered a more specific explanation, pointing not just to the attitudes of a growing population, but also to the power of markets to transform and consume nature. In so doing, they paved the way for the deep suspicion of untrammeled markets that would mark the conservation movement and Progressivism as a whole.

Henry George's explanation of what he saw as a new era typified the historical consciousness of these authors. "There is in all the past nothing to compare with the rapid changes now going on in the civilized world," he wrote in *Social Problems* (1883). Pointing to many developments—the growing concentration of wealth, labor unrest, frequent unemployment and economic crises, the flight from the countryside, the rapid (and his view unsustainable) rate of urbanization—George identified the "rapid changes" of industrial capitalism as the underlying cause. "The snail's pace of crawling ages," he continued, "has suddenly become the headlong rush of the locomotive, speeding faster and faster. This rapid progress is primarily in industrial methods and material powers." But it reverberated in many aspects of social and political life, since "industrial changes imply social changes and necessitate political changes."[51]

The "political changes" that George proposed centered on the taxation of land values, whose increase he saw as the product of society as a whole, and whose unearned acquisition by landowners he saw as a primary creator of economic and political inequality. The "action of the new industrial forces in social conditions not adapted to them" caused what George considered an "unnatural distribution of population" in a hollowed-out countryside and an overpopulated urban sector, just as those forces caused "that unnatural distribution of wealth which gives one man hundreds of millions and makes other men tramps." The diagnosis led to the cure: with a universal tax on the increase in land values, the government would create an incentive for true industry and labor rather than idle profit through rent, as well as "a new surplus which society might take for general purposes." After the implementation of the single tax, there "would ensue a natural distribution of population which would give every one breathing space and neighbourhood."[52]

Urban development, land prices, and regulation lay at the heart of George's political economy and policy proposals. Moreover, he applied the principles of his thought broadly, including to questions of game preservation, which would become important aspects of early conservationist thought and legislation. Recognizing "the common right to land" could lead to environmental sustainability as well as social equity. Writing of fur seals in the Aleutian Islands off the coast of Alaska, George argued that allowing unlimited fishing would soon eliminate the hapless and easily killed (but extremely valuable) animals. The much better alternative was to keep the islands as part of the public domain, where in fact they had remained since the purchase of Alaska from Russia. The islands were leased to the Alaska Fur Company, an arrangement that had "already yielded two millions and a half to the national treasury" and kept the fishery "in unimpaired value (for under the careful management of the Alaska Fur Company the seals increase rather than diminish), the common property of the people of the United States."[53]

Many of George's contemporaries shared his concern about the environmental impacts of unfettered markets, even if they often shied away from his condemnation of inequality or the aggressive remedies that he proposed. The influential forester Bernhard Fernow, for example, focused narrowly on the question of rational and sustainable management of woodland resources, eschewing the engagement with broad questions of class and wealth that animated Henry George. Trained for a year by the forest service of his native Prussia, Fernow advised private landowners before becoming chief of the U.S. Department of Agriculture's Division of Forestry and then going on to found a short-lived forestry school at Cornell University. Yet the genteel and cautious bureaucrat shared much of the firebrand George's explanation for the era's mounting environmental crises. On one hand, building on George Perkins Marsh, Fernow argued that "the natural resources of the earth have in all ages and in all countries . . . been squandered by man with a wanton disregard of the future." Fernow found this destructiveness to be "natural" in the absence of state ownership or regulation, since "private enterprise . . . has only one aim in the use of these resources, namely, to obtain from them the greatest possible personal and present gain." He was caustic about Americans' attitudes toward natural resources such as timber and water, damning the "careless and extravagant use of them" and the "neglect to which they are abandoned as soon as the cream is taken." Drawing on Turnerian notions of the frontier, he also allowed that this was "simply characteristic of all pioneering populations," whose low population density amid natural abundance encouraged profligacy. On the other hand, recent economic developments had exacerbated this long-standing dynamic. With Americans, "the pioneering stage fell into a period when the invention and development of railroad transportation intensified the disproportion of population and resources, opening up new territory and making virgin supplies available more rapidly than the needs of a resident population required." The result was a particularly "destructive competition in the attempts to profit from . . . rapacious exploitation and exportation."[54]

Fernow elaborated on his general theory of environmental destructiveness in his field of specialization, forestry. In *The Economics of Forestry*, he methodically traced the dramatic increase "in the volume and character of the business of forest exploitation" from the 1840s to the last years of the century. The more than 30,000 mills at the start of his period produced slightly over $400 annually per mill and generally "sawed for home consumption, or sent material to the mouth of the river to be carried by vessel to home and foreign markets." The mills became fewer in number—declining to some 21,000 by 1890—but larger, with an average product of $6,500 in 1870 and $19,000 in 1890. They were also more efficient, fifty times more so by his calculations. Yet what might be praiseworthy from a different perspective—the application of improved engineering, capital flow, and market integration to the production of a key good—was as much a problem as a triumph. The nation's timber mills, tied into an increasingly seamless international market, were powerful enough to consume all its trees. Fernow meticulously demonstrated that the capital invested in the industry was by the century's end increasing more rapidly than the lumber that it produced. So with the prices of raw lumber increasing, and returns to labor and capital decreasing, all signs by 1900 were "pointing to the deterioration and exhaustion of supplies."[55] He thus conveyed a message echoing the title of Henry George's most widely read work: progress and poverty.

What Fernow did for the lumber industry, others did for different natural resources. William Temple Hornaday, for example, broadened out from his early work on bison preservation to sound the alarm about threats to wildlife in general. He held an even lower view of Americans' attitudes toward natural abundance than did Fernow. Surveying the extinctions and mounting game shortages of the nineteenth century, Hornaday attributed "the appalling destruction of wildlife" to "greed, slothfulness, and ignorance." But like Henry George, Hornaday pointed to the power of markets to dramatically accelerate the slaughter. He opened a series of lectures at the Yale School of Forestry, later published as *Wild Life Conservation in Theory and Practice* (1914), on precisely this note: "The industrial development of the United States has wrought so many sweeping changes from conditions of the past that the American people are fairly compelled to adjust their minds in conformity with the new conditions." For Hornaday, one of the most pressing "new conditions" was the extraordinary power of markets to decimate populations of wild animals. When the United States was still a rural and agrarian nation, an assumption that wildlife was indestructibly abundant was understandable: "Throughout every state, on every shore line, in all the millions of fresh lakes, ponds, and rivers, on every mountain range, in every forest—aye even in every desert,—the wild flocks and herds held sway. It was impossible to go beyond the haunts of civilized man and escape them."[56]

But by the century's end, the market created by "civilized man" was virtually everywhere. Cataloguing the extinctions of the passenger pigeon, great auk, Labrador duck, and other species, Hornaday urged that "it be remembered for all time" that "*no wild species of mammal or bird can withstand systematic slaughter for commercial purposes.*" The efficiency of modern firearms and the scope of markets meant that his dictum applied "to all wild animals that are killed for their skins or their oil, all birds that are killed for their plumage of their flesh, and all game fishes that are taken for sale." Any animal targeted by "commercial interests" in the new century could "be exterminated . . . in twenty years time, or less." In the face of this stark modern reality, the belief "that the resources of nature are inexhaustible" could only be pernicious, because "it helps to salve the conscience of the man who commits high crimes against wild beasts and birds and forests." The unprecedented power of markets meant that humanity was living in a new historical era that demanded a new environmental understanding.[57]

A Web, Not a Tree

Sixty years after Hornaday delivered his sober message, another era of ferment in American politics was under way. As protests against racism and the Vietnam War roiled cities and campuses, more and more Americans looked to environmental questions as aspects of national policy and culture in need of reform. With oil coating their seashores, the bald eagle teetering on the brink of extinction, rivers catching fire, and the specter of nuclear war looming, environmentalists wondered whether the American past might provide inspiration and guidance. How did some of their predecessors recognize problems and spur their contemporaries to solve them? Recent figures such as the scientists Aldo Leopold and the nature writer Rachel Carson were obviously relevant, but so too were activists and thinkers from the more distant past, especially Henry David Thoreau, John Muir, and Gifford Pinchot. The iconoclastic Thoreau's rejection of materialism and validation of the West as a landscape of freedom spoke to their own rejection of stifling conventions, and the success of Muir and Pinchot in securing federal protection for iconic places and important natural resources seemed like an obvious model for some of their own efforts. Like activists for labor, civil rights, and women, environmentalists could see themselves as the bearers of an honorable tradition.

Resurgent environmentalism inspired historians to write about traditions of American environmental thought and reform. It also structured how they did so, encouraging them to draw straight lines between past and present in a discrete environmental tradition: Ralph Waldo Emerson begat Henry David Thoreau, who begat John Muir, who begat Edward Abbey; George Perkins Marsh begat Gifford Pinchot, who begat Paul Ehrlich. A closer examination of the intellectual precursors of conservation, however, reveals a web more than a tree, multiple lines of overlapping influence rather than linear genealogies. A wide range of writers and scientists argued on different counts that industrial humanity had created for itself a new era of environmental crisis. They saw signs of this crisis everywhere—scarce game, burning woods, flooding rivers, foul cities, and the prospect of full-scale environmental apocalypse. Some, like Marsh, thought of the natural world as their primary subject, but others, like Henry George, addressed alienation from nature as part of what they saw as the social tensions created by industrial capitalism. Most of these thinkers pointed to the power of markets to transform both nature and society, although they differed sharply on how an agrarian republic could maintain its ostensible commitments to economic independence and political liberty in an increasingly urban, industrial, and corporate future. In the twentieth century, their ideas would inform a movement that fervently hoped to solve the problems they had identified.

T • W • O

Landscapes of Reform

An exhilarated Enos Mills strode to the podium in the packed First Baptist Church in downtown Atlanta in early 1908. The Colorado outdoorsman and conservationist was in the midst of his second year as a lecturer for the infant U.S. Forest Service. Mills's persona was more prophetic than bureaucratic: his chiseled and weathered face, bald head with scraggly hair trailing in back, plain outdoors clothes, and minimalist diet evoked a backcountry preacher rather than a government clerk pushing papers across a desk. For more than a year, Mills had barnstormed the country, from New England to the South, the Midwest, and the West Coast, ultimately giving more than two thousand orations to audiences gathered in private homes, municipal auditoriums, courthouse steps, union halls, fraternal lodges, schools, and colleges. He had come to Atlanta at the invitation of the Appalachian Forestry Association. Joined by the Atlanta Chamber of Commerce and the Atlanta and Georgia Federation of Women's Clubs, the association had assembled numerous delegates from a dozen southern states, in large part to agitate for an expansion of the national forest system into New England's White Mountains and the southern Appalachians. Telegrams from President Theodore Roosevelt and the head of the Forest Service, Gifford Pinchot, were read to the delegates, but it was left to Mills to make the case for the expansion directly.[1]

What would the United States look like in fifty years? Like so many

Progressives, Mills depicted a utopian future in order to push his audience to consider the consequences of their choices. He was addressing practical, hardheaded business and political leaders drawn mostly from the South, whose governing class viewed political reform and the legitimacy of an active federal government with greater skepticism than did its counterpart in any other part of the nation. So Mills was sure to emphasize the practical, material benefits that fifty years of forestry could bring. In his vision of America in 1958, national forests were profitably harvested every year, generating a revenue stream for the federal treasury even as they provided the building materials for an ever increasing national population. The science of forestry was so advanced and well funded that areas such as the Dakota Badlands, lost to desert at the dawn of the century, now sprouted young trees that would soon be ready for sustainable harvesting. Widely supported and enjoyed by the American people, forests provided other benefits as well. The water they absorbed and slowly released fed prosperous family farms, buffered them from drought, and sheltered them from violent winds. The reforested and carefully tended national landscape was no longer devastated by the forest fires and floods that the environmental profligacy of the nineteenth century had made so common and unstoppable.

Besides being a paying proposition, forestry was a virtuous one, so Mills invoked the aesthetic and cultural benefits of decades of forestry. The grandchildren of his audience members would be modern and sophisticated, but nonetheless would want to spend much of their time out of doors. Pursuing their "tree-love" and tending to their physical health would be expedited by the "excellent and artistic systems of roads and trails" that would connect cities to forests and open up forests to visitors. The mysterious canyons, high peaks, dark woods, and flowery meadows would attract travelers from across the country and from Europe. Such habitual outdoor recreation would transform both nature and culture: birds would become so accustomed to humans that "one of the pretty common pictures in the forest [would be] children and birds playing together," even as the woods would inspire "immortal poems" and fill "many grand books with strength . . . and . . . majesty."[2]

Mills's utopian vision embodied many of the elements of conservation in the early twentieth century. His sensibility reflected a broad cultural and political program that sought to address what he and so many others understood as an environmental crisis. Mills came as the agent of the federal government to urge the expansion of his employer's power and reach, but he pleaded as much for cultural renewal as for legislative action. He thought that the scientific management of resources and lands would foster both wealth and beauty in places where they already resided and in newly rehabilitated landscapes alike. He assumed that the United States was marching relentlessly toward an urban, industrial future. Yet in his America of the 1950s, urbanites like those in Atlanta would recognize their continuing material dependence on nature even as they reestablished the direct contact with the nonhuman world that their pioneer and rural ancestors had taken for granted. His mention of the prosperous farms made possible by well-tended forests promised the continuation of economic opportunity and even independence for a large portion of the population, a note that other conservationists would sound even more loudly. Mills's optimism showed forth in the generally utopian cast of his remarks, but also in the confidence he had that his diverse audiences—women and men, rural and urban, business and labor, northern and southern—could all find a reason to join his crusade for conservation.

By the time of Mills's speech, which prompted a standing ovation and garnered more support for the ultimately successful bill creating new national forests, the word "conservation" had become shorthand for a robust political program with different but overlapping principles. The transcendent beauty of nature, particularly in its wildest and least tamed faces, deeply moved most conservationists. As did the need to use timber, water, grass, soil, and other resources wisely so that there would plenty for the prosperity of future generations. State power would be one of the means to these ends, by preserving and creating places of refuge and drawing on scientific knowledge to ensure that resources were used with a restraint that the unregulated market could not muster. Grassroots pressure was another means to these ends: an enlightened and engaged citizenry, inspired by the majesties of nature but sobered by humanity's unprecedented ability to destroy, would insist that its government do so. The results, if conservationists had their way in reality, as in Enos Mills's forested utopia, would be seen everywhere: clean cities dotted with parks that evoked the landscape out of which they grew, private homes on lots landscaped along similar lines, prosperous farms and rural settlements, wild parks and forests to provide recreation and sustainable flows of natural resources.

Subsequent events forced Mills to recognize that some of these commitments conflicted with one another. Damming up a valley for a municipal reservoir, for example, might make economic sense even if it destroyed a majestic natural space. The lives of industrial workers and the needs of the urban masses for nature mattered greatly to some of his compatriots, but hardly at all to others. Conservationists came in different stripes. As Mills would discover, they could end up arguing as much with one another as with their enemies. The future he depicted in Atlanta, however, nevertheless represented a coherent solution to the menacing psychic and physical threats of the environmental crisis created by rapid industrialization. Employed by a young federal agency, backed by a charismatic president, and bolstered by the enthusiasm that his speeches evoked in many different quarters, Enos Mills was sure conservation would remake the nation.

Remaking Cities

On its surface, conservation seemed to be concerned principally with the least populated and remotest stretches of the nation. That is indeed how most historians have written about the subject. Lightly settled and rarely traversed mountains and forests were valuable as camping places and timber lots. The majority of the national population, having moved from farms and small towns to cities, and still centered in the East and Midwest, did not visit such places or even live particularly close to them. At the same time, cities and the conditions of urban life deeply shaped conservation. As Henry George and others had argued, the powerful economic forces that gave rise to burgeoning cities deprived urbanites of regular contact with the sights, sounds, and smells of nature. Much of conservation's political program—or its aesthetic or romantic side, at least—was designed to address this deprivation by ensuring that places of natural refuge would remain. Many conservationists took this a step further to propose ways of restoring and preserving nature within cities.

The activism and writings of two figures, Mira Lloyd Dock and Dana Bartlett, embodied the urban aspects of conservation. Born shortly before the Civil War in the East (Dock in Pennsylvania, Bartlett in Maine), both were drawn into social reform circles by their concerns about public health, business monopolies, urban beauty, and the depletion of natural resources. Dock's early adulthood was spent managing her father's household and raising her younger siblings after her mother's early death. In her forties, however, she pursued formal training in environmental sciences—something quite rare for women—studying forestry in Germany and botany at the University of Michigan in the 1890s. This training ensured her credibility with male civic and business leaders and with the women's club leadership in Pennsylvania, which sent her to national club conventions as their representative on the forestry committee. She served on Pennsylvania's State Forestry Commission and lent energetic support to a plan to bring systematic street paving, sewage treatment, and drinking water protection to her native Harrisburg.

Dana Bartlett followed a different trajectory into Progressive activism. He became a Congregationalist minister early in life, tending to flocks in Iowa and Utah before moving to Los Angeles in 1896. There he founded and ran the Bethlehem Institute, which provided educational programming and social services to a heavily immigrant and working-class population, on the model of Jane Addams's famous Hull-House, where he had worked while studying at the Chicago Theological Seminary. Both were active in a variety of progressive and reform causes through the 1920s.[3]

Both reached wide audiences with their lectures and writings. Bartlett published three extended works: *The Better City* (1907), *The Better Country* (1911), and *The Bush Aflame* (1923), all of which discussed conservation in the larger context of Progressive concerns such as municipal ownership of utilities, antimonopoly measures, labor and safety law reforms, and the integration of immigrants into American society. In addition to regularly giving lectures on botany, forestry, and city beautification, Dock published more than a dozen articles on natural history, plants and trees of the Northeast, and forestry practices in the influential magazine *Garden and Forest*. Subtitled "A Journal of Horticulture, Landscape Art, and Forestry," this weekly magazine was pub-

Mira Lloyd Dock (1853–1945), *above,* and Dana Bartlett (1860–1942), *right,* championed the need for urban environmental reform. *(Pennsylvania State Archive and Charles Lummis,* Out West *[1910])*

lished in New York from 1888 until the 1897 death of its editor, William Stiles; much of the financial support and editorial guidance came from a group of Bostonians headed by Charles Sargent, the botanist director of Harvard's arboretum. Dock was in good company: other contributors included the agricultural reformer Liberty Hyde Bailey, prominent landscape architects such as Wilhelm Miller and Charles Eliot, and the founding head of the U.S. Forest Service, Gifford Pinchot.[4]

Dock and Bartlett were advocates of what the historian Shen Hou has called the "City Natural." To be sure, their speeches and writings reflected differences between the regions where they lived: while Dock's central preoccupation was with restoring an urban landscape already marked by decades of industrial development, waste, and pollution, Bartlett cast himself as a westerner intent on preventing Los Angeles and other younger cities from following the path of eastern and midwestern towns. But both the Angeleno and the Pennsylvanian were united in their belief that urban residents' isolation from nature was harmful and could be overcome by changing the design and physical form of cities and by protecting and making accessible remoter, wilder nature. Bartlett opened *The Better City* with an idyllic description of a past California free of the pressures of commercial and urban life. This past was irrecoverable, but nature could still be a refuge from and antidote to city living. His own vantage on the challenges confronting Los Angeles, which he expected to grow in size and population for the foreseeable future, drew on his idea of the city: "[It is] a holy sanctuary, high up in the mother mountains, under a spreading sycamore tree, with the maple, the oak and the spruce as its companions. The walls of this nature's sanctuary are lined with ferns and moss and beautiful flowers. The squirrels and the birds in the bush are of more value than their caged fellows in the city park. The babbling of the mountain brook is nature's own medicine for tired nerves. Slow of heart, indeed, is he who cannot recognize the imminent God in the life and voices around him."[5]

Bartlett held a vision of his adopted city in which all its residents would meet this "imminent God." "There is so little in a great city that speaks of the spiritual," he continued, "but on the mountain top it seems to press in at every pore. You can draw it in at every breath. You can dip down deep into the great ocean of spiritual power and be made strong.

The writer longs for such changes in our economic life, that all the city workers may have this opportunity of becoming acquainted with 'our brothers and sisters, the birds,' and receive this mountain-top inspiration for the better life." Not all urban conservationists used his explicitly deist invocation, but they shared Bartlett's goal of giving urbanites respite from an entirely human-made environment. Mira Dock spoke of flowers and trees rather than God and spiritual power. The "Botanical Talks" that she started delivering in the 1890s embedded a discussion of native plants and their study within a larger consideration of the "means by which they may be protected and preserved from extinction in thickly settled communities," implying that nature's splendors ought to be fostered and admired close at hand, not just far away. Dock's fellow Pennsylvanian and frequent collaborator Horace McFarland, whose American Civic Association promoted urban beautification across the country, sounded a similar note in the *Sierra Club Bulletin*. Asking his readers to "consider wealthy Pittsburg, busy Cincinnati, proud Chicago, with their wasteful smoke, their formless streets, their all-pervading billboards and grime," he argued that in "parks lies the answer . . . for it is incontrovertible that peace and health and good order are best fostered in the parks including the most natural scenic beauties."[6]

Conservationists of McFarland's stripe pinned much of their hopes on parks. Great commercial metropolises could and should incorporate large parks as part of their urban fabric and their citizens' daily lives. The Boston journalist and utopian socialist Sylvester Baxter, for example, advocated both the creation of a metropolitan government that would transcend the growing urban region's divided and balkanized municipalities, and the creation of an accompanying metropolitan park system. A devotee of Edward Bellamy's *Looking Backward*, Baxter insisted that nature ought to be part of a more humane urban future (an insistence almost entirely absent from Bellamy). In 1893, Baxter cautioned Bostonians that "acres and acres of streets and houses" filled places "where a few years ago were only pastures and woodland." Without aggressive park planning, Boston would become "a vast desert of houses, factories, and stores, spreading over and overwhelming the natural features of the landscape." Writing in *Garden and Forest,* he laid particular emphasis on the value of woodlands situated with "the densely populated and bustling city close at hand." Los Angeles should take better care of its existing parks, Dana Bartlett similarly argued, acquire new ones, and hire a nationally renowned urban planner such as Frederick Law Olmsted Jr., Charles Robinson, or Daniel Burnham to draw up a comprehensive plan for a metropolitan park system. He was particularly enthusiastic about the potential of the Los Angeles River to serve as a "line of beauty" uniting much of the city. If "placed under a special commission empowered to carry out a definite plan for its reclamation from base uses," the river could be spanned by beautiful bridges and lined with "a pleasant promenade beautifully lighted at night by light clusters on ornamental posts, forming a natural boulevard that might reach even to the sea." Nearby factories and warehouses could "be hidden behind a wealth of climbing vines and roses."[7]

Urban parks blossomed in this period, thanks in part to the ideas of urban conservationists such as Mira Lloyd Dock, Sylvester Baxter, and Dana Bartlett. There were no managed urban parks in 1850, but by century's end, of the 157 cities with more than 30,000 residents, all but one had a park. Moreover, these parks were more evocative of wild nature than were their predecessors. Urban park design became more naturalistic as designers aimed to evoke nearby ecosystems by choosing native plants in natural associations rather than relying on geometric forms, formally delineated playing spaces, and gymnastic and playground equipment. Prominent landscape architects, especially those such as Ossian Cole Simonds and Jens Jensen from the Midwest, articulated the principles and practices aimed to make the golf courses, subdivisions, parks, and estates they designed appear "to be the work of nature alone, untouched by human hands." Simonds, whose designs provided for minimal tree and shrub pruning, and who often insisted that leaves not be raked, wanted his creations to evoke the "charm which we feel when we go to the woods" and the "uncultivated prairies which glow with wild sunflowers, asters, and goldenrod." "In a word, we have turned our backs on the artificial and are grasping eagerly for the natural," summarized one observer of landscape architecture, "because that alone can satisfy the wants and secret yearnings of populations cabined, cribbed and confined for six days out of every seven within the walls of the work-shop or the city's narrow streets."[8]

In the early twentieth century, landscape architects increasingly modeled parks after natural landscapes, as suggested in Jens Jensen's photograph of a midwestern prairie stream in 1911, *above,* and his re-creation of it in Chicago's Humboldt Park, *below. (Courtesy of the Sterling Morton Library, Morton Arboretum)*

Boston's park system was widely considered the most ambitious and successful in urban environmental circles. Within a decade of its creation in 1893, the city's Metropolitan Park Commission—Sylvester Baxter's brainchild—controlled almost sixteen square miles of land, most of it wooded. The commission routinely destroyed remaining houses, farmhouses, and work buildings in the parks, fostering the impression that the parks represented untouched nature surrounded by a dynamic modern city. The Los Angeles businessman and philanthropist Griffith J. Griffith, whose three-thousand-acre gift to his city became a large park named after him, extolled Boston for integrating this style of park into a system of large, connected, accessible, and wilder parks. "It is apparent that Boston's aim has not been to furnish her citizens with set and artificial gardens, as was the ancient fashion," he wrote, "but to bring them into immediate touch with nature, placing at their disposal a vast range of mountain, sea and river scenery, amid which they may roam at will. In other words, a genuine effort has been made to offset the admittedly deteriorating effect of congested urban life."[9]

Much of the appeal of Boston's system lay in the fact that its reach extended well beyond the developed portions of the city. Conservationists motivated by a desire to alleviate the conditions of urban life looked outside the city as well as within it. The countryside was important to urban-oriented conservation both as an idyllic retreat and as the source of critical natural resources such as clean water. As Mira Lloyd Dock wrote in 1910 on the occasion of Arbor Day, "We need not only play-grounds and parks, but we need woods,—great, wide, far-reaching woods . . . the hunter becomes more primal; the strong gain greater strength and clearer purpose; the weary soul achieves serenity." Griffith J. Griffith, Dana Bartlett, and other supporters of a robust park system for Los Angeles were also deeply committed to preserving and making more accessible the San Gabriel Mountains looming to the city's north. One of the principal advantages of Los Angeles, Bartlett believed, was that the "workers in the mill and the toilers in the factories" had the "opportunity of entering the silences of the mountains and there hear the still small voice that cannot be heard in the noise and rush of modern commercialism." Mountains and canyons lay "within easy reach of rich and poor alike, by trolley or car," and ought to be preserved as something of a city common. Most cities, unlike Los Angeles, were ringed by farm fields, pastures, and orchards rather than mountains and forests, so their residents had to go farther to find the succor lauded by Bartlett and his compatriots. The citizens of Boston, New York, Philadelphia, and other northeastern cities—or at least those who had the time and money—turned to the woods and mountains of Vermont, New Hampshire, and Maine for their respite, a task made easier by the dense railroad network that made what was once an arduous journey by carriage or horseback into a comfortable and possibly even luxurious weekend jaunt. Wealthy and influential citizens of these cities, in turn, played key roles in protecting their vacation hinterlands from deforestation. Organizations devoted to the protection of Vermont and New Hampshire forests, founded around 1900, regularly included prominent New Yorkers, Philadelphians, and Bostonians in leadership positions.[10]

These metropolitan networks of conservation reflected how forests and mountains had become hinterlands of recreation, places where, in a sense, nature was consumed by tourism and hiking. Metropolitan integration also operated on a material level, in which nature could be managed to produce critical resources. Securing clean water for cooking, washing, and drinking was one of the leading practical challenges facing cities in the late nineteenth century. Industrial and human waste in cities of any appreciable size fouled the wells, ponds, streams, and rivers that earlier residents had relied upon. Starting with Philadelphia in 1801, cities began to build municipal water systems. By 1890, nearly three-quarters of American cities had large-scale water supplies, either public or private. These generally worked by taking clean water from upstream portions of a river flowing through the city (the Schuylkill, in the case of Philadelphia) or another source and then pumping it high enough to flow into the city's heart, where it was again pumped up a water tower to be distributed under pressure to mains and taps. Waterworks thus linked the health and cleanliness of city residents to the conditions around the water source.[11]

Most recognized the necessity of keeping these sources free from industry and residential development in order to minimize pollution and contamination. By the 1880s, however, new understandings of the connection between forests and waterways prompted many city officials to think more extensively about their entire watersheds. Drawing on George Perkins Marsh's widely read account of the impact of deforestation on rivers and springs, foresters in the late nineteenth century urged the preservation or reforestation of extensive tracts as a means of protecting the quality and increasing the quantity of water. Such was the rationale for the Forest Law of 1882 in Massachusetts, which allowed municipalities to buy or condemn land inside their corporate limits in order to protect forests or water supplies, and for New York's creation of an upstate forest preserve in 1885. Similarly, Abbot Kinney in 1900 titled his treatise on American and California forestry *Forest and Water.* He listed "the guarding of water-sheds as natural forest reservoirs to secure perennial flow of springs and streams" as a key goal of professional forestry, second in importance only to the production of a renewable timber crop. This aspiration led city leaders to support the creation of state and federally managed forests in their cities' hinterlands, perhaps most notably in Pennsylvania, where the protection of municipal water supplies justified the creation of more than three million acres of forest preserves. Theodore Parker Lukens of Southern California similarly made the interdependence of city and forested hinterland the centerpiece of his 1915 tract *Forestry in Relation to City Building.*[12]

If too little water could be a problem, then so could too much: particularly in the arid West, sporadic torrential downpours combined with shallow soil and scarce ground cover to produce devastating urban floods. "A denuded water-shed delivers the rainfall on it suddenly and always with detritus, such as sand, gravel, and boulders," warned Kinney, invoking a threat that would have been familiar to any reader of George Perkins Marsh. Kinney pointed out how damaging these deluges could be for agriculture, particularly the kind based on irrigation systems that could be wrecked by such debris and heavy flows, but cautioned "city people" that "no part of the community stands in more immediate and greater danger from forest destruction" than cities themselves.[13]

In the Countryside

The mix of aesthetic and material concerns that drove urban-oriented conservation similarly marked the push to bring vast tracts of rural

America under state environmental supervision. This quest came to be so closely identified with conservation, especially as a set of federal policies, that it would later stand for the whole of the movement in popular memory and much scholarship, obscuring its more polyglot urban preoccupations and adherents. In some measure, this later eclipse of urban conservation was the product of the tremendous charisma and influence of John Muir and Gifford Pinchot. Neither man had much to say about the environmental circumstances of city life, but along with Theodore Roosevelt, they were the most nationally known conservationists, and the ones who would leave the largest imprint on the countryside.

Little in John Muir's early life suggested that he would become the romantic prophet of wild places, the wide-eyed bard who sang to Americans of the majesty of nature untamed. Born in Dunbar, Scotland, in 1838, Muir came to America at age eleven with his family and soon settled on a farm in central Wisconsin. His boyhood was marked by the physical demands of farm labor and the psychological challenges of an austere and unforgiving Protestantism. A few years at the University of Wisconsin—particularly his friendship with Jeanne Carr and her husband, Professor Ezra Carr, then the university's only scientist—deepened his fusion of a scientific and romantic understanding of nature. But Muir was not on a straight path to environmental sainthood. Working in an Indianapolis wood-products factory in the mid-1860s, he gained rapid promotion by throwing himself into the task of improving mechanical efficiency and more closely monitoring the factory's workforce. He split Sundays between church services and teaching Sunday school, on one hand, and rambling walks full of botanizing and drawing in nearby woods on the other. Holding together these sometimes clashing devotions to Protestant piety, industrialism, and awe of nature was difficult, but for a time he managed.[14]

A terrible accident soon put him on a different path. One day at work, while removing a tightly woven saw belt, Muir's hand slipped, sending a file into his right eye. As liquid dripped out of his eye and into his cupped hand, sight departed with it. Soon he was entirely blind in both eyes, lying in his boardinghouse room, despairing that he would never again see "a single flower, no more of lovely scenery, not any more of beauty." But his sight returned over the next month. Bolstered by

Jeanne Carr's insistence that he should use his God-given gift of "the eye within the eye, to see in natural objects the realized ideas of His mind," Muir turned down the opportunity to manage a new shop being opened by his employer. Instead, he began a series of extraordinary journeys, first walking some thousand miles from Indianapolis to the Gulf of Mexico, crossing the Isthmus of Panama, and sailing to California. In 1868 he entered the Yosemite Valley, which he called "nature's landscape garden, at once beautiful and sublime." The next summer, spent herding sheep and exploring the Sierra Madre, forever made wild nature his central preoccupation and inspiration, a source of wonder, curiosity, and spiritual and physical renewal. Increasingly distant from Christian theology, Muir began to seek redemption in nature: as he wrote to Jeanne Carr, "I will fuse in spirit skies . . . I will touch naked God." The tallest of trees were "lordly monarchs proclaiming the gospel of beauty like apostles." He found this divine essence abundant in California, but also sought it afar. Even after marrying, fathering two daughters, and assuming the active management of his father-in-law's prosperous orchards, he pursued the wild in Alaska's glaciers and mountains, on the Nile, in the Himalayas, in Australian eucalyptus groves, on New Zealand lava plains, on the Amazon, in Japan's gardens, and on Hawaiian cliffs.[15]

Muir's life might have remained a personal and individualistic discovery of meaning and transcendence in nature had it not been for the extraordinary influence of his force of personality, his writings, and, ultimately, his turn to environmental politics. In the 1870s, he began publishing articles about the Sierra Nevada. His passion for nature and his scientific theories about glaciers and other shapers of the landscape drew major cultural, scientific, and political figures to seek him out, including the botanist Asa Gray, the journalist Robert Underwood Johnson, Ralph Waldo Emerson, Gifford Pinchot, and Theodore Roosevelt. By his death in 1914, his writings, totaling more than three hundred articles and a dozen books, had reached millions of readers in the United States and across the English-speaking world.

The mounting threats to the places he loved led Muir into political involvement in his later decades, despite his private disposition and his aversion to public life. He was so politically unengaged as a young man that he lived in Canada for a few years in order to avoid conscription into the Union army, and never seemed troubled by having done so. Some of his articles from the 1870s about his journeys made passing reference to the depletion of fisheries and to deforestation, which would later become widely seen as pressing conservation issues. In the next decade, concern that timbering, sheep grazing, and haphazard tourist developments would mar the Yosemite Valley and other jewels of the Sierra Nevada led him to advocate governmental protection of such places as national parks. His calls were heeded in late 1890 with the congressional establishment of Yosemite and Sequoia National Parks, which joined with Yellowstone (1872) as the country's first national parks. A year later, Congress authorized the creation of forest reserves by presidential decree. Little discussed, this measure concerned the protection of watersheds from timber harvesting. The statute placed the federal government in charge of a large and growing domain (forty-six million acres by 1900) that was protected from homestead entries and could be managed for a range of environmental purposes. Indeed, the first reserve established under the legislation encompassed areas around Yellowstone that faced no apparent threat from logging.[16]

These national parks and forest reserves were created in advance of the mass movement for conservation. But Muir was an important player in their creation as writer, activist, and explorer. And his participation anticipated the role that an engaged citizenry would soon play in expanding the federal role in environmental protection. In 1892, he presided over the meeting of San Francisco academics, scientists, and professionals that created the Sierra Club. The new organization was devoted to both advocacy ("preserving forests and other natural features of the Sierra Nevada Mountains") and wilderness recreation (dedicating itself to "explore, enjoy, and render accessible the mountain regions of the Pacific Coast"). Muir received unanimous support as the new group's president, an office that he occupied until his death. His status and the later growth of the Sierra Club into a national organization obscure its metropolitan origins and concerns: almost all members were drawn from greater San Francisco's scientific and educational circles, and they focused on the city's recreational hinterland in the northern Sierra Nevada. Important as the club's establishment was, its metropolitan cast marked it as a counterpart of the Appalachian Mountain

Club (founded in Boston in 1876 to protect and foster the enjoyment of New Hampshire's White Mountains), the Trustees of Reservations (also founded in Boston, in 1891, to preserve places of particular natural and historical importance in Massachusetts), and the Association for the Protection of the Adirondacks (founded in New York City in 1901). Urban networks, interests, and institutions deeply shaped the nascent conservation movement.[17]

Muir's brand of conservation, like that of Dana Bartlett, Mira Lloyd Dock, and other urban conservationists, grew in the shadow of industrial civilization. In *Our National Parks* (1902), Muir aimed "to show forth the beauty, grandeur and all-embracing usefulness of wild mountain forest reservations and parks" so that people would "come and enjoy them, and get them into their hearts, that so at length their preservation and right use might be made sure." Almost all of the text lovingly portrayed North America's natural splendors, particularly its forests, whose sights, sounds, and history he described with great detail and passion. The proposals to improve urban environments that that animated Dock and Bartlett were of no concern to Muir. Yet he shared urban conservationists' belief that the nation had reached the point of environmental crisis, of the real and foreseeable possibility of the destruction of its remaining wild places. Muir interrupted his pages-long ode to trees with a stark declaration: "When the steel axe of the white man rang out on the startled air, their doom was sealed. Every tree heard the bodeful sound, and pillars of smoke gave the sign in the sky." The waste of Muir's America was in a sense the continuation of European settlement, since "the invading horde of destroyers called settlers" expanded across the continent "until at last it has reached the wild side of the continent, and entered the last of the great aboriginal forests on the shores of the Pacific." But it was also the reflection of a new historical era in which the country had run out of frontier, and in which people needed wild nature all the more precisely because of the dreary, dangerous, and unhealthy circumstances in which they lived and worked. "Few in these hot, dim, strenuous times are quite sane or free," Muir wrote. "Choked with care like clocks full of dust, laboriously doing so much good and making so much money,—or so little,—they are no longer good for themselves." Thus, people's need for wild nature, in conjunction with the new historical era, meant "it should not be wondered at that lovers of their country, bewailing its baldness, are now crying aloud, 'Save what is left of the Forests!' Clearing has surely now gone far enough." Past assumptions of "inexhaustible abundance" had to give way to an unavoidable realization: "Quick measures must be taken if ruin is to be avoided. Year by year, the remnant is growing smaller before the axe and fire, while the laws in existence provide neither for the protection of the timber from destruction nor for its use where it is most needed."[18]

Yet Muir held views of the industrial and urban life different from those of Bartlett, Dock, and most other urban conservationists. Or at least he did by the 1890s, when he had made his turn toward politics. Some of his earlier writings, especially his accounts of Arctic exploration, were more harrowing than his later works in their portrayal of the life-threatening harshness of nature and the smugness and casual brutality of American culture. The older Muir, however, the conservationist leader and exemplary writer, was not so much a critic of industry, cities, or the cult of money—indeed, in his work as an orchardist he was a prosperous and conventional horticultural businessman—as an advocate of vacations away from them. "I suppose we need not go mourning the buffaloes," he wrote in *Our National Parks,* deliberately refraining from a full-scale jeremiad. "In the nature of things they had to give place to better cattle, though the change might have been made without barbarous wickedness. Likewise many of nature's five hundred kinds of wild trees had to make way for orchards and cornfields." Those who lived in landscapes of orchards and cornfields—even more, the burgeoning ranks of those in "hot, dim, strenuous" cities—restored something of themselves when they indulged in the "tendency nowadays to wander in wildernesses." Muir insisted that those on both sides of the class divide could benefit from such restoration, "awakening" themselves from "the stupefying effects of the vice of over-industry and the deadly apathy of luxury." Where urban conservationists drafted blueprints for reform, Muir sang songs of escape.[19]

Muir's appreciation of the restorative power of nature for human beings did not blind him to the economic benefits of its protection. Staving off destruction for the country's remaining wildlands, he noted in passing in *Our National Parks,* as he did in other writings, "will yield plenty of timber, a perennial harvest for every right use . . . and will continue to cover the springs of the rivers that rise in the mountains and give irrigating waters to the dry valleys at their feet, prevent wasting floods and be a blessing to everybody forever."[20]

Gifford Pinchot, Muir's sometimes compatriot and later foe, became both the chief proponent of a utilitarian approach to conservation in the countryside and the conservation movement's most important institution builder and political figure. Pinchot and Muir met in 1896 during the Forest Commission's survey of potential reserves, for which Muir served as informal adviser and Pinchot the travel coordinator. The two men seemed fast friends and camped together near the rim of the Grand Canyon. Born in Connecticut in 1865, nearly thirty years Muir's junior, Gifford Pinchot was the scion of prominent New York families. His educational career reflected his family's social standing: he attended high school at Phillips Exeter and then college at Yale, where he was inducted into the elite secret society Skull and Bones. Encouraged by his father, much of whose fortune had come from lumbering and real estate development, and who gave his son George Perkins Marsh's *Man and Nature* as a birthday present, the young Pinchot sought professional training in forestry. So undeveloped was the discipline in the United States that his confidant Bernhard Fernow, the forester in charge of the minuscule federal forestry department, cautioned him not to, believing that the limited reach of the American state, compared with its European counterparts, meant that the profession was unlikely to provide a way to reach the kind of power and influence that Pinchot sought even as a young man. With no formal education in forestry available in the United States, he went to Europe, where he established contact with leading foresters, including Sir Dietrich Brandis, who founded England's India Forestry Service and a few years later served as informal adviser to another American environmental pilgrim, Mira Lloyd Dock. Pinchot acquired more formal training at the French National School for Forestry, where he studied for a year.[21]

The combination of ambition, family connections, a keen political sense, and a veneer of professional training allowed Pinchot to make himself the most influential forester and then, in short order, the most powerful conservationist in the nation. He began writing articles on continental forest management for *Garden and Forest* while still in Europe, ensuring himself an audience of some of the most environmentally engaged Americans. In a talk on the same subject delivered to a joint gathering of the American Economic Association and the American Forestry Association shortly after his return to the United States, Pinchot argued for a greater role for the federal government in forestry. Emphasizing the long life cycle of trees and forests, he concluded that "only the supervision of some imperishable guardian; or in other words, of the state," could ensure the most efficient management and harvesting of timber resources. Pinchot seemed to agree with Fernow that a weak central state limited the reach of forestry. Unlike his elder, however, he did not despair. Pinchot anticipated that the American state might soon come into its own.

His first real work as a forester was designed to demonstrate the potential of scientific management of large acreages as well as to burnish his own reputation. Pinchot secured a position at Biltmore, the sprawling North Carolina estate of George Vanderbilt. Managed by the renowned landscape architect Frederick Law Olmsted, one of the designers of Central Park in New York, Biltmore was intended to showcase not only its owner's wealth and cultivated sensibilities, but also a modern and systematic approach to land management that stressed both beauty and economic productivity. In the words of the Pinchot biographer Char Miller, modern forestry techniques would be "an emblem of a new, more rational form of land management for a nation already better known for its rapid and unrestrained exploitation of natural resources than its sustainable development," meaning that "Biltmore, despite its architectural excesses, would serve as an antidote to the Gilded Age." Pinchot surveyed the growing estate (which soon reached 125,000 acres) and developed a plan for selective harvesting, forest reproduction, and tree planting. Although the plan was far more Olmsted's than his own, and though his claims that the revenue from timber sales paid for the management were based on deceptive bookkeeping, in articles for *Garden and Forest* and the book *Biltmore Forest* Pinchot trumpeted his results as proof that "it is not necessary to destroy a forest in order to make it pay."[22]

This flurry of work allowed Pinchot to make himself a key player in national-level U.S. environmental management at its inception. He was a part of the Forest Commission's survey of western lands for appropriate forest reserves. Heavily influenced by Pinchot, the commission warned that the United States was falling badly behind other countries in the scientific management of its forests and that to rectify this, outgoing president Grover Cleveland should create thirteen new reserves totaling more than twenty million acres (which he did in 1897), and that the army should manage forest reserves until a permanent bureau could be established. This bureau would hire professional foresters and rangers to fight fires, tend to forest health, and plan and supervise timber harvesting. Pinchot managed to get himself appointed head of this new bureau in the incoming administration of William McKinley. The ascension of Theodore Roosevelt to the presidency after McKinley's 1901 assassination elevated an avid outdoorsman, conservationist, and close confidant to the office. By 1905, Pinchot's staff had grown from sixty to five hundred, and he and Roosevelt secured the transfer of the nation's forests to the Department of Agriculture, to be managed by the newly named U.S. Forest Service. The Forest Service was one of the first modern federal bureaucracies, a permanent agency that relied on a loyal cadre of trained professionals. Many of the first forest rangers came from the Yale School of Forestry, whose establishment the Pinchot family had funded in 1900. The school became the most important source of foresters in the United States. No longer would ambitious young men like Gifford Pinchot need to go to Europe for such instruction. Pinchot himself, still in his early forties, presided over a public domain of 150 million acres, or nearly twice the size of Germany today. He was the world's most powerful conservationist.[23]

He focused most of this influence on the countryside, where the federal government's strength was the greatest and where Pinchot and many other conservationists felt that environmental problems were the most pressing and solutions the most promising. Pinchot's conservation policies and his widely read writings and speeches focused on the depletion of natural resources and the need to use, protect, and sometimes augment them. Like Muir in his depiction of the need for wildness in an increasingly urban era, Pinchot forcefully argued that industrialization had brought humanity into a new historical era. "As a people," he proclaimed of Americans, "we have been in the habit of declaring certain of our resources to be inexhaustible. . . . We are in the habit of speaking of the solid earth and the eternal hills as though they, at least, were free from the vicissitudes of time and certain to furnish perpetual support for prosperous human life." But the nation could no longer afford such thinking: the increasing consumption of coal and timber, the rapid erosion of farming soils, the degradation of grazing pastures, and the fouling of water supplies confronted America with the prospect that "those who come after us will have to pay the price of misery, degradation, and failure for the progress and prosperity of our day."[24]

In his public life and policy proposals, Pinchot looked to the countryside not as a refuge from the grind of modern urbanity, as did Muir, but rather as the arena where the nation's future prosperity would be secured by a cautious and self-conscious use of resources. Efficiency would make Americans wealthier, and their country more powerful on the world stage. In this regard, Pinchot channeled both the emphasis on comprehensive management in emerging disciplines such as engineering and forestry, and the commitment to making the United States a world power, a goal that animated much of its governing class. He was resolutely focused on the United States, but saw the country in a global context. To avoid the decline of past great powers such as Rome and China, the United States needed to forestall the kind of environmental destruction that had contributed to their fall. Internal reform was part of power exercised abroad.[25]

Pinchot did not discuss urbanites' lamentable lack of regular contact with wildness, and was less disturbed by the social changes brought by industrial development than were Henry George, Mira Lloyd Dock, and Dana Bartlett. Like urban conservationists, he aimed for reform rather than escape. Far from invoking misery, degradation, or squalor, his manifesto *The Fight for Conservation* (1910) opened with the proclamation that "the most prosperous nation of to-day is the United States." But precisely because "our unexampled wealth and well-being are directly due to the superb natural resources of our country," maintaining American prosperity and power in the face of environmental limits required change. This was a hallmark of what might be called the rhetoric of conservative Progressivism: the achievements of America could be preserved and extended only by change. "Perhaps the most striking characteristic of the American people," he wrote in the early pages of *The Fight for Conservation,* "is their superb practical optimism, that marvellous hopefulness which keeps the individual efficiently at work. This hopefulness of the American is, however, as short-sighted as it is intense. As a rule, it does not look ahead beyond the next decade or score of years, and fails wholly to reckon with the real future of the Nation." That future lay in the efficiency and farsightedness that enlightened leaders like him could bring.[26]

Like most elite Progressives, Pinchot fervently hoped that the "future of the Nation" would look much like its present, a continued growth in wealth and power. He did acknowledge some troubling aspects of American economic life. Pinchot repeatedly warned of the dangers of the "great oppressive trusts" and presented the challenges that they posed as the most recent chapter in the story of "the everlasting conflict of the few to grab, and the many to keep or win the rights they were born with." A heightened role for the state in administering and developing natural resources, he insisted, would help address these problems even as it augmented economic development and national strength. Pinchot shared Muir's focus on the countryside, but his sensibility was starkly different. Rather than losing themselves in the majesty of wildness, Americans should recognize that the "first principle of conservation is development, the use of the natural resources now existing on this continent for the benefit of the people who live here now." The "prevention of waste," which Pinchot articulated as conservation's second principle, "is an industrial necessity," one that would not only augment growth but also help extend it across generations by producing the greatest wealth from the least amount of resources. In the end, nature was the critical substrate for progress and social justice, and thus "the first duty of the human race is to control the earth it lives upon."[27]

Conserving the Past

Numerous conservation writers and political leaders took up the great themes of Muir's and Pinchot's pronouncements—that protecting rural nature would secure the future of humanity's spiritual health and material prosperity alike. To these themes other writers added a third: that the conservation of the countryside preserved not only nature, but also the history of the nation.

New Englanders pursued this endeavor with particular fervor and ambition. In the late nineteenth century, many sought to preserve and celebrate the region's colonial years and Puritan heritage. Old-stock New Englanders turned to antiques, depictions of colonial times in paintings and literature, and a revival of colonial architecture and cooking out of a concern that profound changes in their own time threatened to cut them off from ancestral virtues such as thrift and independence, and menaced their power and social standing. Decades of urbanization, the supplanting of farm and town life by factory wage labor, and extensive immigration from Catholic Ireland marked the advent of a new and perhaps less auspicious era. While New England's cultural elites hardly rejected what they saw as economic progress, they nonetheless developed a nostalgic and self-conscious view of New England's past as the seedbed of American ingenuity, self-reliance, and democracy.

This cultural impulse gave rise to the founding of such organizations as the Daughters of the American Revolution, the Colonial Dames, numerous local history societies, and historical preservation organizations. It deeply informed other political projects as well, such as immigration restriction (which in New England centered on the Irish) and conservation. New England conservationists saw the parks and forests established in this period as valuable not only for preserving nature, but also for maintaining elements of their colonial past for present and future generations. In this sense, what they sought in preservation was not only nature primeval, but also a world that nurtured the best New England virtues. As one writer noted of Massachusetts parks, "the fathers with their Aryan ways, their patient oxen, and their demon wolves have gone," but through conservation they "are being restored to the common inheritance of their children's children." Naming practices for natural features in protected areas reflected a similar sensibility. Eager to preserve "memorials of the simple and toilsome life of the pioneers," New England parks administrators and Appalachian Mountain Club leaders drew on local colonial figures rather than more recent political leaders, Civil War heroes, or widely used local colloquial names. They thereby erased the naming practices and landscape uses of Irish immigrants, which had deeply marked many of Massachusetts's parks for forty years. The colonial past was honored in other ways as well. Park commissioners in Lynn illustrated their annual reports with images of early settlers; one celebrated the fact that the lands under their protection, "with the wood-choppers kept out of them for ten years, look more like the forest that the Puritan fathers saw." As the historian Michael Rawson concludes, "Despite all the concern about providing adequate recreational space and safeguarding timber resources," New England conservation "was as much about history as it was about nature."[28]

New England conservationists were not the only ones protecting nature as history. In New York, the Trustees of Scenic and Historical Places and Objects, founded in 1895, sought protection both for natural areas such as the Hudson River Palisades and for "colonial forts, town commons, historic homes," and even the names of settlements and streets. The Association for the Protection of the Adirondacks was oriented toward environmental protection, but it also invoked the "wealth of legendary and historical association" of many of the state's mountains as a reason to bring them into state ownership. The identity of the Empire State was bound up in both human and natural places.[29]

The writings of Charles Francis Saunders also marked an imperiled nature with national history, but in a more critical way than did New York and New England forest advocates. In a series of books and numerous periodical articles published in the 1910s and 1920s, Saunders extolled the virtues of California as a civilization in close harmony with nature. He honored John Muir by acknowledging that "the prose poet who has written this region into enduring literature is John Muir, and to go mountaineering through the Sierra country with his 'Mountains of California' or 'Our National Parks' in one's satchel is a liberal education." Saunders occasionally sang the praises of an untouched nature, for example, conferring the title "the real California" on the "immensity of almost unexplored mountain, desert, cañon, and flowery plain." Yet his poetic voice was distinct from Muir's in its consistent invocation of human history alongside natural splendor. Moreover, in contrast with New Englanders' ethnocentric approach to preservation, Saunders found the Native, Spanish, and Mexican pasts deeply compelling. Riding past the town of Ramona in the desert east of San Diego, he relayed the details of Indian life—past and present—alongside a description of the stunted but hardy trees. He described not only his reactions to the desert, but also the diet of the region's Indians, testimony to their ability to live off the land. A visit to Yosemite Valley prompted him to describe the Yosemite Indians as well as the trees and cliffs of the stunning place that bore their name.[30]

For Saunders, the past haunted all these places, marking them with human as well as natural histories. History echoed not just with happy tales of triumph but also with darker stories of death and dispossession. In the midst of the Tejon Pass

> gleams Castaic Lake, a pond of harsh, mocking waters, which, in the summer of a dry year, may disappear, leaving a bottom of white, choking dust across which you can ride your horse. It is a lake of gruesome memory; for old timers will tell you that once upon a time some exasperated white men, of the type that modern lynchers are made of, drove a whole village of Indians, men, women, and children, into it, because it was assumed that some of the number was responsible for the murder of the cook and a boy at Fort Tejon.

In Castaic Lake, Saunders continued, "they drowned like rats, and the bodies of the dead wretches, mummified by the mineral in the hard water, are said to have bobbed up at intervals for a long time, a ghastly reminder to other redmen that on occasion their white brethren can be savages, too." Nearby mountains made him ponder the exploits of Tiburcio Vasquez and Joaquin Murrieta, known to white Californians during the Gold Rush as bandits and to many Mexicans as heroes. Nor were the conflicts of this land entirely relegated to the past: living Mexicans and Indians appeared in Saunders's writings as interlocutors, guides, and sources of botanical wisdom. The canyons near his Pasadena home were splendid "examples of unspoiled rugged wilderness at the very edge of one of the best-groomed little cities in the United States," but also home to refugees such as

> a Teuton of some tripe, who, during the Great War, sought shelter from spy hunters. . . . One of the gentlest of men, he

would kill not even a mouse, and with greatest reluctance
could be brought to throw a stone at a marauding dog, and
then not to hit but to frighten it. . . . He had a neat little camp
under an oak at the head of a dry arroyo, in a retired pocket
of the hills, where he could count on being little disturbed by
ramblers and busybodies.

In the end, Saunders knew that all nature was touched by history: "I
doubt if there is an absolutely solitary spot in all the world. Some touch
of pervading humanity will attach to it, even if it be but a flower tagged
by an 'Adam of science.'"[31]

Saunders and his New England counterparts differed from Muir
in their sustained blending of the natural and human, but found themselves drawn to nature writing and conservation by the same romantic
impulse to lose one's self in the larger world that animated the trans-
planted Scotsman. Another important group of rural conservationists
partook mainly of Pinchot's materialist approach in their blend of conservation and rural revitalization. Liberty Hyde Bailey, a Michigan-born
botanist and horticulturalist who founded Cornell University's College
of Agriculture, became the most prominent leader of what came to be
called the "Country Life" movement. These reformers sought to revitalize rural America, which they believed was being drained of vitality by
migration to cities, the cultural appeal of urban life, adverse economic
circumstances in agriculture, the backwardness and stubbornness of
many farmers, and mounting environmental threats. Invoking the nation's agrarian roots, Country Lifers insisted that the United States could
not be true to its heritage with a decimated countryside.

Country Life gave rise to 4-H programs, agricultural extension
agents, and a host of rural self-improvement publications that marked
agricultural life for decades to come. The movement is not generally
associated with conservation, but in fact the two impulses overlapped
considerably, particularly in the person of Bailey. As with Muir and even
more so Pinchot, Bailey's influence flowed from his writings and his institutional position. His most important book, *The Holy Earth* (1915),
opened with an elegant statement of the conservation critique of the
dangers of obliviousness to continued dependence on nature. "So boun-

tiful hath been the earth, and so obscurely have we drawn from it our substance," he wrote, "that we have taken it all for granted as if it were only a gift, and with little care or conscious thought of the consequences of our use of it, nor have we very much considered the essential relation that we bear to it as living parts in the vast creation." This attitude was not only morally obtuse, but also downright dangerous in an era when humanity possessed unprecedented power to alter nature. "In the past," he wrote, humanity's power to "ravage" the earth was "small in amount because the engines of destruction were weak, but with the perfecting of the modern enginery the havoc is awful and brutal. While we have to our credit the improvement of agriculture and other agencies of conservation, it is yet a fact that man has never been so destructive as now."[32]

As head of the Commission on Country Life, Bailey worked closely with Pinchot, who served as a commission member even as he began convening state governors and private-sector leaders in a series of national Conservation Congresses. The commission was created by President Theodore Roosevelt in 1908 in the typically Progressive hope that a group of experts could reach consensus on ways to make rural life more appealing, and that the publicity generated by presidential support might inspire the public as a whole to implement these findings. Although the report was more successful in highlighting the "deficiencies" that prompted so many to abandon the countryside than it was in proposing remedies, it pointed to the materialist side of rural conservation as a key part of revitalizing the countryside. Farmers would be "vastly benefited by a systematic conservation and utilization, under the auspices of the State and Federal Governments, of our waterways," the commission argued. In addition to such state supervision and development—being pursued aggressively by Pinchot even as the report was crafted—forest protection would preserve the material basis of prosperous agriculture: "The conservation of forests and brush on watershed areas is important to the farmer along the full length of streams, regardless of the distance between the farm and these areas. The loss of soil in denuded areas increases the menace of flood, not alone because of the more rapid runoff, but by the filling of channels and the greater erosion of stream banks when soil matter is carried in suspension." Conservation would help revitalize the countryside.[33]

The Country Life Commission's call for state conservation neatly justified Pinchot's growing domain. Indeed, some scholars have argued credibly that the commission's emphasis on economic development and the adoption of business practices by farmers represented a coercive, top-down imposition of the mores of industrial society on farmers, much as Pinchot's validation of efficiency seemed to apply industrial practices to forests and grasslands. Yet in other respects, Bailey and some of his agrarian fellow travelers emphasized an aspect of environmental reform in which individual conscience and cultural change were as important as state power and scientific expertise. This generally neglected and underappreciated strain of conservation deeply influenced later thinkers such as Aldo Leopold and Wendell Berry, who similarly rooted a sustainable economic system in a reverence for the earth rather than in technical mastery and efficiency. Bailey strongly advocated the dissemination of scientific knowledge to the tillers of the land, seeing it as liberatory. He was one of the popularizers of Mendelian genetics in the United States, encouraging farmers to work with universities such as his own Cornell in developing improved orchard and crop varieties; the agricultural extension service, whose creation the Country Life Commission endorsed, was designed precisely to inform farmers of the best crop varieties and growing practices. But whereas subsequent generations were more likely to assume that rationality and religion stood in opposition, for Bailey they complemented each other. Science and conservation needed the companionship of religious reverence, as suggested by the title of *The Holy Earth*. "Our relation with the planet must be raised into the realm of spirit; we cannot be fully useful otherwise," he wrote in the book's early pages. "We must find a way to maintain the emotions in the abounding commercial civilization." The world in which Americans lived was the product of human ingenuity and nature, but the increasing complexity of the former, especially in cities, made it easy to forget the latter.[34]

City life and its increasing allure troubled Bailey because they seemed to epitomize a soulless materialism in which wealth was lionized over all other virtues, but also because daily life in an industrial metropolis made it easy to lose sight of the ultimate basis of human sustenance. "There are two kinds of materials," he argued, "those of the native earth and the idols of one's hands. The latter are much in evidence in modern life, with the conquests of engineering, mechanics, architecture and all the rest. We visualize them everywhere and particularly in the great centres of population. The tendency is to be removed farther and farther from the everlasting backgrounds. Our religion is detached." The environmental historian William Cronon later described nineteenth-century capitalism in very similar terms, arguing that the "new corporate order, by linking and integrating the products of so many ecosystems and communities, obscured the very connections it helped create." Americans who bought their flour and meat in grocery stores easily forgot the wheat fields and cows that produced their sustenance. The fact that Bailey articulated his version of this critique so forcefully at the time underscores the importance of Cronon's insight. Bailey's insight and his influence also suggest the shortcomings of later environmental historians: these scholars imagined that they saw much more clearly than their historical subjects, that they had powers of discernment and insight unavailable to Americans at the time. In fact, conservationists were quite aware, and often quite critical, of the alienation produced by large-scale markets.[35]

At its most intellectually probing, as in Bailey's work, conservation grappled with the problem of alienation, not as mere intellectual achievement, but also as a spur to cultural and political reform. Bailey argued that an engaged "religion"—by which he meant not so much a particularly Christian theology as a spiritual commitment to and reverence for creation—could give conservation a reach and a power that a mere reliance on state power and scientific expertise could not. Since private landownership dominated the American landscape, and since almost half the population lived on farms and in small towns, the daily choices of farmers and other landowners had enormous consequences. For some, the commitment to maintaining a large percentage of the American population as country folk, which strongly animated Bailey and Country Life, reflected sentimental nostalgia, often accompanied by an ethnocentric disdain for urban populations. Bailey's commitments, however, ran much broader: he intended for agricultural reform to preserve the kind of economic freedom that farm ownership could bring, and to foster an environmental vision in which those whose labor was most directly and obviously blended with nature should serve as the nation's environmental conscience. Ultimately, an agriculture awakened to its spiritual and material connection with the earth "should express itself in all the people and not exclusively in farming people and their like." Economic growth was not a substitute for moral refinement: "No system of brilliant exploitation, and no accidental scratching of the surface of the earth, and no easy appropriation of stored materials can suffice us in the good days to come. City, country, this class and that class, all fall and merge before the common necessity" of cultivating a reverence for creation.[36]

New Landscapes

Bailey's extraordinarily long life and career—he died in 1954, at age ninety-six—allowed him to witness profound changes in the fabric of American life and to rearticulate his core beliefs accordingly. The collapse of farm commodity prices in the 1920s and the wrenching Depression of the 1930s deepened the crisis of agricultural overproduction, driving millions more from the farming life whose virtues he extolled. Accordingly, gardening by urbanites and suburbanites grew to become the most important subject of his writings and speeches in the last three decades of life. His involvement with Horace McFarland's magazine *Suburban Life* (later *Countryside Magazine and Suburban Life*) presaged this later application of his philosophy. Backyard and small-scale gardening could not deliver the prosperity and independence that agrarians hoped would continue to characterize farming, but it could cultivate the kind of conservationist consciousness that Bailey had long advocated. As he wrote in his book *The Garden Lover* from 1928: "Every soul should be put in contact with the mystery that stands stark before us but which we do not apprehend. It is in every leaf, every tender shoot, every opening flower and growing fruit, every pulse of life on the planet. The wonder of life is the greater as our knowledge grows." Suburban life, which contemporary environmentalists regard with horror, was once infused with agrarian environmental visions.[37]

Even before the hopes of Country Lifers were dashed on the rocks of rural depression, some conservationists argued that people could wed economic prosperity and natural beauty by creating new kinds of land-scapes that were not urban, suburban, or rural. In much of the industrial world in these decades, a diverse group with roots in urban reform, irri-gation, conservation, and agricultural reform found themselves drawn to model settlements that combined productive agriculture and horticul-ture with the sociability and opportunities of urban life and the beauty of nature. Heavily influenced by two Americans—Edward Bellamy and Henry George—the Englishman Ebenezer Howard offered the most influential advocacy for such settlements in his books *To-Morrow: A Peaceful Path to Real Reform* (1888) and *The Garden Cities of To-Morrow* (1902). Howard intended for his garden cities to be self-sufficient settle-ments of about thirty thousand, with relatively dense housing nestled within large parks and agricultural fields. Graceful boulevards would allow for easy access to factories located in the garden cities, and rail lines and roads would link the settlements to somewhat larger central cities. In the rest of the industrial world as well as the United States, urban and environmental reform often walked hand in hand.[38]

Howard and his devotees across the Atlantic world anticipated that garden cities would combine the virtues of rural and urban life. Why should the citizenry of industrial nations have to choose between cities devoid of nature and a countryside strangled by lack of economic oppor-tunity? As if channeling Henry George, Howard condemned "this unholy, unnatural separation of society and nature," believing instead that "human society and the beauty of nature are meant to be enjoyed together." So they would in the garden cities, whose residents would have the social and em-ployment opportunities provided by cities along with the "free gifts of Nature—fresh air, sunlight, breathing room and playing room."[39]

American conservationists were among those who found How-ard's proposals compelling. These new settlements seemed to promise a solution to the urban environmental crises that Dock and Bartlett high-lighted, and to the rural problems Bailey and Pinchot addressed. *Cali-fornia Outlook,* the mouthpiece of Golden State Progressivism, whose pages featured extensive coverage of urban and rural conservation, called for a "workable compromise between the extreme conditions of congested city life and the isolated farm." Pointing to garden cities and similar schemes, the editors urged that "the salvation of the soil lies in combining the advantages of the city and country, without their dis-advantages."[40]

In the western United States, the massive expansion of state-sponsored irrigation in the early twentieth century created fertile ground for the planting of such visions. Since little of the western half of the nation received enough rainfall to make conventional agriculture viable, residents had long turned to damming and siphoning off waterways fed by springs and winter snowpacks. Several Indian peoples, Spanish and Mexican settlers, and Mormon and other white American colonists succeeded in building local irrigation networks that gave rise to productive and comparatively dense agrarian settlement. Larger rivers and tracts of arid lands, however, proved impervious to private and community irrigation endeavors. In the late 1800s, a growing chorus of development-minded westerners therefore began clamoring for the federal government to become the nation's chief irrigator. They achieved their goal with the passage of the Newlands Reclamation Act in 1902, which established the Bureau of Reclamation and charged it with building dams and reservoirs along with the canals and ditches needed to bring their waters to fields and orchards.

Conventional economic boosters found it easy to support mass irrigation—or reclamation, as it came to be called, a term that implied that the natural state of land was agricultural. Conservationists likewise found themselves drawn to the crusade for reclamation, seeing it as a way to create agricultural communities that were both environmentally responsible and economically modern. Gifford Pinchot considered irrigation to be an important part of his materialist vision of conservation. Especially when combined with forest conservation's enhancement of water supplies, the engineering of waterways for navigability, and dams for flood control and hydroelectric energy, irrigation could maximize the efficient use of natural resources. Pinchot accordingly invited leading irrigation advocates and officials from the Bureau of Reclamation to the Conservation Congresses that he organized from 1909 to 1915. In his own writings, he held up "such rural communities as those of the irrigated West" as "useful examples for the consideration of regions in which life is more isolated, has less of the benefits of cooperation, and generally has lacked the stimulus found in irrigation farming."[41]

Irrigation boosterism often took on a nearly utopian cast. William Ellsworth Smythe, a Nebraska journalist who became the leading American exponent of irrigation agriculture, embodied this utopianism. He offered a sober assessment of the social and environmental problems of conventional agriculture: Americans "have wasted the bounty of nature where they should have conserved it; defaced the landscape where they should have beautified it; dissipated their strength in fighting each other where they should have combined their strength and worked together; degraded toil where they should have ennobled and glorified it." The landscapes of irrigation, in contrast, would embody a productive and beautiful relationship with the land. "The great cities of the western valleys," he prophesied, "will not be cities in the old sense, but a long series of beautiful villages, connected by lines of electric motors, which will move their products and people from place to place. In this scene of intensely cultivated land, rich with its bloom and fruitage, with its spires and roofs, and with its carpets of green and gold stretching away to the mountains, it will be difficult for the beholder to say where the town ends and the country begins."[42]

The hybrid landscapes that Smythe inspired secured the admiration of many conservationists. Charles Saunders's appreciation of them suggests how a Muirian admiration for wild nature could also lead to an appreciation of cultivated lushness. "Magnificent rows of palms, grevilleas and peppers, miles of them, line and often overarch the streets and make a grateful shade in summer days," he wrote of citrus-enveloped Redlands, California. "Of all the riotous growth of trees and shrubs that makes the Redlands of to-day the paradisaical garden that it is, not one is indigenous; all have been planted by the Pauls and watered by the Apolloses of the last quarter century." Saunders appreciated the austere beauty of deserts, noting that "prophets of all time have found inspiration and strength in desert regions" because in them the "veil between this world and the spiritual seems thinner than elsewhere." Yet in such places as Redlands, the presence of deserts underscored the fragility and beauty of the landscapes of irrigation: "Just across the line which marks the high tide of cultivation, the parched, treeless slopes of the desert borders lie as if in wait for man's care to be withdrawn, when the desert will sweep in again and claim its own," vanquishing the "artificial wildwood of eucalyptus, deodars, pines, palms, peppers, acacias, olives, oranges, bamboos and a perfect wilderness of roses."[43]

Latter-day environmental sympathizers might find it odd to call one of Smythe's irrigation colonies or Saunders's horticultural suburbs "natural." Indeed, one of the largest differences between those who called themselves conservationists in the early twentieth century and those who embraced the label "environmentalist" a few generations later was the indifference or hostility of the latter to these created places. How could a place be natural if human artifice had created it a scarce few years earlier? Surely these landscapes had been more created than conserved. Saunders acknowledged the existence of such a view in his own time, writing in the 1920s of the Big Bear Reservoir in California's San Bernardino Mountains. He called the lake "one of the loveliest sheets of water in California," even as he freely acknowledged that it "was created by damming the outlet of the valley, into which many streams drain." Big Bear's human origin, "this fact of artificiality[,] . . . is a defect in the view of some," he acknowledged, but "for reasons which I leave to philosophers to explain." Saunders's sardonic tone suggested that he did not see any point in a protracted and complicated consideration of the paradox of considering a landscape made by human artifice to be "natural." Indeed, the corpus of his nature writing consistently and subtly suggested that even places less obviously human than Big Bear Lake were just as human as they were natural. Saunders was typical of the aesthetic-minded reclamationists in his willingness to remain content with "the pure beauty of this upland mere in its green forest setting." Writing of the landscape of orchards that California had created in the last few generations, he acknowledged that "much wild beauty" had been "buried by the plow forever," but found some consolation in the thought that "if California has lost some of the aboriginal loveliness that clothed her fertile valleys before the white occupation, she had but put on another charm in her cultivated areas, soberer but still very appealing."[44]

Irrigation landscapes were not the only places conservationists sought to make from whole cloth. Since bringing the country's remaining forests under federal supervision was a major conservationist goal, why not take the next step and create forests where there were none? Although the very term "conservation" implied maintaining or shepherding what

already existed, many conservationists saw such large-scale landscape engineering as perfectly consistent with their central goal of profitably and
beautifully uniting humanity and nature. For a generation before the
blossoming of conservation, some developers and agricultural boosters promoted the dubious notion that "rain follows the plow," or that
agricultural settlement itself would change climate and, in turn, vegetation. Arbor Day, the tradition of reflecting on and often planting a tree,
began in Nebraska in the 1870s, in part out of the similar hope that the
human cultivation of trees would create enough rainfall to make the
Plains more viable for traditional agriculture. The Timber Culture Act,
passed by Congress that same decade, awarded 160 acres to settlers who
managed to grow trees on a quarter of their grant in ten years. Although
these efforts made little headway—the Timber Culture Act was such a
failure that it was soon repealed—early foresters and public lands managers embraced their ambitious goals. During his time as head of the
Division of Forestry, Bernhard Fernow argued in his annual report for
1886 that "a forest department might be properly extended to the creation of new forests, so as to produce beneficial results upon the agricultural conditions of the arid and semi-arid regions of the Western States."
His successor, Gifford Pinchot, saw to it that the nation's burgeoning
forest system would in fact undertake such efforts. In 1902 he helped persuade President Theodore Roosevelt to create two forest reserves in the
Nebraska Sandhills based on the proposition that they would soon be
forested. Conservationists made similar efforts in Southern California,
where much of the San Gabriel Mountains were covered by a low chaparral of shrubs rather than a proper forest of taller trees. Here for decades
Theodore Parker Lukens, an early Sierra Club member and close confidant
of John Muir, struggled to create a lush forest that would produce more
timber and water. Enlisting local chambers of commerce, conservation organizations, botanists from around the world, and the Forest Service in his
crusade, Lukens insisted that "every acre of our bare mountain slopes can
be successfully planted to trees, and at a nominal expense."[45]

These efforts to create new environments met with mixed results.
On one hand, thousands of farms and orchards sprouted across the
West—a total of perhaps three million acres by 1912. The reservoirs and
canals that watered this vast domain reshaped much of the local envi-

ronment, sometimes in deleterious ways that would receive recognition only decades later, but also by creating new habitats for birds and other wildlife. One such area in Idaho became so important to migratory birds that in 1909 it became a federally managed wildlife reservation. Reclamation boosters thus had some justification for describing irrigation as "the one thing needed to complete nature," and irrigation engineers as "understudies of the creator." Reforestation, however, was much less successful. Theodore Lukens's hopes that a forest of tall pines would carpet Southern California never came to fruition. Early successes with a few trees prompted a note from John Muir congratulating him on "a good beginning" that might turn into something "far reaching." It did not. Low germination rates, drought, and predation by birds, rabbits, and squirrels hampered his planting efforts. By the time an irate Lukens turned to advocating their wholesale slaughter—"there has been a lot of sentimentalism in regard to squirrels in the mountains," he wrote in 1910, "they look very cunning leaping from branch to branch of the trees, but they are a great menace to our forests of Southern California"—the Forest Service and many of his prior collaborators had come to think his goal quixotic. The Great Plains efforts were more mixed. The initially unforested Nebraska National Forest eventually included about thirty thousand acres of woodlands. Although the millions of dollars and years of labor that went into creating this woodland were not enough to deliver more rainfall to the Cornhusker State, the hunters, cattle ranchers, and hikers it attracted over the course of the twentieth century seemed untroubled that its amenities were as artificial as natural. In a sense, then, sometimes conservation succeeded in creating an attractive and bounteous nature as well as protecting it.[46]

Eugenics

Some conservationists looked at the human body as another arena where planning and scientific expertise could deliver social improvement. Eugenics, the deliberate "improvement" of humans through the control of heredity, appealed to conservationists for reasons analogous to those calling for the state management of resources such as timber and water. Dana Bartlett explicitly drew this parallel in *The Better Coun-*

try: "We have passed in review the wonderful work of the Department of Agriculture," he wrote, "in breeding plants and animals, in preventing disease, in creating better environment, in improving the quality of food for man and beast, in teaching the farmer how to grow his crops, in adding millions of dollars to the value of farm products; the thought must have suggested itself that if a like amount of work and thought were applied to humankind, even greater results might be produced." Bartlett foresaw that "choice strains in men as well as in plants and animals" could be the result if the country established a "bureau of eugenics, or of health and development."[47]

The potential of deliberately manipulating human heredity deeply appealed to intellectual classes, political elites, and social scientists across much of the world in this period—in North America, western Europe, Australasia, Japan, and Latin America. Much of its attraction derived from the assumed possibility of eugenics to preserve a supposedly racially superior ruling caste. In the United States, Madison Grant was one of the chief advocates of the most racist and social Darwinist versions of eugenics. His stark warnings of America falling into a "racial abyss" that would leave citizens of northern European descent outnumbered and destroyed by breeding with their supposed inferiors made his book *The Passing of the Great Race* (1916) a key text for modern American white supremacy—as well as the basis for the restrictive immigration laws of the 1920s. So enormous was his influence on racist thought and policy that Grant has been dubbed "the high priest of Racialism in America" and the "great patriarch of scientific racism."[48]

Grant was also an active and influential conservationist. Alongside Gifford Pinchot and Theodore Roosevelt, he was a member of the Boone and Crockett Club, a small organization limited to one hundred elite hunters, which lobbied for the protection of endangered animals and their habitats. Much of his adult life was spent founding and running organizations devoted to natural history and conservation, which in addition to the Boone and Crockett Club included the American Bison Society, the American Society of Mammalogists, the American Museum of Natural History, the League of American Sportsmen, the National Conference on Outdoor Recreation, the National Audubon Society, the National Parks Association, the New York Zoological Society, and the

Woodcraft League of America. Grant was particularly enamored of red-wood trees; in 1918, with fellow eugenicists John C. Merriam and Henry Fairfield Osborn, he helped found the Save-the-Redwoods League. For Grant and his compatriots, the redwoods were singularly magnificent trees whose disappearance and replacement by lesser species would be a tragic degradation of the American landscape. Protecting superior trees from the encroachment of undesirable ones found direct analogy in American society. "A rigid system of selection through the elimination of those who are weak or unfit—in other words, social failures—would solve the whole question" of the disappearance of the "Great Race," just as it would "enable us to get rid of the undesirables who crowd our jails, hospitals, and insane asylums." As Grant once explained to his friend and collaborator Henry Fairfield Osborn, eugenics and conservation were both "attempts to save as much as possible of the old America."[49]

Grant was a singularly influential figure, but hardly alone in seeing a coercive and unabashedly racist eugenics as, in a sense, an extension of conservation to human reproduction. Abbot Kinney, a key advocate and popularizer of professional forestry in California, advanced similar arguments in the 1890s. Noting the rise of French-Canadian and Irish immigration, he warned of "an extinction of the old American stock" and lamented the prospect that "their intelligence, self-reliance, capacity for a liberal form of self-government, their religion, and perhaps their language will go with them." In 1911, during a period of much more active conservation politics, Mrs. Matthew T. Scott, president-general of the Daughters of the American Revolution (DAR), echoed Kinney's concerns to a national gathering on conservation. Offering the assembled delegates a lengthy description of the work of the DAR, Scott was at pains to emphasize that "the mothers of this generation have a right to insist upon the conserving not only of soil, forest, birds, minerals, fishes, waterways, in the interest of our future home-makers, but also upon the conserving of the supremacy of the Caucasian race in our land." Scott emphasized immigration restriction, rather than forced sterilization, as a way to "protect the stream of human life . . . from pollution. We must not so eagerly invite all the sons of Shem, Ham, and Japhet wherever they may have first seen the light, and under whatever traditions and influences and ideals foreign and antagonistic to ours they may have been reared, to trample the mud of millions of alien feet into our spring. We must conserve the sources of our race in the Anglo Saxon line, Mother of Liberty and Self government in the modern world."[50]

How tightly linked were eugenics and conservation? There were strong intellectual congruencies: regulation based on scientific expertise could preserve an imperiled and degraded race as well as an imperiled and degraded nature. On the other hand, plenty of eugenicists had no interest in conservation, and plenty of conservationists no interest in eugenics. Those with the most overlap, such as Madison Grant, were conservationists of a very particular type, those with a deep interest in iconic places and species, but virtually none of the strong urban focus and concern with monopoly that animated many other conservationists. Perhaps Gifford Pinchot's cautious and measured response to an invitation to take an active part in the affairs of the "Eugenics Section" of the American Breeders' Association best embodies the relationship between conservation and eugenics. A close associate of Madison Grant asked him to join a study of "the problems connected with the conservation of the best blood lines in the American population" and the "efficacy and feasibility of sterilization of hereditary degenerates and defectives." Pinchot politely declined.[51]

The extensive use of eugenicist thought (particularly Madison Grant's work) by the Nazi regime in Germany in the 1930s and 1940s, and the horrors of the Holocaust, deeply discredited eugenics and led many of its American advocates to renounce it or deny their past advocacy. This discrediting made it more difficult for later observers to see the different political ends to which hereditarianism had been put. Black leaders such as W. E. B. Du Bois and Marcus Garvey, for example, adamantly rejected notions of white supremacy but nonetheless expressed their concerns that African Americans risked decline if their better or "more fit" members were outreproduced by the lesser ones. So eugenics could be used to resist white supremacy as well as to justify it. And expressions of concern about heredity did not have to be coupled with coercive measures against the supposedly unfit. Bartlett, for example, invoked hereditarian concerns as part of his vision of conservation even as he rejected the ethnoracial chauvinism that was part and parcel of most eugenics. He dismissed the "survival of the fittest, which is the law in the animal world," as unacceptable, in favor of the "more Godlike" "making fit to survive." Environment, not birth, created criminals and paupers, and thus "the recovery of defectives to citizenship and power is part of the program of those whose souls are stirred by the thought of universal love and a truer manhood." Bartlett made it clear that this "recovery," like the rest of his political program, ought to include all segments of the population. Categorically rejecting the bigotry of the DAR, Madison Grant, and other opponents of immigration, he flatly asserted its ahistorical basis: "There never has been a time when this was a white man's country with common ideals and a universal language. The nation, its people, and its language have always been in the making, for new elements have been constantly introduced. If the earlier settlers were English, they were quickly followed by Dutch, German, Spanish, French, African, each with its own national offering for the composite life of the new nation."[52] The hereditarian strain in conservation was neither universally shared nor always used for racist ends.

The overlap between conservation and eugenics suggested just how broad a field of action conservationists saw: the protection and cultivation of nature could occur in cities, suburbs, the countryside, and in the human body. In the end, however, conservation was no more tainted by eugenics than was any other political movement that enjoyed substantial support among the native-born white population of the country. Indeed, the political principles that informed conservation were of a quite different nature.[53]

The Crisis of Capitalism and the Progressive State

The language of heredity and eugenics employed by some conservationists was a young one, having come into wide circulation only in the late nineteenth century. In many other respects, conservationists drew on familiar, even commonplace American and more broadly Western traditions. The suspicion of urban life and the identification of national virtues such as independence, egalitarianism, and sincerity with the countryside were in a sense a continuation of Thomas Jefferson's celebration of agrarian civilization. Jefferson's assumption, widely though generally hypocritically shared even by urban writers and business leaders in the young republic, stretched back to the pastoral tradition in Western antiquity. Much younger but also exerting a powerful influence on the minds of conservationists was the Transcendentalist philosophy developed by Ralph Waldo Emerson and others in the 1830s, in which humans could access the divine by directly experiencing the wholeness of nature. Further elaborated by Henry David Thoreau, this belief clearly animated John Muir and Charles Francis Saunders as well as a host of other conservationists and nature writers.

Another striking but less well known influence was what the historian Aaron Sachs describes as "Arcadian America." More a sensibility than a philosophy, and not at all an organized movement like conservation, Arcadianism was at heart an appreciation for the blending of culture and nature. Sachs sees an Arcadian sensibility in the ways that "antebellum Americans established kinship with the land," including parklike cemeteries that seemed to place human mortality in the larger cycle's of nature's perpetual death and rebirth; actual parks such as the Boston Common or New York's Central Park, where human creations were balanced with invocations of wilder nature; and in some of the ways that writers such as Hamlin Garland and Henry George portrayed farmers as simultaneously altering, placating, and submitting to nature. Sachs emphasizes the disjunction between the sensibilities of Arcadians and conservationists, stressing the latter group's mania for "rational management, an orderly efficiency, utilitarianism, statistics-driven maximization, a grid-like regularity." He is right that some conservationists departed from Arcadianism: Gifford Pinchot was overly invested in efficiency and productivity, and John Muir viewed the orchard that came with his marriage as an onerous distraction from his pursuit of pure and wild nature. On the other hand, many conservationists were deeply indebted to this tradition: Dana Bartlett, Mira Dock, William Ellsworth Smythe, Charles Francis Saunders, and conservation-minded architects and landscape architects happily swirled together nature and artifice in their work and politics.[54]

The connections between Frederick Law Olmsted Sr. and environmental politics demonstrate the influence of Arcadianism on conservation, but also a divergence between the two traditions. Olmsted achieved some repute for his writings about the slave-owning South in the 1850s, and catapulted himself to national fame by winning, with Calvert Vaux, the competition to design New York's Central Park. Olmsted and Vaux made Central Park a pastoral landscape, re-creating an idealized countryside and avoiding such features as sports fields and geometrically arranged plantings. The idea that such a landscape would provide urbanites with a natural respite from the world of artificiality and commerce animated their design, much as it animated urban conservation decades later. Later in the 1860s, Olmsted suggested keeping Yosemite Valley in the public domain to serve as a national park, believing that its sublime scenery would draw thousands and ultimately millions. He joined Gifford Pinchot and Liberty Hyde Bailey as a frequent contributor to *Garden and Forest*.[55]

Olmsted was clearly an Arcadian, although one more taken with the grandeur of raw nature than were most of his contemporary landscape architects. His close association with parks and conservationists make it easy to claim him as a conservationist; indeed, his Wikipedia entry describes him as "an important early leader of the conservation movement." Yet he never expressed the sense that industrialization posed new hazards to humans and nature alike, particularly in contributing to resource scarcity, an idea that lay at the heart of conservation. Perhaps he would have embraced this view if he had lived longer (he died in 1903 after suffering years of dementia). Yet it seems a stretch to identify him as a conservationist. Not so for his son, Frederick Law Olmsted Jr., who imported the Arcadian sensibility of his father, and therefore much of American landscape architecture, into the conservation movement. The younger Olmsted continued his father's practice as a landscape architect, designing numerous parks, campuses, and suburban developments, but also vigorously embraced political action: in the 1890s, he became an early member of the Appalachian Mountain Club, the American Forestry Association, and the Society for the Protection of New Hampshire Forests. In the 1910s he advocated protecting Yosemite National Park's Hetch Hetchy Valley from use as a reservoir and wrote key passages of the law establishing the National Park Service; and in 1940 he became a member of the Council of the Wilderness Society. Olmsted Jr. never lost his Arcadian sensibility, but his turn to politics demonstrated that he also evolved into a conservationist.[56]

Conservation, as the trajectory of the Olmsteds indicates, brought with it earlier understandings of nature, beauty, city, and country, and then added to them much of the political culture of Progressivism, particularly that larger movement's commitment to restraining and humanizing the power of capital. In one way or another, almost all conservationists thought of themselves as addressing not only environmental but also social problems. John Muir was perhaps the most understated in this regard. Rather than reforming society, his brand of conservation was about maintaining places where people could escape from it. Still, even Muir acknowledged the yawning class divide of the age as part of its environmental crisis, warning of the "indifference" of the rich ("sleepy with wealth") and the poor ("sleepy with poverty, most of whom never saw a forest"). And most conservationists went much, much further. Gifford Pinchot attributed Americans' careless waste of natural resources not so much to a generalized environmental profligacy as to the dangerous power that concentrated wealth had come to exercise over the life and politics of the nation. "We have allowed the great corporations," he proclaimed, "to occupy with their own men the strategic points in business, in social, and in political life." By allowing for the monopolization of natural resources, the "unholy alliance between business and politics" denied economic freedom to millions, making it "the most dangerous fact in our political life."[57]

Urban conservationists similarly emphasized the problems of monopoly and the aggrandizement of political power by the wealthy. The architects of the forest reserves around Lynn, Massachusetts, in historian Michael Rawson's words, "framed their entire park enterprise as a rescue of the old town commons from private hands and a restoration of its ancient form and public purpose." Dana Bartlett, who frequently invoked Pinchot as a hero of the fight against monopoly, similarly drew parallels between U.S. politics in his own time and British politics in earlier centuries. Just as Americans were finding that the wildness and resources of nature were slipping from their grasp, so too in England had "the commons [been] gradually wrested from the people by the nobles" until "they had very little of what could be called common land." Bartlett pointed to the landscape of cities (particularly their luxurious private dwellings and businesses but deficient or absent parks) rather than woods and water, but like Pinchot, he attributed the problem to the victory of wealth over democracy in his lifetime. The "downward course of the city" commenced after the Civil War: "A few men began to amass large fortunes, importing cheap labor and exploiting the working class in their own interest. It was then that the tenement house and the slum seemed necessities, the public not realizing that to sow a slum meant to reap an epidemic."[58]

Because most conservationists believed that the wealth accumulated in the Gilded Age lay behind the environmental problems that faced the nation, it made sense that their proposals reflected critical elements of Progressivism, which sought to check that wealth. In particular, despite many differences on specific issues, and the great variance in their interest in urban environments, conservationists hoped that an active state could help Americans regain opportunities taken from them. Muir was pithy and matter-of-fact about this, but typically eloquent. The closing lines of *Our National Parks* made a plea for vigorous state intervention. "Through all the wonderful, eventful centuries since Christ's time—and long before that—God has cared for these trees," he proclaimed, "but he cannot save them from fools,—only Uncle Sam can do that." Pinchot made an active state role in the economy a major feature of his conservation platform. As he argued in *The Fight for Conservation:* "This country has achieved political freedom. What our people are fighting for now is industrial freedom." Like other Progressives, Pinchot attached the adjective "industrial" to "freedom" to underscore the point that the nominal formalities of political democracy—the vote, due process of law, adherence to the Constitution—were necessary but not sufficient for actual freedom. A worker denied a living wage or even physical safety by his employer was no more truly free than a farmer or small workshop forced to pay monopoly rates for rail shipping or fuel oil, or an electorate whose senator was bribed by the same company. Conservation, Pinchot and most of his compatriots believed, was a part of this larger struggle for real freedom. If natural resources were to be "developed and preserved for the benefit of the many and not merely for the profit of a few," then a strong state was needed to guide the use of such critical commodities as pasture, timber, and water, or else the property rights "so strongly entrenched" in America's constitutional order would prevent "the people" from gaining "their fair share of the benefit which comes from the development of the resources which belong to us all."[59]

Whether writing about reclamation, urban reform, or the rural resource issues so central to Pinchot's career, conservationists regularly emphasized the ways that an active state was a critical part of maintaining industrial freedom. Smythe's passion for reclamation, for example, was driven not just by the expectation that it would create lovely and profitable farms, but also by the belief that "the essence of the industrial life which springs from irrigation is its democracy." If a central state rather than a speculative market limited the acreage allotted to each farmer, it would represent adherence to, "the first great law which irrigation lays down," namely, that "there shall be no monopoly of land." Moreover, irrigation fostered the kind of economic independence that Smythe, Liberty Hyde Bailey, and other agrarian conservationists thought imperiled at the dawn of the urban age. Comparing an irrigated farm to the fields of a Texas cotton or Dakota wheat farmer, Smythe argued that "in the one case we see the little unmortgaged farm, its crops insured by irrigation, systematically producing a variety of things required for the family consumption." Such a life was likely to bring not great riches or fame, but something though more modest, more appealing: "a generous living . . . within the control of the proprietor." The other, unirrigated farms were both more vulnerable nature's whims and subordinated to larger economic power. "In the other case we see the single crop exposed to the mercy of the weather and the markets, its owner employing many hired hands, and going to the town to buy with cash nearly all that is necessary to feed his family and laborers." Bartlett made a similar point with respect to urban development. "Why should it be left to the caprice of a few individuals to decide whether the land outside of a growing city should be held as vacant property waiting for larger returns," he asked, "without regard to the interests of the rest of the city?" Here again the government, in this case at the municipal level, could protect a common good threatened by the economic power of a few: "Far better for the city itself to decide in advance the character of all the surrounding neighborhoods, buying and laying out in advance, for parks and playgrounds; establishing industrial, residential and agricultural districts, all with an idea to beauty as well as to utility." Freedom was not merely the absence of state control, but rather the product of a democratic political and economic system.[60]

Critiques of Conservation

Bartlett's Los Angeles, like most American cities, and perhaps even more so, did not follow his advice. Private property, not a municipal plan or government, determined the explosive growth of the metropolis in subsequent decades. City fathers set aside very little park space. Later generations of the very Angelenos on whose behalf Bartlett labored so much—its recently arrived immigrants, congregating in the urban core, out of easy reach of the beach and mountain retreats—ended up the most deprived of regular contact with the larger rhythms of nature. The Los Angeles River, which Bartlett and other conservationists envisioned as a key public space and environmental amenity became, in the nature writer Jennifer Price's words, "an outsize open sewer that carved a no-man's-land through many of the city's most fragmented and park-starved areas."[61]

At a certain point in the twentieth century, the surviving organizations bequeathed to America by the conservation movement seemed to have little to say about this situation. Muir's Sierra Club and Pinchot's Forest Service were still in full force. The club fought battles on behalf of such iconic places as Yellowstone and the Grand Canyon, defending them from mining development and damming. The Forest Service continued to manage much of L.A.'s mountain hinterland, providing for some modest logging, fire control, fishing, and hiking. Yet neither the Muirian nor Pinchotian side of conservation—which so often stand in for the whole movement—seemed to have any solution to, or even interest in, the environmental challenges facing the least advantaged Angelenos.

By the 1990s, environmental historians and other environmental scholars were pointing to precisely this kind of gap between the urban masses and environmental agencies and organizations as a symptom of the deep flaws and weaknesses in American environmentalism. By focusing on a pure nature that lay outside cities and by relying on bureaucracies and laws rather than mass political engagement and mobilization, these critics argued, environmentalists spoke mostly to the concerns of a disproportionately white and wealthy minority. Many of the historians among the critics traced this flaw to the founding of American environmentalism and the environmental state, arguing that the conservation movement's emphasis on protecting a supposedly pure nature from defilement (Muir) and its reliance on bureaucratic power to manage natural resources (Pinchot) locked in this pattern early on. Moreover, some critics charge, the racism of conservationists—and indeed, of conservation itself—undergirded the kind of neglect that allowed a river flowing through the most heavily Latino and African American neighborhoods of a rich and environmentally conscious city to become a noxious drainage ditch. Jake Kosek, for example, argues that such key environmental thinkers as Marsh and Muir "fed" on "racial and class fears surrounding purity and degradation" in their arguments for "the importance of maintaining in perpetuity the purity of the nation's environment—the very environment that embodied white nationalism." From this vantage, conservation sought to preserve whiteness as much as nature.[62]

Recognizing the full breadth of conservation makes it difficult to attribute all the later narrowness of American environmentalism to its founding generation. Conservation contained more commitments and ideas than its critics allow. It is true that John Muir was moved the most by majestic and seemingly lightly touched nature, and that Gifford Pinchot believed in bureaucracy, efficiency, and order much more than in grassroots democracy. Yet other figures offered different visions: Charles Francis Saunders was as enraptured by carefully cultivated beauty as much as by the purely wild variety, and Dana Bartlett and Mira Lloyd Dock emphasized remaking urban environments. Many conservationists, none more so than Pinchot, saw their proposals as addressing the economic opportunities and dignity of Americans, whether urban wage earners or small farmers. Their politics drew no line between the social and environmental. It was as concerned with inequality between people as with the protection of nature.

The critique of conservation on the count of race is more convincing. Most conservationists—or at least white conservationists—were indeed invested in whiteness. They assumed that other races were inferior to their own, and their environmental proposals reflected this chauvinism. It was no accident that park authorities in Massachusetts erased Irish place-names, or that Henry George championed the exclusion of Asians as part of his attack on land monopolies. The implementation of Jim Crow and the move toward comprehensive immigration restrictions mark the early twentieth century as a high point of white supremacy, so it should be no surprise that white conservationists partook of this. Perhaps it is more surprising that some did not: Saunders's landscape was not so much witness to the rise of Anglo-Saxon greatness as haunted by the terrors of white racial violence; Bartlett wanted Los Angeles made a city natural for the benefit of all its residents. Believing in conservation did not require believing in white supremacy.[63]

Breadth characterized the range of landscapes that conservation addressed (wildlands, the countryside, suburbs, the city, even the human body) and its proponents' ideologies, and also characterized the means by which conservationists sought to implement their vision. Conservationists built laws and bureaucracies, but tried to animate them with a vigorous awakening of conscience as well. They created a vibrant culture of conservation.

T • H • R • E • E

Back to Nature

"On its face the Conservation Movement is material—ultra material," noted W. J. McGee in 1910. "At first blush the moral and the social in which cults arise and from which doctrines draw inspiration may not appear." "Yet in truth," the influential scientist continued, "there has never been in all human history a popular movement more firmly grounded in ethics, in the eternal equities, in the divinity of human rights! Whether we rise into the spiritual empyrean or cling more closely to the essence of humanity, we find our loftiest ideals made real in the Cult of Conservation." McGee's commitments to science and progress drove his career, which included service for the U.S. Geological Survey, the directorship of the Bureau of American Ethnology, and the presidency of the National Geographic Society. Yet his invocation of "ethics" and "human rights" as key aspects of a "popular movement" points to the ways in which conservation relied on passionate moral commitments as well as scientific rationality.[1]

What McGee approvingly labeled a "cult" impressed others as well. "More Americans go back to nature for one reason or another, annually, than any civilized men before them," noted the literary critic Henry Canby. The essayist Louise Willcox similarly argued that the huge number of "outdoor books"—novels with an outdoors theme, gardening and horticultural manuals, works of natural history—meant that "the depravity of doors has been proven finally by the present generation."

What Willcox called a "return to nature" was an old theme in Western civilization, as she knew. Yet since "the progress of civilization began to house man more and more, and to stifle him with treasures and things . . . there had to be a revival, a definite call 'back to nature,' and artificial means thereto sprung up, sports and landscape-gardening, voyages of discovery, Arctic expeditions, and nature poetry and nature study, a hundred or more magazines of outdoor life, and countless books to remind us of the delights of living in the open, and loving the closest, most obvious, and more blessed gifts of heaven." By the early twentieth century, this impulse was not merely the concern of a literary and artistic sliver, bur rather, as Willcox noted, a mass phenomenon: "The thought of it has penetrated and impregnated the world with its healing power, first men, and then women, till at last the average bank clerk has learned the value of a side-issue resource that binds him to the great sphere twirling underfoot, and the busiest of mothers has stretched her sense of duty beyond the bounds of a sewing-machine." Henry Canby was also struck by how many Americans were drawn to nature: "In the West, the very day laborer pitches his camp in the mountains for his two weeks' holiday. In the East and Middle West, every pond with a fringe of hemlocks, or hill view by a trolley line, or strip of ocean beach, has its cluster of bungalows where the proletariat perform their *villegiatura* as the Italian aristocracy did in the days of the Renaissance."[2]

McGee, Canby, and Willcox captured a powerful truth, although one that has largely fallen out of scholarship on the subject: conservationists pursued their central goal—a material balance and psychic renewal with a nature they thought imperiled—in private lives as well as public actions. In a time when the built world had grown so complicated and consuming as to alienate many from the natural world, conservationists sought a "return to nature" in outdoor recreation, the study of nature in schools, literature, and domestic architecture. Conservation was as much about cultural change as it was an economic doctrine or a set of policies. Like conservation politics, conservation culture was aimed at escaping the artificiality and destructiveness of industrial life. By hiking, studying wild plants and animals, reading novels about reconnecting with nature, and living in homes deliberately crafted to evoke the natural world, conservationists hoped that Americans would revitalize themselves and deepen their appreciation of nature. As with so much of the rest of Progressivism, institutional reform and cultural change would reinforce each other: America would be different because Americans would be different.

Outdoor Recreation

The simplest way for Americans to "get back to nature" was to travel from a city or suburb, where humanity's imprint lay all around, to a place that seemed less touched or even untouched. Recreational hiking, canoeing, and camping became markedly more popular in the Progressive era. The contours of an outdoor recreation industry took shape in this period, catering to countless Americans who never joined a conservation organization or perhaps never considered themselves conservationists. National forests and parks aggressively marketed their rugged and remote attractions, as in the boast of a promotional pamphlet for northern Minnesota's Superior National Forest: "Fine camping sites are abundant, and the voyageur can always pitch his tent wherever night overtakes him—at places others have camped before, or perhaps where the ring of a woodsman's ax has never broken the forest silence."[3] These sorts of calls fell on receptive ears. Visitation to parks and monuments administered by the U.S. government grew tenfold from 1906 to 1915. The scant sixty-nine thousand visitors to national parks in 1908 grew to more than a million in 1921.[4]

Regional sporting magazines and national venues such as *Forest and Stream* described the virtues of particular parks, forests, and trails. Hardware stores near outdoor destinations began advertising camping gear. Residents of many cities organized outdoor clubs and cooperatives, including the Seattle outfit that would later become REI (Recreation Equipment Incorporated). These organizations pushed for easy access to public lands and sometimes pooled members' resources to buy and rent camping equipment at affordable prices. Indeed, outdoor recreation became a major feature of genteel urban culture. Edward Bok, editor of the *Ladies' Home Journal*, urged his readers to rent a remote cottage rather than stay in resorts, or at least to hike in the woods. Bok and others organized "Fresh Air Funds" to subsidize vacations for urban children whose families could not afford to pay for their own trips. The *Journal* ran a regular column, "American Woodcraft for Boys," by the naturalist Ernest Thompson Seton, which offered practical camping advice.[5]

John Muir's Sierra Club epitomized the fusion of environmental politics and outdoor recreation. It was as much a hiking organization as an advocacy group; its newsletters routinely described the pleasures of excursions to the California Sierra, complete with photographs of enthusiastic trail parties. A *Sierra Club Bulletin* article in 1909 memorializing a young member who died on the trail captured members' faith in the restorative potential of wilderness hiking: "Young, vigorous, gay, eager for adventure, she loved the outdoor life among the forests and mountains of her native State. She bloomed like a flower in this wilderness, vivid with life, brilliant with color, responsive to winds from the heights. She had the spirit of an explorer; she would put her foot on untrodden soil, would test the inviolate vastness of Nature in her secret and protected places, in the haunts reserved from eye and foot of man."[6]

The Boy Scouts of America (BSA) likewise fused outdoor recreation and aspects of conservation. Founded in 1910, the BSA aimed to foster the healthy development of boys into mature, devoted, independent citizens. Camping and the development of outdoor skills aided in this endeavor by fostering toughness, self-reliance, and group bonding. The organization soon absorbed other outdoor-oriented youth organizations, such as Ernest Thompson Seton's Woodcraft Indians. Conservation was a metaphor through which BSA leaders understood their work. "You have seen a lot in the papers about conservation of our resources," wrote Dan Beard, the national scout commissioner, in 1913. "The most valuable resource we have are the boys of America. Every boy who goes astray and becomes a misfit and a failure is a great loss to the assets of this country. Every honorable, brave, efficient boy is a tremendous asset to this country. The Boy Scouts of America is the greatest conservation society in the world, for we are working to conserve the boys."[7]

Some of the practices and ethos that Scouting troops used to "conserve the boys" would have given devoted conservationists pause. White American pioneers were role models for Scouts, who were to emulate the virility and patriotism that their forebears supposedly demonstrated by exploring and developing the wilderness. Accordingly, chopping down

trees and erecting buildings and bridges with the logs were major activities and even requirements for boys to earn merit badges. On the other
hand, an increasingly loud chorus of voices within Scouting called for
aligning its ethos with natural resource conservation. In 1917 the chief
dendrologist for the Forest Service penned an article in the magazine
for Scout leaders that criticized the legend of the young George Washington chopping down a cherry tree. He urged Scouts instead to use
dead and down timber, and to learn tree taxonomy well enough to cut
down only trees worthless as timber, if they had to be cut at all. Scouting
publications during World War I called for a wide range of conservation
measures, including food conservation and the extermination of the
destructive tent caterpillar (which it compared to the quashing of German sabotage and propaganda that threatened the "Liberty Tree" of the
United States). By the 1920s, Scout handbooks featured environmental
critiques of pioneers, who, the handbook said, thought of forests as "an
obstruction in the path of progress . . . [to be] cut and burned as rapidly
as possible." Tests for moving up the ranks and earning merit badges
came to include repairing trees and planting seedlings.[8]

The kind of extended camping trips so important to Scouting were
beyond the reach of most wage earners, given the cost of a long trip
to a remote destination and the rental of specialized equipment. But
strenuous hiking in preserves near cities could be viable and had its appeal for those of modest circumstance. Oregon's *Labor Press,* for example, reported on the growing ability of the state's union families to visit
parks and forests by car; by the 1920s, it regularly ran advertisements for
outdoor gear. Its columnist "The Dreamer" used Muirian language to
urge readers with "lungs cramped and half suffocated from the continual laboring with the 'civilized' air . . . that has come through countless
clouds of smoke, past reeking garbage cans, through office buildings and
stores until any semblance it once had to freshness has been extracted
from it" to "enjoy the day as it was meant to be enjoyed—out in the
open, beneath God's wind-swept sky, in the woods' temples built by His
hands."[9]

Similar calls to the wild could be found in California's *Western
Comrade,* the mouthpiece of the Golden State's socialist movement. "In
fastnesses and shaded nooks, by brookside or seaside, in song of bird

or care-free life of animals, Mother Nature spreads her bounty of life, light, and beauty" ran one piece in 1913 titled "Nature's Banquet Table." The author urged California socialists to go beyond a superficial contact with the outdoors, to seek the same kind of transcendence that the more upper-crust Sierra Clubbers sought:

> Most travelers follow routes laid down in guide books and visit resorts well known. Not many leave the beaten paths for the solitude of mountain fastnesses, where such close access to the heart of the All-Mother is permitted that its pulsing may be felt and one's own should be attuned to its eternal rhythm. In the dark of silent gorges, amid the awful silence of a mountain canyon, alone, afar from the haunts of men on some broad expanse of ocean shore, let him who would wrest Nature's secrets from her, woo her there. Let him pitch his tent and hearken to myriad voices speaking in myriad tongues. Such communion is for all if all will it.[10]

Not all may have sought such "communion," but many did. "This is the land of the pedestrian and the mountain climber," Charles Frances Saunders wrote of California's mountains in 1913. "All summer long parties big and little and of both sexes, their blankets and camp kits slung upon their backs, come gaily up from the cities of the coast and the plain, from the schools and counting houses and shops, living Arcadian days and weeks in shady cañons by never-failing waters, and sleeping beneath the sky." John Muir was impressed by the pull of mountain retreats on nearby urbanites, but by the twentieth century he had been startled by what heavy visitation could do to wilderness solitude. He wrote of his disappointment that the mosses and ferns that had once lined Eaton Falls in the San Gabriel Mountains bordering Los Angeles had been trampled bare by a constant stream of visitors. Muir's beloved Yosemite Valley was subjected to similar heavy visitation. "There were actually thousands of tourists in the Valley this summer," wrote a correspondent to Gifford Pinchot. "Decent camp grounds were difficult to find; meadows for campers' horses were grazed to the ground before the middle of July." Conservationists feared that ignorance and greed led to the despoiling of nature, but they were learning that love of wildness could wreak its own destruction.[11]

Educating for Conservation

Advocates of outdoor recreation often invoked conservationist themes, and the proponents of "nature study" were even more explicitly conservationist in their goals. Nature study was a curricular program to acquaint students with the natural world by teaching them to grow schoolyard gardens and to identify and explain the characteristics of animals and plants. Spearheaded by the American Nature Study Society, founded in Chicago in 1908, nature study proliferated across the primary-school curriculum. By 1915, it was being explicitly taught in elementary school in fourteen states and incorporated into the curriculum in one way or another in almost all states. Educators who drew on nature study believed it was an effective way to further the goals of cultivating the imagination, developing powers of observation, and learning basic scientific principles. At the same time, they expected that it would give "the child a sense of companionship with life out-of-doors and an abiding love of nature," in the words of Anna Botsford Comstock, a Cornell University professor of nature study. Writing in his influential book *Nature Study and the Child* (1902), the educational theorist Charles B. Scott explicitly linked this goal to the historical moment, which cried out for conservation: We have stripped "our land of its forests, our air of its birds, our waters of our fish, by using up in the most reckless manner our natural resources," he wrote. "Nature has been our slave, from whom we could take anything, to whom we owed nothing . . . [but] we are learning that such adaptation is in the end unprofitable, unwise, utterly wrong . . . We are discovering as a nation that we must protect our forests, and are just beginning to plant where we formerly used our energies in destroying our trees." Inculcating knowledge of and respect for nature contributed to this reversal, Scott argued. A properly educated child would realize that he "owes something to the world around him. He protects what he once destroyed. He takes care of the flowers which before he trod upon . . . He is adapting himself to his physical environment; not merely ap-

propriating, but giving in return." This form of education aimed at moral
and political transformation as much as mere knowledge.[12]

Nature study blended scientific rationalism and aesthetic Roman-
ticism, two key ingredients of conservation as a whole. On one hand, the
curriculum's central aim was to guide students in the direct investigation
of nature around them. Accuracy and attention to detail were to be fostered, and nature study educators prided themselves on their scientific
literacy. On the other hand, the approach to nature was also Romantic
and mystical. Plants and animals were to be encountered outdoors, not
in books or as preserved laboratory specimens. They were to be identified with and loved, not simply studied. Fostering an emotional attachment to nature was as important a goal as memorizing technical
knowledge. "When the child has watched the bean and pea grow from
seed to fruit, and noted how each part has a work, and how well it does
its work," wrote Scott, "when he has *seen* the buds emerge from their
protecting scales, throw out leaf and flower, and go to work; when he has
listened to the song of the robin or bluebird, and peered into her nest as
she has fed her little ones,—he appreciates, as he cannot be led to appreciate in any other way, the beauties of the his natural environment." In
this holistic emphasis on direct experience, nature study circles partook
of the critique of narrowly technical knowledge that ran in some conservationist circles.[13]

In the end, the architects of nature study used and embraced scientific expertise, but subordinated it to a larger, more holistic vision of education and nature. "Nature came to be seen as a spiritual and aesthetic
antidote to modern life," the historian Kevin Armitage writes in his
history of nature study, one of the few works to recognize the cultural
breadth and richness of conservation. "Contact with nature became not
just a pedagogical method but also a way to ameliorate the stresses and
anxieties of the modern world," he notes in an observation that applies
as much to the culture of conservation as a whole as to nature study in
particular.[14]

Nature study and fiction merged into each other as conservation
themes appeared in some of the most widely read novels of the era. In
these works, as in reality, those suffering from the ills of industrial and

urban life found healing by renewed contact with nature. Marjorie Benton Cooke's novel *The Girl Who Lived in the Woods* (1910) was a good example. The novel opens with the glum and nearly loveless marriage of two modestly wealthy heirs, Anne and Richard Barrett. Discontented with their lives, they move from the city to a wooded tract north of Chicago. Here they meet the young Cecilia Carné, whose marked appreciation for nature they soon come to admire and emulate: "[Cecilia] made her way along the path worn by her feet through the wood, and her quick eyes took in every twig and tree. . . . She marveled at the blue-gray of the water, resigning herself, as it were, to the softening influence of spring winds. She delighted in the first faint green of the trees against the background of spruce and pine." Living in the sort of environs advocated by conservation-minded landscape architects—where native trees and wild animals are constant reminders of the larger patterns of nature —soon improves Richard and Anne's marriage. The couple spends more time together, falls in love again, and, with their young son, come to delight in their garden, the trees that surround their house, and distant glimmering Lake Michigan. The contrast throughout the novel is between the healing power of nature, on the one hand, and urban life— deadening to the spirits of the fortunate Barretts and the impoverished Carné alike—on the other.[15]

No explicit advocacy or discussion of the political program of conservation emerged from novels such as *The Girl Who Lived in the Woods*. Other authors, however, were much more direct about conservation. The midwestern realist writer and future Pulitzer Prize winner Hamlin Garland published *Cavanagh, Forest Ranger: A Romance of the Mountain West* in 1910, with an introduction by Gifford Pinchot. The entwined dramas of *Cavanagh* are the romance between the protagonist whom the book is named after and a local girl recently returned from the East, and the violent conflicts over the range that culminate in the grisly murder of Basque shepherds. Cavanagh, an English immigrant, performs numerous feats of manly heroism in the course of his public service as a forest ranger. He is sensitive enough to be moved by the transcendent beauty of nature, as on a high midnight ride: "He parted the layer of mist and burst into the moonlit heights above. He drew a deep breath of awe as he turned and looked about him. Overhead the sky was sparkling with innumerable stars, and the crescent moon was shining like burnished silver, while level with his breast rolled a limitless, silent, and mystical ocean of cloud which broke against the dark peaks in soundless surf and spread away to the east in ever widening shimmer." (Garland later echoed these sorts of passages in his memoir *A Son of the Middle Border,* when he remembered how the midwestern farm families he grew up with could be moved by "the marvel of a golden earth beneath a crimson sky" even in the midst of backbreaking labor.)[16]

Despite this sort of occasional invocation of the sublime qualities of nature, the antimonopoly aspects of conservation loom larger in the novel than does environmental protection. Garland, an early disciple of Henry George and a onetime Populist stump speaker, portrays Cavanagh and the federal government he serves as bearers of order and stability to the crude and violent community around the Colorado national forest. "Cattle-barons" and "sheep-herders" wage a bloody struggle for control of the range, overgrazing and poaching when supervision becomes lax. This frontier community is unable to govern itself, its feckless citizens and sheriff too cowardly and corrupt to stop the murderous thugs in their midst. At one point Garland directly compares a dying cowboy to the West itself: "He was going as the Wild West was going, discredited, ulcerated, poisoned, incapable of rebirth, yet carrying something fine to his grave."[17]

In contrast, Cavanagh's labors in taming the West allow him to join a larger, glorious story of national power and achievement. "The English empire to him was falling apart," Garland has his protagonist reflect in a moment when the loneliness and physical rigors of his work force him to consider its meaning. "Its supremacy was already threatened by Germany, whereas the future of the States appealed to his imagination. Here the problems of popular government and of industry were to be worked out on the grandest scale. The West inspired him. 'Some day each of these great ranges will be a national forest, and each of these canons will contain its lake its reservoir.' There was something fine in this vision of man's conquest of nature."[18]

The works of Gene Stratton-Porter presented a more aesthetic and romantic vision of conservation. A founding member of the conservation and outdoor recreation organization the Izaak Walton League, Stratton-Porter wrote novels, nature study tracts for the *Ladies' Home Journal* and other mass-circulation publications, and natural history books. Of the fifty-five novels published between 1895 and 1945 that sold more than a million copies in the United States, five were hers. Her most widely read work was the novel *Freckles* (1904), which was turned into a movie by Paramount Studios in 1917. *Freckles* was set in the swamps of Stratton-Porter's native Indiana, where the orphan Freckles becomes a forest guard for a timber company. The "Limberlost," as the area was known, awakens deep sympathy and curiosity in the young man, particularly for its birds. "Through fall, when brooding was finished and the upland birds sought the swamp in swarms to feast on its seeds and berries, Freckles was content with watching them and speculating about them. Outside of half a dozen of the very commonest, they were strangers to him. The likeness of their actions to humanity was an hourly surprise." Freckles revels in the spring return of migratory birds, the birth of a luna moth, and his discovery of a rare pair of nesting black vultures (the last seemingly patterned after the author's own early experience as a naturalist). Soon he turns to ordering nature-study books with his modest savings.[19]

The two central tensions of *Freckles* are the romance between the title character and the "Angel," a beautiful girl from a nearby town, and the possible destruction of the Limberlost by timber poachers. Freckles works for a private timber company rather than the federal government (unlike his counterpart Cavanagh in Hamlin Garland's novel), but Stratton-Porter presents the company managers as environmentally benevolent. The thieves with their eyes on the swamp's timber are another matter. As Angel puts it, "They'll clear out roads, cut down the beautiful trees, and tear up everything. They'll drive away the birds and spoil the cathedral. When they have done their worst, then all these mills close here will follow in and take out the cheap timber. Then the landowners will dig a few ditches, build some fires, and in two summers more the Limberlost will be in corn and potatoes." Vigilance is required to protect the natural treasures of the Limberlost from greed and rapaciousness. In the book's melodramatic climax, Freckles's heroic willingness to sacrifice himself for the Limberlost and the Angel saves the former and wins him the love of the latter. As in *Cavanagh,* the public triumph of conservation accompanies the private romantic triumph of the protagonist.[20]

Stratton-Porter viewed her novels as means to advance the conservation movement. Writing in the *Ladies' Home Journal,* she declared that she became a writer in order to "lead women back to the forest"—to cultivate a sense of wonder and adventure in the face of nature. The historical moment seemed right for this quest: "There was no need for many of them to wrest a living from the forest; they, from the work of three generations were frequently prepared to spend a fortune on it; but in the course of accumulating that fortune the forest had receded until it was sometimes difficult to find, while wild life had been wantonly sacrificed until deer were scarce, buffalo and wood pigeons exterminated and many other birds rare." Her initial draft of *Freckles* was "another book of woodlore, straight nature stuff, through which I ran a slight romance as a sugar coating, in my effort to entice the household afield"—in fact, "the sole purpose of the book was to put the nature stuff it contained before the people." Once *Freckles,* supplemented with a conventional romantic storyline and happy ending, became a popular success, Stratton-Porter secured the consent of her publisher to alternate between a "nature story" such as *Freckles* and "any kind of nature book I chose." She thus secured the wide circulation of what might be called "conservation novels" and nature-study books on such topics as birdsongs and moths.[21]

Conservation Architecture

Schools and novels became important ways of fostering conservationist values. Private homes and their grounds or lots became an even greater preoccupation of conservationists. Architects, real estate developers, and women's clubs hoped to infuse private homes and their grounds or lots with many of the same values that wilderness and urban parks systems were designed to protect. With properly skilled negotiations between humans and nature, these places, the provinces of individual and family life, could ameliorate the social harms of industrial life and restore authenticity and physical vigor to daily existence. Given the environmental destruction that suburban sprawl would bring after World War II, it is understandable that the close connection between conservation politics and certain types of real estate development and home designs has been obscured. But it in its own time, this connection was one of the most important aspects of the culture of conservation.

The bungalow and similar styles of homes owed much of their appeal to their apparent congruence with the environmental values associated with conservation. An English adaptation of village houses on the Indian subcontinent, the bungalow in North America came to refer to a "comfortable-looking, one or one-and-one-half story dwelling usually preceded by a spacious front porch . . . [that] dispensed with the formal separation of public spaces seen earlier in the Victorian house." Its informality, frequent use of sleeping porches, and emphasis on light and ventilation were designed to blur the once heavily policed line between outdoors and inside. The first American bungalow appears to have been constructed on Cape Cod in 1880, and as late as 1900 the handful of these homes in the United States were summer retreats in the mountains or by the sea in northeastern states. In the first decade of the twentieth century, however, the bungalow spread across the country, in the process developing into several different regional styles. It had become so ubiquitous by the 1920s that cultural critics associated it with Babbitry and middle-class blandness. In the same period, the Chicago architect Frank Lloyd Wright turned to bungalow-like elements in his home designs— open floor plans, strong horizontal lines, long windows that integrated the interior and external nature. Like the bungalow, this "prairie style" of architecture relied on modern construction techniques to build homes that merged with and evoked the surrounding landscape.[22]

The bungalow retained much of its original connection with a retreat to the wholesome simplicity of outdoor living. Exponents of the bungalow frequently advocated that it be constructed on lots as undisturbed by construction as possible. Trees should be left standing (which Wright also emphasized), and exterior materials selected to foster, in the words of one such advocate, "the intimate relationship between home and surroundings that always conveys an impression of peace and stability rather than strife and unfitness." The bungalow was a favored home of devotees of the Arts and Crafts movement, which reacted against industrialization and its tidal wave of mass-produced goods by revitalizing traditions of craftsmanship that united art and labor. On both sides of the Atlantic, Arts and Crafts devotees produced furniture, ceramics, and textiles that they thought of as typifying a simpler, wholesome, more natural society. Gustav Stickley, editor of the *Craftsman,* the mouthpiece of the American Arts and Crafts movement, praised the way the bungalow's typically low profile ensured "that the countryside is no longer *affronted* with lean, narrow, two-story houses"; appreciated how its wooden shingles "came to look like autumn leaves"; and argued that proper design and detailing could "tie the building to its surroundings and give it the seeming of a growth rather than a creation." He considered the bungalow an excellent domestic counterpart to "the new wilderness areas being used by vacationers." Stickley's writings about the bungalow fit comfortably into the broad range of environmental topics in his magazine, in which readers could encounter John Muir extolling the virtues of primitive wilderness on one page, female Audubon Society leaders condemning the slaughter of majestic birds on the next, and gardeners advocating the use of native plants later in the same issue. These endeavors, in one way or another, reflected the sense that industrial civilization had alienated people from wild nature. Decisions about home design and recreation were the private counterparts to the public actions of conservation laws and policies.[23]

In a less obvious way, bungalows reflected the values of efficiency that animated some varieties of conservation. The straightforward, rectangular shape of the bungalow lent itself to simpler and thus cheaper construction, one of the reasons it made for such affordable housing. The open floor plans allowed heat from a single basement furnace to circulate throughout the home, eliminating the need for multiple stoves and fireplaces. Even the numerous large windows of bungalows had their analogues in factory construction, which in the early twentieth century generally featured large expanses of windows out of the belief that fresh air and sunshine would maximize worker productivity. Smaller kitchens more easily reached from other rooms required less movement and energy for cooking and cleaning, and the exposed wood floors and surfaces and lack of heavy drapes made for easy cleaning and sanitation. Bungalows were paradoxically modern and antimodern.[24]

Perhaps only in Chicago, where about a third of the city's housing stock consisted of bungalows, did this style mark the landscape as much as in Southern California. Bungalows had so impressed themselves upon the Los Angeles landscape by 1914 that the writer Mary Austin concluded that "in this group of low hills and shallow valleys between the Sierra Madre and the sea, the most conspicuous human achievement has been a new form of domestic architecture." For Austin, the omnipresent bungalows suggested that Anglos had become at home in this region, for "with their low and flat-pitched roofs, they present a certain likeness to the aboriginal dwellings which the Franciscans found scattered like wasps nests among the chaparral along the river—which is only another way of saying that the spirit of the land shapes the art that is produced there."[25]

Southern California was notable for other house designs premised on bringing nature into daily living. "Here homes are built with reference to the climate," boasted Dana Bartlett of Los Angeles in 1911, "with large porches used as living-rooms, with open-air bedrooms, with patios filled with blossoms and rare plants—the joy of every season." The designs of the architects R. M. Schindler and Richard Neutra looked little like bungalows, instead featuring concrete walls and sliding-glass panels. But these designers embraced the new construction materials made possible by industrial technologies for the same reasons that the bungalow was so alluring: they could take maximum advantage of sunlight, fresh air, and scenic views.[26]

Schindler's Kings Road House, built in West Hollywood, California, in the early 1920s became a widely celebrated example of such modernist domestic architecture. Its design was inspired by a trip to Yosemite that Schindler took in late 1921 with his fiancée; on their return to Los Angeles, in the words of an ecological architect in the twenty-first century, "they decided to try to recapture the freedom they had felt camping out in the wilderness and sleeping under the stars." "Our rooms . . . will descend close to the ground and the garden will become an integral part of the house," Schindler wrote of his Kings Road design, comparing its elements to "the basic requirements of a camper's shelter: a protected back, an open front, a fireplace and a roof." His design was informed by a belief that humanity had entered a new stage in its relationship with the wider natural world, the same assumption that conservationists used to argue for more state control over natural resources. "The machine has become the ripe symbol for man's control over nature's forces," the Viennese native wrote in 1912. Whereas previous dwellings were constrained by the need for structural bulk, the technology of reinforced concrete broke that chain, if only people could realize their newfound power. "The man of the future does not try to escape the elements," Schindler confidently predicted. "He will rule them," he continued, in a flourish reminiscent of Pinchot's declaration that "the first duty of the human race is to control the earth it lives upon." For Schindler, this meant that "his home is no more a timid retreat: the earth has become his home."[27]

Environmentally sensitive buildings seemed to hold a particular allure for conservation circles. The managers and principals of the national parks embraced the notion that park buildings needed to fit in with their natural surroundings. The architects and landscape architects they hired to develop park infrastructure put into practice the aesthetic principles touted by Stickley, Schindler, Austin, and others. Yellowstone's Old Faithful Inn, built in 1903–4 a few hundred yards from the famous geyser from which it took its name, departed from the previous pattern of relying on the kind of conventional architecture that might have been found in any city, suburb, or resort in any region. Constructed of enormous peeled logs and featuring large stone fireplaces, the building employed a style that evoked the structures of Blue Ridge and Adirondack resorts. At the same time, its boulder masonry, deliberately coarse textures, and "pseudo-pioneer construction techniques" made it fit especially well with the rugged landscape of the remote park. Other park structures took on an Arts and Crafts feel, as in the Grand Canyon administrative building, whose lower level was made of coarse local limestone, with an upper level of exposed dark boards and intersecting roof gables. By the mid-1910s, the notion that park buildings ought to speak to their larger natural setting had become a commonplace among landscape architects. "If a landscape character is to be dominant in the scene," wrote Henry Hubbard and Theodora Kimball in a chapter on buildings in parks in their widely touted *Introduction to the Study of Landscape Design* (1917), "then the building must be in some way subordinated . . . [and] related harmoniously to a landscape which as a whole expresses its own natural character." Hubbard and Kimball advised designers to pay particular attention to the texture and color of their creations, and to the ways in which these qualities could evoke the surrounding landscape.[28]

The private dwellings of conservationists often reflected the architectural culture of the movement. Charles Francis Saunders extensively praised the bungalow, along with the wilder places close to his heart. "The ample windows fill the house with light," he noted, "and there is the perfume of the violets or roses, or both, in the air . . . Opened doorways and windows admit the breeze with manifold fragrances from hedge and garden." In his own bungalow, Saunders and his wife, Mira, "made an outdoor living-and-dining-room of our rear veranda, a quiet, retired spot on whose roof and sides were climbing roses and honeysuckles that hid us from our neighbors. From this flowery bower we looked out upon our little 60 × 90 foot garden, and beyond to the Sierra Madre, with its lovely lights and shadows and exquisite colors in the evening glow. Old-hickory chairs and settees, with a similar table or two, indifferent to the weather, make a suitable furnishing to such a nook."[29]

Charles and Mira Saunders drew inspiration for their home from an earlier resident of Pasadena, California—Jeanne C. Carr. Carr remained devoted to her husband's former student John Muir: she introduced Muir to Louisa Strentzel, who later became his wife, and she and Muir remained active correspondents for nearly forty years until her death, in 1903. Yet her passion lay with the cultivated, domesticated nature close at hand rather than the majestic wilderness. After relocating to what was then the small town of Pasadena in 1877, Jeanne and her husband Ezra began planting a small acreage that they dubbed "Carmelita" with trees, flowers, and plants from around the world. Their first home at Carmelita was soon engulfed in vines. Their friend Helen Hunt Jackson called Carmelita an "inspiration" wrought by "a person whose only relations with nature were of the closest, and of long standing." Ultimately the estate was incorporated into Pasadena's municipal park system.[30]

In the very different environment of the boreal forest along the Minnesota-Ontario border, Ernest Oberholtzer, a founder of the Wilderness Society, created dwellings that similarly made the most of their surroundings. Drawing on his knowledge of landscape architecture learned at the feet of Frederick Law Olmsted Jr., Oberholtzer ensured

The California naturalist Mira Saunders relaxing outside the bungalow she shared with her husband, Charles, in the 1910s. Their appreciation for the bungalow style was widely shared among conservationists. *(Courtesy Huntington Library)*

that "all of the buildings are of local material in the character of the country . . . and fit attractively into the landscape." On Mallard Island, he employed local craftsman and indigenous materials in the construction of small dwellings made of rough boards, exposed log rafters, and stone walls and foundations. Christened with such names as The Bird House, Old Man River House, and Cedarbark House, the buildings were linked with unpaved paths and placed in order to maximize their vistas of Rainy Lake, its swirling currents, and the constellations, sunsets, and moonrises. Oberholtzer devoted other portions of the small island to vegetable and flower plots. The overall result of his efforts was the preservation and cultivation of his island home into what Oberholtzer's biographer describes as "an integration of nature with civilization."[31]

The interest of Saunders, Carr, and Oberholtzer in melding their homes with their interest in the wider natural world also appeared in real estate advertisements in Progressive magazines and newspapers. Some of these advertisements placed particular emphasis on the environmental aspects of intelligent home design and planting, suggesting

that developers and architects believed that these political circles were
concerned with such values in their own lives. (*Progressive Los Angeles*
went so far as to offer special deals on home sites in "Beautiful Paradise Park" to new subscribers.)[32] An advertisement for summer homes
in the Sierra Nevada deployed a staple conservationist trope in its jux-
taposition of artificial urbanity with the wholesome and peaceful life
in the outdoors. "Do you remember," the California-Pacific Investment
Company asked, "you footsore plodders along man-made canyons, the
happy yesterday of youth, when, lithe limbed and care free, you stood
at Nature's knee and learned from her beneficent lips the secret way to
the open trail she imparts only to the young?" The company assured
"brain-fagged business and professional men" that "you can leave the
hard heart of the city and within a few hours' railway journey snug-
gle yourselves against the breast of old Mother Nature and grow young
again in body and in mind"—simply by purchasing one of their Sierra
homes.[33]

Other companies invoked conservationist themes to sell home
tracts. In 1912, the L. D. Loomis company advertised for home sites in
Santa Monica, California, in nearly every issue of *California Outlook*,
ensuring that its pitch would appear alongside discussions of irrigation,
the management of national parks, timber harvesting, and the management of the city parks of Los Angeles and San Francisco. The primary
selling point of the ad was the "invincible" combination of beach access
and canyon. The crashing waves of the Pacific and the sharp elevation
changes and mountain views were both the sorts of sublime landscapes
that the more romantic conservationists wanted to preserve as public
land. The assumption of this ad was that such a landscape could also
be sold as a private natural amenity. So confident of this were the ad's
authors that they felt it effective to identify "THE NATURE LOVER" as one
of their target markets.[34]

Although they offered sites for the construction of homes, the developers presented the canyon as a natural place. The top picture contained no human beings—let alone enough level ground to easily envision a home being constructed there—and the path was clearly too
small to be a road. The man in the lower picture allowed readers to envision themselves in this rustic and tranquil setting, but he remained a

A real estate advertisement in the Progressive magazine *California Outlook* in 1912 allowed prospective customers to envision themselves in surroundings of natural beauty, reflecting both the environmental impulse in home design and its commodification. *(Courtesy Huntington Library)*

small presence in the image, thereby reinforcing the emphasis on the area's natural amenities. Just as urbanites tired of the grind of modern industrial life could find refuge in Yosemite or Yellowstone, so too could home buyers "enjoy life in the right way—out close to Nature." Theodore Roosevelt's call for the "strenuous life" found its echo in the argument that living in the Santa Monica canyon would provide home buyers "the opportunity to improve the physical welfare of their children through outdoor life."[35]

Even those not fortunate enough to own a home in a canyon could see to it that their homes and lots reflected a conservationist sensibility about the place of humans in nature. Popular magazines such as *Suburban Life, House Beautiful, House and Garden,* and *American Homes and Gardens* counseled their readers to protect the large trees of their suburbs and cities. The more environmentally engaged articles in these publications advocated the use of muted, natural colors that made homes blend into their surroundings, rather than the traditional stark white that embodied the farmhouse's triumph over the wilderness. The Philadelphia architect Henry Saylor developed this theme in a 1915 homebuilder's manual on bungalow design, construction, and planting advice. A bungalow should "be in its proper environment, blending with the grays and greens and browns of the surrounding trees," he wrote. Saylor was not against conventional color schemes and finishes, because "the smooth white stucco of a permanent home is beyond criticism where the immediate surroundings have felt and show the unmistakable marks of man's dominion over the natural—in smooth lawns and clipped trees, in geometrical lines of formal gardening and its architectural accessories." But "when we take up our abode by choice in Nature's own domain we should have the good taste to conform to her general color scheme for the whole place rather than introduce a blatant note of discord, just to show our independence." The architect Irving Gill, whose home designs blended Spanish Revival and modernist aesthetics, struck a similar note the same year in the *Craftsman* magazine. "We should build our house simple, plain and substantial as a boulder," he declared in one of his few published essays, "then leave the ornamentation of it to Nature, who will tone it with lichens, chisel it with storms, make it gracious and friendly with vines and flower shadows as she does the stone in the meadow."[36]

Saylor's and Gill's kinds of aesthetic considerations could be adapted on a much larger scale and in service to a different vision of conservation. The California author, conservationist, and real estate developer Abbot Kinney was a case in point. The New Jersey–born citrus grower, one of the largest landholders in Los Angeles County in the 1880s, became vice president of the American Forestry Association, president of the Southern California Forest and Water Association and of the Southern California Academy of Sciences. Kinney argued for decades that scientific forestry was particularly crucial to Southern California's development because it could prevent forest fires and ensure the regular supply of water needed for productive fields and crops. He was also instrumental in the development of the town of Venice, California, and nearby Santa Monica. Eucalyptus trees, native to Australia, played prominent roles in his vision for the region. He believed that they could turn desolate spaces into productive agricultural and residential landscapes. "The introduction of this tree," he wrote of the eucalyptus, "has done more to change radically the appearance of wide ranges of country in California than any other one thing. In the reclamation of many arid plains of the central and southern parts of California the blue gum has worked almost like magic. It modifies the winds, breaks the lines of view all so quickly that one can scarcely realize that a valley of clustered woods and lines of trees was but a year or two before a brown parched expanse of shadeless summer dust." Kinney also touted the health benefits of the eucalyptus, even speculating that it could prevent malaria. Neighborhoods benefited as much from such forests as did the countryside. Kinney portrayed the beauty of his own estate as a model for other property owners and urged uniformity of plantings on his readers.[37]

Other conservationists appreciated the virtues of Kinney's style of forested boulevards. Charles Saunders waxed rhapsodic about similar landscapes, which for him embodied the potential of conservation to create lush, comfortable neighborhoods. In places such as Pasadena, Riverside, and Redlands, "the proximity of the desert, indeed, is at the bottom of the marvel [that] . . . illustrates the transforming power of water when directed by man's intelligence and taste in an arid land." The fact that this was a created rather than a preserved landscape only enhanced Saunders's admiration. Deserts could strike Saunders with awe; he once wrote of them as places where "the veil between this world and the spiritual seems thinner than elsewhere." But in the forested neighborhoods of Southern California, it was the contrast between the created and the wild that struck him: "Just across the line which marks the high tide of cultivation, the parched, treeless slopes of the desert borders lie as if in wait for man's care to be withdrawn, when the desert will sweep in again and claim its own."[38]

In the well-watered Midwest there was no danger that a desert would swallow up a civilization. But conservationists there also went to great lengths to develop an aesthetic of home plantings, one they thought of as preserving and restoring nature rather than transforming it. The Illinois landscape architect Wilhelm Miller explicitly linked the formal political agenda of conservation to the private aesthetics of the culture of conservation. In a lengthy bulletin from 1915, *The Prairie Spirit in Landscape Gardening,* Miller proclaimed that "'Conservation' is the First Principle of the Prairie Style of Landscape Gardening." For Miller, the "Prairie Spirit" was "a new style of architecture, interior decoration, and landscape gardening" advocated by landscape architects such as O. C. Simonds and Jens Jensen as well as architects, particularly Frank Lloyd Wright. Miller detailed the achievements of Wright and others like him: "He has put the house not outside the woods but inside. . . . For the same reason he has made the house long and low, instead of tall and narrow. Also he has used more wood and less stucco than for a house in the open. Finally he has stained the siding brown and the roof green to harmonize with tree trunks and foliage." Homeowners, gardeners, and landscape architects could take their cue from Wright's aesthetics by preserving or planting native vegetation in a way that emphasized "the horizontal line of land or sky which is the strongest feature of prairie scenery." The invocation of the prairie fostered a spiritual reverie parallel to the Muirian wilderness ecstasy:

> When you stand upon a high place overlooking the prairie, what seems to you its deepest meaning? Some say the dominant note is peacefulness—that this middle-western country will never be invaded by a foreign foe, and the landscape expresses this sense of security. Others declare that it is an expression of God's bounty. The horizon is but a symbol of a religious idea which each person may express in his own way, just as everyone may make his own interpretation of a piece of music . . . So, every Illinois citizen, no matter what his religion, can express the modern, intimate, and joyful relation with the Infinite by planting some stratified trees or bushes that symbolize the great horizon which in turn is but a symbol of the great reality that underlies all religions.[39]

Miller urged political lobbying and organizing as counterparts to the private decisions about landscaping yards and grounds. His conservation politics embraced the full spectrum of conservation organizations, ranging from the local to the national, the material to the aesthetic. In a

12-14. Three Ways by which Every Illinoisan can Bring the Prairie Spirit into his Home Grounds in Country or City
12. Idealize the farm view, e. g., frame it with   13. Conventionalize the prairie, e. g., put into   14. Symbolize the prairie, e. g., plant Illinois
haws, crabs, or honey locust.   the formal garden some flat-topped flowers.   or prairie roses beside the front door.

The Illinois landscape architect Wilhelm Miller praised the invocation of the prairie landscape in these home plantings. "Every home in Illinois can connect itself with the greatest source of inspiration in middle-western scenery," he wrote, "by preserving, restoring, or repeating some phase of the prairie." *(Miller, The Prairie Spirit in Landscape Gardening; courtesy Newberry Library)*

section entitled "Everyone Can Apply the Principle of Conservation," he advised saving trees on private properties, along nearby thoroughfares and waterways, and in state preserves. Under "Organizations Devoted to Conservation," the listings included the National Conservation Association, the American Civic Association, Friends of Our Native Landscape, and the Conservation Department of the General Federation of Women's Clubs. His checklist labeled "I will" fused much of the culture and politics of conservation:

> Write to national, state, and local organizations interested in conservation, study their literature, and help them all that I can.
> Work and vote for the extension of the state park system to include all types of Illinois scenery.
> Ask the county highway superintendent to save trees, shrubs, and flowers on state and country roadsides.
> Work and vote to help our community extend its sys-

tem of local parks and reservations, and to save the street trees.

> Give the people some piece of scenery to enjoy forever.
>
> Save the permanent native vegetation on my farm or home grounds, as far as possible.[40]

Wilhelm Miller was uncommonly specific about the connections between conservationist aesthetics and politics, but the aesthetic practices he advocated circulated widely in landscape architecture circles. Frank Waugh's *The Natural Style in Landscape Gardening* (1917), widely influential on garden designers, cited Miller's work as an example of how designers could capture "the spirit of the native landscape" to create grounds and plantings that would speak to the love of landscape engrained in Americans by their pioneer past. Waugh saw this spirit as an animating force in American culture. "Men break away from big cities year by year and seek the wilderness," he wrote. "They go to the farthest solitudes. They spend the longest vacations they can capture in hunting, fishing, tramping. They find a fierce joy in the wilderness. The landscape to them means freedom. It means release from a strenuous civilization which at best they find only partly good." Landscape architects could bring something of the American landscape of freedom into private yards by modeling their designs after wild places. Here Waugh went further than the already venerable landscape architecture tradition epitomized by Olmsted. Waugh advocated that designers not only embrace the "picturesque"—the avoidance of straight lines and geometric forms in favor of gentle curves and seemingly unplanned clusters of stones and plants—but also follow ecological principles in their selection and placement of plantings. "It is readily observed that very few species of plants exist in nature alone," he noted, after explicitly referring to "that branch of botanical science known as ecology." And since "practically every [plant] associates habitually with certain other species . . . these friendly associations based upon similarity of tastes and complementary habits of growth should not be broken up." "If we as landscape gardeners desire to preserve the whole aspect of nature with all its forms intact," he concluded, "we will keep all plants in their proper social groupings." As in Wilhelm Miller's more explicitly political vision, Waugh's aesthetic sensibility placed domestic landscapes in the larger natural context that nurtured culture.[41]

The Culture of Conservation

One morning as he hurried across Boston Common, the writer Dallas Lore Sharp was detained by a significant crowd at the intersection of two paths. Wondering what had caused other commuters to slow, Sharp joined the onlookers. "It was not a Mormon preaching, not a single taxer, not a dog fight," he wrote. "It was Billy, a gray squirrel, taking peanuts out of a bootblack's pocket. And every age, sex, sort, and condition of Bostonian came around to watch the little beast shuck the nuts and bury them singly in the grass of the Common." For Sharp, the sight was a reminder of what to him was one of the most significant cultural developments of the day. "This crowd on the Common is nothing exceptional," he continued. "It happens every day, and everywhere, the wide country over. We are all stopping to watch, to feed, and—to smile. The longest, most far-reaching pause in our hurrying American life to day is this halt to look at the out of doors, this attempt to share its life; and nothing more significant is being added to our American character than the resulting thoughtfulness, sympathy, and simplicity,—the smile on the faces of the crowd hurrying over the Common."[42]

Sharp saw signs of the "nature movement" in many places: the displays in bookstore windows, the nature study taught in schools, the enthusiasm for camping, a five-year-old visitor's ability to identify flowers by scientific name. He also recognized the connections between this cultural awakening and the formal political program of conservation. "Few laws can be enacted, fewer still enforced, without the help of an awakened public conscience," he noted. "As a nation, we need a popular and a thorough education in ornithology, entomology, forestry, and farming, and in the science and morality of corporation rights in public lands."[43]

Many leading conservationists shared Sharp's assumption that laws and their enforcement depended on the support of an educated and engaged public. The culture of conservation fostered just such knowledge and engagement. William McGee articulated this in his pithy observation that "whatever its material manifestations, every revolution is first and foremost a revolution in thought and in spirit." Anna Botsford Comstock similarly argued that "keeping wild and natural the thousands of acres of our beautiful forests and lake regions, and the conservation of wild life there will prove to be a futile effort if the people to whom the parks belong have no intelligent interest in them."[44]

Scholars have downplayed and sometimes altogether ignored this emphasis on cultural change, stressing instead the laws that conservationists passed and the expanded state powers they secured to implement those laws. Perhaps it was easy for environmental historians to marginalize or overlook the culture of conservation because they wrote from political commitments (and in political eras) more indebted to liberal notions of expertise, state power, and rights than to Progressive and older republican notions of virtue and character. In the century since the Progressive era, liberals have largely ceded the language of character and public virtue to the Right. Moreover, conservationists did indeed embrace state power as a potential check on the power of unregulated and voracious markets—and as we will see, some were quite comfortable with an authoritarian and coercive state.

Yet recognizing the importance that so many conservationists placed on private cultural and aesthetic practices helps us not only understand conservation, but also see the ties between conservation and Progressivism more broadly. Comstock and McGee were hardly alone in arguing that democratic politics grew the strongest when it was nourished by the fertile soil of culture. A wide range of Progressive reformers and thinkers embraced this idea and attempted to implement it. Temperance advocates, for example, relied on moral suasion, lurid stories of the harms of drunkenness, and recreation not centered on intoxication, in addition to bans on the sale of alcohol. Muckraking journalists hoped that accounts of meatpacking would so disgust the public that lawmakers would be forced to act. Many Progressives pinned their hopes for labor reform on widespread revulsion at the grim and dangerous conditions of work, and on the similarly widespread fear of revolution if those conditions were not ameliorated. Walter Weyl, a founder of the magazine the *New Republic* who was widely recognized as a key Progressive intellectual, generalized from these sorts of reform movements:

"The end goal of the democracy is thus a social goal. It is the improvement, physical, intellectual, and moral, of the millions who make up the democracy. It is such an advancement and increase of the progressive masses that the gains made on the political and industrial fields may be increased, retained, and wisely utilized."[45]

The commitment to the reform of Americans, as well as to changing laws and business practices, compelled many conservationists to enlist not only the powerful few, but also Weyl's "progressive masses." This quest enjoyed more success than has generally been portrayed.

Fighting for Conservation

As the first decade of the twentieth century wore on, conservationists seemed more and more optimistic about their influence and accomplishments. "The movement," Gifford Pinchot wrote in 1910, "has gathered immense swing and impetus. In 1907 few knew what Conservation meant. Now it has become a household word. While at first Conservation was supposed to apply only to forests, we see now that its sweep extends even beyond the natural resources. . . . Conservation has captured the Nation."[1]

Pinchot was not alone in his optimism or in his use of the term "movement." By 1910, it had become common for conservationists to use the word in both their public announcements and, un-self-consciously, in their private correspondence. Pinchot, for instance, used it as early as 1907 in a letter to an American forester working in India, and routinely a few years later. Beforehand, he employed the narrower and more technocratic term "management" to refer to the judicious use and stewardship of natural resources. Harvard president Charles Eliot was giving public lectures entitled "The Conservation Movement" by 1909, by which point J. Horace McFarland was regularly employing a similar term. An admirer writing to Pinchot after his dismissal from the presidential administration of William Howard Taft for leveling charges of corruption against the interior secretary gushed that "we are proud that our daughter is the very happy wife of a 'forester'" and offered his congratulations "on your new position as head of the people's movement for 'Conservation sans politics.'"[2]

The word "movement" succinctly conveyed the idea that conservation involved a wide range of policies, attracted a diverse set of passionate supporters, and was converting the dubious and inspiring the apathetic. Americans had once used resources with no sense of tomorrow, conservationists thought, but now the prophets of restraint and self-consciousness seemed to be making some headway. In national politics, conservation reached its height during the presidency of Theodore Roosevelt (1901–9). With the aid and guidance of his trusted adviser Gifford Pinchot, Roosevelt made conservation one of his leading causes. The two convened a national meeting of governors to discuss conservation in 1908. In the following years, the first and second National Conservation Congresses brought together elected officials, scientists, conservation advocates, and journalists from across the nation for extended discussions of natural resource and other environmental issues. Roosevelt spoke frequently and passionately of the dangers of resource exhaustion and of the majestic beauty of such places as Yosemite and the Grand Canyon. The power of the federal government to conserve resources and protect such places expanded dramatically on his watch. The Lacey Act of 1900 forbade the transport of birds or other wild animals killed in violation of state game laws, effectively nationalizing wildlife protection. When Roosevelt left office, the federal government was managing some 230 million acres—nearly a tenth of the nation's territory—as game preserves, bird reservations, national monuments, and national forests. Within a few years, the Reclamation Service, founded in 1902, boasted that it its dams, reservoirs, and canals provided irrigation water to over 2 million acres of farmland divided among 35,000 farms, and it had projects under way to double reclaimed areas. Soon after its birth, the environmental state grew vigorously.[3]

As the intellectual rationale for the political program of conservation became coherent, it achieved wide circulation in the late 1900s and early 1910s. Academic specialists wrote works intended to persuade small but highly influential audiences of their fellow professionals of the virtues of conservation. Bernhard Fernow's *The Economics of Forestry: A Reference Book for Students of Political Economy and Professional and*

Lay Students of Forestry (1902), for example, synthesized the economic, silvicultural, and legislative aspects of forestry. The establishment of the first schools of forestry in the Western Hemisphere—short-lived efforts at George Vanderbilt's Biltmore estate and at Cornell University in 1898, followed by enduring schools at Yale in 1900 and Pennsylvania State University in 1903—ensured that Fernow had an audience of professional foresters, many working for the U.S. Forest Service, established in 1905 as an agency of the Department of Agriculture.

The young field of economics was also influenced by conservation. In *The Foundations of National Prosperity: Studies in the Conservation of Permanent National Resources* (1917), Richard Ely, one of the era's most influential economists, made the case that the rational, orderly use of natural resources was a critical part of ensuring continued economic growth and national prosperity. He went to considerable lengths to locate conservation in the history of economic thought, particularly within the German academy, which was highly influential among academic economists in the United States. In Ely's telling, Americans had only recently begun using the term "conservation" to refer to the careful use and augmentation of natural resources. That adaptation was no radical departure from tradition, but rather built on decades of careful study by European economists of how "the natural inheritance of the human race" could be protected and enhanced to the benefit of all.[4]

One did not have to be a university professor or a forester to encounter extended arguments for conservation. Gifford Pinchot's *The Fight for Conservation* (1910) was an accessible, pithy articulation of his vision of a materialist and staunchly antimonopolist management of public lands. University of Wisconsin president Charles Van Hise made a more extended case for essentially the same program in *The Conservation of Natural Resources in the United States* (1910), which he wrote "to put into a handbook of moderate size the essential information which an intelligent citizen might desire in reference to conservation." (Not all who perused his 393-page tome may have found its size "moderate.") John Muir's romantic and ecstatic vision of conservation reached its widest circulation at the same time. Houghton Mifflin brought out his book *My First Summer in the Sierra* (1911), an account of his youthful wanderings in the California mountains that invoked the powerful spiritual harmony of nature, just as he was inducted into the American Academy of Arts and Letters and accepted an honorary doctorate from Yale University. William Temple Hornaday's darker tone similarly reached the general reading public. By then head of the New York Zoo, Hornaday focused on the dangers of extinction in *Our Vanishing Wild Life* (1913), which urged "every possible means of preservation,— sentimental, educational, and legislative"—in the defense of "the beauty of nature."[5] Conservation messages also resonated outside the realms of politics and books. The popularity of the Boy Scouts and the national reach of nature study in primary education ensured that hundreds of thousands were exposed to at least some of the principles of conservation every year.

Why did the culture of conservation and its political program make so much headway in this period? Answering this question requires paying attention both to the internal dynamics of conservation and to its relationship with Progressivism as a whole. The internal breadth and heterogeneity of conservation was a source of enduring strength, allowing conservation to attract supporters from a wide range of demographic backgrounds and ideological perspectives. At the same time, conservation was deeply marked by Progressivism and its simultaneous ascendance in this period.

In a sense, the basic message of conservation contained little that was new. George Perkins Marsh had warned of resource scarcity since the 1860s, Henry George of alienation from nature since the 1870s. Painters and novelists had portrayed wild landscapes as antidotes to overcivilization since the Hudson River School of painting in the 1820s. Yet conservation did not become a powerful force until the twentieth century.

Progressive justifications of expanded state power allowed conservation, or rather some conservation ideas, to become a set of policies instead of remaining in the realm of ideas and culture. Most conservation measures could not be implemented without a state capable of performing such tasks as administering vast tracts of land as national forests and parks, or in the absence of a politics that supported such state power. Richard Ely thus deemed the state "a first condition of conservation" and credited "a broad view of the state" as one of the contributions that Progressive economists made to the cause of conservation. By contrast, laissez-faire—the doctrine that the state should leave private economic actors free to do as they saw fit—was "in its very essence . . . fatal to conservation." Indeed, belief in the inadequacy of laissez-faire was an article of faith among conservationists; as Fernow wrote, "private enterprise . . . knows only the immediate future—has only one aim in the use of these [natural] resources, namely, to obtain from them the greatest possible personal and present gain."[6]

Only when American Progressives commenced their assault on laissez-faire and built the capacity of the state to regulate the economy could conservation thrive. By the 1910s, Progressives had passed a wide range of laws, at both the federal and state level, to limit child labor, enforce workplace safety, break up or regulate monopolies, inspect food processing, label food and drugs, limit workplace hours, create the Federal Reserve to manage the national currency, and provide pensions to Civil War veterans. Not all who supported such efforts called themselves Progressives, and not all who called themselves Progressives supported all these measures. Indeed, Progressives argued and fought with one another often enough for one exasperated historian to claim that "the concept of a 'movement' seems very much like a mirage." But people who considered themselves Progressives had a sense that they belonged to a larger, even if fractious, movement. In different ways, they all believed that an awakened people could check the dangers of industrial life and inequality by revitalizing themselves, reclaiming their government from vested economic interests, and using it for constructive good to protect against concentrated economic power. As the political scientist Benjamin De Witt noted in 1915, "in so far as conservation of natural resources is considered, the progressive movement in the nation is of the utmost importance because of the aid which the national government, and it alone, can give." De Witt saw conservation as one of the three most important issues requiring the intervention of the federal government "to enact remedial legislation," ranking along with taxation and "the protection of men, women, and children engaged in industrial work." The conservation movement could not have happened without the wider Progressive impulse.[7]

The career of the term "conservation" reflects the deep connections between conservation and Progressivism as a whole. The word itself long predated the rise of anything resembling environmental politics. It was a part of English usage by the fifteenth century, conveying the general sense of maintaining something or keeping it together (the Latin prefix con and verb servare, meaning "to keep"). Sir Thomas More used it in this sense in 1533 in the phrase "conseruacyon of the catholyque fayth." Until the twentieth century, the only particular association that the word had with natural processes was the physicists' idea of the "conservation of energy," one of the most frequent uses of the word in magazine and newspapers. More often, "conservation" was used in the general sense of preserving something for the future, as in the "conservation" of architecture, rainwater, honor, interests, an urban waterfront, or "the pure antique style of church music." George Perkins Marsh used it in this generic sense, all of two times in 577 pages, in his seminal *Man and Nature* (1864).[8]

Because periods of rapid transformation made it particularly challenging to maintain something, the word "conservation" was useful for those who wanted to express the need for some kind of continuity amid change. A newspaper editorial condemning the Pullman railroad strike of 1894 thus argued that "our reliance for the conservation of our institutions is upon the law-abidingness of the great majority of the people, and this reliance has for more than a century held good."[9] The American intellectual and civil rights pioneer W. E. B. Du Bois used the word in his 1898 manifesto *The Conservation of Races* to capture the importance of African Americans shepherding their power, culture, and institutions in the fact of virulent white supremacy. "It is our duty," he wrote, "to conserve our physical powers, our intellectual endowments, our spiritual ideals."[10]

Organizations and individuals concerned with natural beauty or natural resources occasionally used the word "conservation," but in the same way that others used it, with no particular resonance or special sense beyond the meaning usually conveyed. When the New York State Forestry Association proposed to create state forest preserves in 1891, for example, the *New York Times* described the organization as seeking "to arouse sentiment in favor of the preservation and conservation of the

forest areas of the state." But both the reporter and the association repeatedly used "forestry," "forest protection," and "forest administration"
rather than "conservation" to describe the organization's goals. "Conservation" invoked the general act of maintaining something, whether
some aspect of the natural world or something else. Bernhard Fernow
used the word in *The Economics of Forestry* (1902), but only three times
in five hundred pages.[11]

Gifford Pinchot made conservation shorthand for the movement
to protect nature in general from humanity's newfound power. In February 1907, while riding his horse in Rock Creek Park late one day in
Washington, D.C., he found himself preoccupied by a bevy of natural
resource questions. The political and technical challenges of managing
forests loomed the largest in his mind, since he was trained as a forester
and charged with running the young U.S. Forest Service. "The forest and
its relation to streams and inland navigation, to water power and flood
control; to the soil and its erosion; to coal and oil and other minerals;
to fish and game; and many another possible use or waste of natural resources—these questions would not let [me] be," wrote Pinchot decades
later. "What had all these to do with Forestry? And what had Forestry
to do with them?" He knew that these "were not isolated and separate
problems," but wondered, "What was the basic link between them?"
Then followed what struck him as a revelation:

> Suddenly the idea flashed through my head that there was a
> unity in this complication—that the relation of one resource
> to another was not the end of the story. Here were no longer
> a lot of different, independent, and often antagonistic ques-
> tions, each on its own separate little island, as we had been in
> the habit of thinking. In place of them, here was one single
> question with many parts. Seen in this new light, all these
> separate questions fitted into and made up the one great cen-
> tral problem of the use of the earth for the good of man . . .
> here was one question instead of many.

There still remained the question of what word to use: "There had to be a
name to call it by before we could even attempt to make it known, much

less give it a permanent place in the public mind." In a conversation with another forester, the fact that "large organized areas of Government forest lands in British India were named Conservancies, and the foresters in charge of them Conservators" came up, and so they decided to "apply a new meaning to a word already in the dictionary, and christen the new policy Conservation."[12]

The word came into wide usage almost immediately. In 1908, the American Forestry Association changed its magazine's name from *Forestry and Irrigation* to *Conservation*. Pinchot dubbed the national gatherings he began convening in 1908 "Conservation Congresses" and titled his 1910 book *The Fight for Conservation*. His use of the term spread quickly and easily among those involved in environmental policy and politics. Horace McFarland, a tireless champion of urban parks and city beautification, began using it, as did the foresters, engineers, and economists whose focus on material resource issues was closer to Pinchot's. Hamlin Garland employed it in his novel *Cavanagh, Forest Ranger* (1910). The popular press began using the term much more frequently, helping make it a one-word shorthand for efforts to regulate the use of nature. In 1908, newspaper appearances of the term were five times as frequent as in the period 1890–1904; by 1910, "conservation" was being used in daily newspaper articles fully twenty times as often as before Pinchot's revelation. The ubiquity of the term was the product of both the increasing momentum of conservation politics and the usefulness of the term that Pinchot had bequeathed to the movement.[13]

Even as it came to communicate a coherent and wide-ranging approach to environmental issues, the word "conservation" never became the sole and exclusive possession of the conservation movement, or wholly associated with environmental matters. It could still convey its older, more general meaning, as in an economic historian's 1910 assertion that "national peace always means the cessation of waste and the conservation of energies along protective lines."[14] This double valence—both a general meaning and a shorthand for a specific movement—made "conservation" a useful term for Progressives to describe their stances on a host of issues, including some that historians would assume had nothing to do with environmental matters. The labor advocate Maude Nathan, for example, wrote to Pinchot about the importance of "the conservation of the human resources of this country," using phrasing that became increasingly common in Progressive circles. Similarly, the theorist and *New Republic* editor Walter Weyl, one of the most influential exponents of Progressivism as a coherent movement and political philosophy, made "social conservation" a central motif of his book *The New Democracy* (1912). "The phrase 'the conservation of human resources' has attained a considerable popularity because of the vogue of the analogous policy of the conservation of natural resources," he wrote. Weyl used the phrase frequently to convey the sense that "the democratic ideal is not only to maintain, but vastly to increase and improve, the life, health, intellect, character and social qualities of the citizenry."[15]

Pinchot welcomed this sort of broadening of the use of the term "conservation" by Weyl, Nathan, and others. In the context of debates over forestry and public lands, he would cling doggedly to his own particular vision of conservation, first frustrating and then deeply embittering onetime allies with broader, more aesthetic, and urban visions of what conservation demanded. But he nevertheless welcomed the extent to which conservation informed the rest of Progressivism. In 1910, he stated:

> The principles of conservation thus described—development, preservation, the common good—have a general application which is growing rapidly wider. The development of resources and the prevention of waste and loss, the protection of the public interests, by foresight, prudence, and the ordinary business and home-making virtues, all these apply to other things as well as to the natural resources . . . These principles, which arose in forestry and have their bloom in the conservation of natural resources, will have their fruit in the increase and promotion of national efficiency along other lines of national life.[16]

Conservation seized the Progressive imagination not only for its own sake, but also as a model for all kinds of reform.

Progressives, particularly female activists such as Maude Nathan, often pointed to childhood as a key "resource" in need of conserving. "If lobsters or young salmon become scarce or are in danger of perishing," argued Florence Kelley, head of the National Consumers' League and labor advocate, "the United States Fish Commission takes active steps in the matter. But infant morality continues excessive from generation to generation." Similarly, the prominent suffragist Lillian Wald called for the federal government to monitor the well-being of children "with as much care as it tells of the trees or the fishes or the cotton crop." Women such as Wald and Kelley who sought to protect children from exploitative employers chose to call their organizations "child conservation leagues." Many of the state governments that heeded these calls for close attention to the health and living conditions of children created agencies or departments of "child conservation," such as Minnesota's Division of Child Conservation of the State Board of Health or the Massachusetts Commissioner of Health's Committee of Child Conservation.[17]

If childhood needed "conserving," then so too might manhood and womanhood. Pittsburgh's H. D. W. English wanted Pinchot to read a pamphlet entitled *Practical Propositions for Purposeful Men,* which, in his description, "means the conservation of men and boys." At the National Conservation Congress of 1911, Governor Robert Vessey of South Dakota touted the breadth of his administration's conservation efforts, which ranged from irrigation, drainage of wetlands, and soil fertility programs to efforts "to conserve manhood and womanhood by making them more efficient in the great agricultural work by sending out into their community and out in their neighborhoods teachers along the line of agricultural and domestic science and other matters pertaining to make the home more efficient and more modern." Reformers pressing for the aggressive care and rehabilitation of disabled soldiers returning from World War I similarly cast their efforts as "part of the great human conservation movement," in the words of Harry Mock. By healing maimed soldiers, Mock and his compatriots believed they were restoring their manhood to them. In his article "Human Conservation and Reclamation" in 1918, he argued that the circumstances of the war would only bolster his case: "The loss in man power, both in this country and in all other warring nations, will force the peoples of the world to conserve the man power remaining to them."[18]

Conservation also became a lens through which to see issues of

immigration and ethnic diversity. The charge that Italians and other immigrants wantonly slaughtered songbirds was an article of faith for many
conservationists. By the twentieth century, the American landscape had
become an important feature of American patriotism. First published as
a song in 1910, Katharine Lee Bates's "America" began by invoking "spacious skies," "amber waves of grain," and "purple mountain majesties /
above the fruited plain." Nativists therefore pointed to an alleged lack of
appreciation for natural beauty as evidence that eastern and southern
Europeans could not be assimilated. In her novel *A Listener in Babel,*
set in a Boston settlement house, Vida Scudder had an anti-immigrant
character recall immigrants "saying the country was so horrid because
you couldn't see anything but spaces." Another demanded, "What do
they know about mountainsides and rocks and rills? They never saw a
rill except in the gutter."[19]

On the other hand, those who welcomed immigration could also
invoke conservationist ideals. Dana Bartlett compared the pluralist
version of Americanization that he advocated to the kind of gardens
and plantings that irrigation had made possible in Southern California. "Much of my life has been spent in social service with foreign-born
neighbors from many lands," wrote the Angeleno. "In creating a home
garden it seemed quite natural to gather about us plants and trees,—
immigrants from many climes. Growing on this little ranch I have al-
monds from Spain, the passion vine, sapote and cherimoya from Mexico, the avocado from Guatemala and Mexico, nectarine from New
Zealand, feijoa from Brazil, bottle-brush, acacia, eucalyptus and hakia
from Australia, flowering peach from Japan, pistache, hawthorn and
persimmon from China. All of these have become as good Americans
as my human friends in the big city."[20]

The conditions of American workers—their wages, their physical
safety on the job, the long periods of unemployment and insecurity that
they endured—were a central object of Progressive reforms, which included workers' compensation, the minimum wage, maximum hours,
and workplace safety legislation. Progressives often explained their
approaches to these labor issues by reference to conservation. Samuel Gompers, head of the American Federation of Labor, did so in his
address "Conservation in Relation to Labor" at the first Conservation

Congress, in 1908. Gompers argued for "wise measures . . . for the conservation of economic energies," particularly the "energy of the laborer
in production for the welfare and well-being of the Nation." The waste
of wood, coal, and other resources was a staple of conservationist rhetoric, which he employed in his charge that "the greatest form of waste
from which we suffer at this time is the waste involved in the unemployment of immense numbers of our people." Conservation's call for
efficiency also gave Gompers a platform for condemning the toleration
of workplace injury. "What is more wasteful, what is more the antithesis
to the conservation of our natural resources," he demanded to know,
than "the myriads of workers whose bodies are maimed or whose lives
are destroyed in industry and commerce by ignorance, incompetence,
or greed." By no means did all conservationists share Gompers's stance
on labor issues, but his position nonetheless made some headway. The
following year's Conservation Commission, chaired by Gifford Pinchot,
pointed to the connections between "conservation of health and conservation of wealth."[21]

Urban reformers also used "conservation" to describe the benefits
of playgrounds and the organization of such activities as plays, concerts,
and sports leagues. John Collier, writing in the *Playground,* argued that
the orderly use of leisure time by urbanites was "the last problem of
conservation." He declared, "The 20th century problem is the conservation, which means the utilization, of the leisure time of the people."
Only by getting people to use properly their time when not sleeping,
working, or attending school "shall we get an educated people, and only
through an educated people can we hope to secure economic justice,
responsible political freedom, or the conservation of the resources of
the earth." Here Collier invoked the importance of culture; Americans
would become more efficient and wholesome because they were taught
to, not simply forced to. He made his case for urban playgrounds, organized recreation, and the regulation of saloons and movies by reference to
Progressive policies on natural resources.[22]

The Progressive choice to fly the banner of conservation in order to
advance a host of issues was more than mere linguistic opportunism.
Conservation was premised on the idea that industrial civilization

threatened wildness, natural beauty, and key resources. But the explosive growth of the American economy subjected other aspects of life to wrenching transformations as well. As Gompers put it at the Conservation Congress in 1908: "We are standing at the meeting and parting of ways. We are preparing to take hold upon a new form of national life. . . . We are to set our faces toward the oncoming prodigious development of our country." Industrial development brought millions of strangers to the nation's ports and cities, sucked millions more out of small towns and the countryside into the same cities, and placed men raised to think of themselves as independent at the mercy of their supervisors and bosses. The hard labor of a farmwife or farmer was now more likely to be replaced by the exhaustion of sewing all day in a crowded and dusty loft or shoveling coke into a blast furnace. Those accustomed to growing and preparing their own food now ate meat, grain, and vegetables of uncertain origin and packaged by anonymous hands. The word "conservation" captured the sense that what had once come easily or naturally— warmth from a fireplace, water from a stream, soil in a field—now had to be carefully watched, studied, and used judiciously. In this sense it was the perfect metaphor for reckoning with this new era.[23]

Yet conservation was more than a metaphor to Progressives who used the word to describe such issues as labor reform, playgrounds, and the protection of children. In some meaningful sense, they thought of human bodies as parts of the nature that conservation was designed to protect. By applying the term "conservation" so broadly, reformers called attention to the institutions and relationships that stunted or nurtured those bodies—employers, food processors, households, neighborhoods, parks—just as warning of deforestation or overhunting lead to a reckoning with economic forces, policies, and culture. The emphasis in recent scholarship on the narrow way in which conservationists understood "nature" fails to account for their deep concern with the body.

The Quest for a National Conservation Organization

At the same time "conservation" emerged as an overarching term for the judicious use and preservation of nature, some leading conservationists began to explore the feasibility of forming a similarly capacious national organization to advance the cause of conservation. If conservation was "a single question with many parts," as it struck Pinchot, then might not a single national organization best advance its cause?

"Important work is going on in forming a broader national organization," Horace McFarland wrote to the University of California professor and Sierra Club leader William Badé, "probably under the title of the American Conservation Association, to handle all these things in a more influential way than we have been able to do." His message referred to an ongoing conversation with Gifford Pinchot. Pinchot was still head of the Forest Service, but maintained an active role in the American Forestry Association, as he had since 1890. McFarland served as the publisher of *Suburban Life* and president of the American Civic Association, an organization with chapters across the nation that focused on city parks, the beautification of urban areas, and the creation of state and national parks. The association's publicity campaigns to defend such places as Niagara Falls from runaway development sought to reach a mass audience, enlisting the public at large as an ally for conservation and scenic preservation. The two men considered joining their forces by merging McFarland's American Civic Association with an organization—perhaps the American Forestry Association—oriented toward natural resource conservation and the protection of federal lands.[24]

This prospective joining of forces would have produced an organization that reached across much of the spectrum of causes that conservationists advocated. Both men shared a heady sense of optimism at the progress of the conservation movement, but also a sense of frustration that conservationists had yet to figure out an effective way of marshaling their forces, in part because there was no one organization that captured the breadth of environmental politics. McFarland was the more adamant of the two on this point. "The conservation movement is now weak," he wrote, "because it has failed to join hands with the preservation of scenery, with the provision of agreeable working conditions. . . . The man whose efforts we want to conserve produces the best effort and more effort in agreeable surroundings. . . . The preservation of forests, water powers, minerals and the other items of national prosperity in a sane way must be associated with the pleasure to the eye and the mind and the regeneration of the spirit of man." With Congress seemingly intent on sharply limiting funding for new conservation agencies such as the Forest Service, Pinchot looked for a way to broaden the political base of conservation, and McFarland's initiative presented an intriguing opportunity. Pinchot shared the frustration that professional organizations like the American Forestry Association were incapable of vigorous lobbying and the mobilization of their membership on behalf of a robust conservation agenda. He thus welcomed the thought that his circles and the American Civic Association "ought to work together hand in hand like two brothers," and seemed open to McFarland's broad vision of conservation. "I am realizing more and more the value of the esthetic side of conservation, and by and by you will make a complete convert of me," he wrote amiably in late 1909.[25]

McFarland and Pinchot could contemplate a conservation organization of national scope that would tap the growing public sentiment for conservation precisely because they had witnessed the rise of a host of civic and political organizations in the previous decade. Writing in 1920, the political scientist Charles Edward Merriam observed that one of the most striking recent changes in the nation's political system was the "development of great numbers of volunteer political organizations undertaking the function of instructing, advising, exhorting, menacing, obstructing and assisting the government and the electorate." Less detached observers shared his sense that civic associations lay at the heart of Progressive democracy. The social worker and political theorist Mary Parker Follett began her book *The New State: Group Organization the Solution of Popular Government* (1918) with the dire warning that "our political life is stagnating, capital and labor are virtually at war, the nations of Europe are at one another's throats." But hope could be found in "group organization," which would become "the new method in politics, the basis of our future industrial system, the foundation of international order" and would "create the new world we are now blindly feeling after, for creative force comes from the group, creative power is evolved through the activity of the group life." By fostering engagement with formal politics even as they led their members in transformative learning, the kinds of organizations to which Progressives were so committed offered hope for American democracy.[26]

The apparent structure of the organization that Pinchot and Mc-

Farland contemplated was also familiar. Early in the nineteenth century, the national federation model—a network of local chapters organized into state federations that in turn worked with a national leadership and staff—emerged as the dominant way of structuring civic associations in the United States. While national leaders helped local chapters to organize and remain active, the lifeblood of such organizations as the Woman's Christian Temperance Union (WCTU), the Rotary Club, or the Daughters of the American Revolution was the willingness of ordinary people in hundreds of towns and cities to join, pay dues, and attend meetings. This civic landscape—neither a purely spontaneous reflection of an unorganized grassroots nor a top-down creation of a central state—deeply impressed observers of American social and political life. Writing in his classic *Democracy in America* (1835), Alexis de Tocqueville placed an earlier iteration of it at the heart of American democracy. "If the inhabitants of democratic countries had neither the right nor the taste for uniting for political objects, their independence would run great risks, but they could keep both their wealth and their knowledge for a long time," he argued. "But if they did not learn some habits of acting together in the affairs of daily life, civilization itself would be in peril." Progressive intellectuals like Follett agreed with his emphasis on the importance of association. Although they validated the role of the state against the advocates of a pure laissez-faire approach, most valued the national state for its ability to coordinate and channel grassroots energies as much as to simply dictate policy. As one observer put it, "The essential characteristic of state actions . . . is that it is preeminently a co-ordinating power. It is a special form of associative action."[27]

These sorts of federated groups entered formal national politics more and more frequently in the early twentieth century, for exactly the reasons that prompted Pinchot and McFarland to explore founding a national conservation organization: the Progressive turn to the powers of the federal government. One measure of this was the appearance of new organizations offering testimony at congressional hearings: 216 in the 1890s, up to 622 in 1900–1909, and more than 1,000 in 1910–17. By the 1910s, groups such as the National Audubon Society, the Immigration Restriction League, and the WCTU appeared before Congress nearly as often as labor unions and business organizations. And the civic organizations were much more likely to be national in scope than their labor and business counterparts. They also pioneered the practice of drawing upon and cultivating academic and policy expertise, convening special commissions of panels to generate publicity and an intellectual rationale for particular policies, much as Pinchot and Roosevelt had done with the national Conservation Commissions and Conferences. As Charles Merriam concluded in 1920, "Much of the current legislation came from this group, and much of the demand for effective administration; much of the vital public discussion by which public opinion is shaped and made." Conservationists called for and relied upon an expansion of state power, but like other Progressives, they hoped to embed that state in a vigorous grassroots civic culture.[28]

The Broad Tent of Conservation

Pinchot and McFarland never united their organizations, although for several years they continued to work in concert, with McFarland at times suggesting they revisit the question.[29] The experiences of both continued to suggest the potential mass constituency for the conservation movement. With requests for speaking engagements, article reprints, and updates on legislation from all corners of the country, from individuals and local organizations alike, reaching them in quantities difficult to acknowledge, let alone to meet, both men were in a position to appreciate the enormous range of people attracted to conservation. Men and women of different ideologies, races, and economic classes found that the shared belief that industrial civilization imperiled nature and thus humanity was enough to try to make common cause. The differences between conservationists sometimes came to the fore and proved insurmountable, as they soon did for McFarland and Pinchot. But at the same time, the very breadth of conservation helped it become as powerful as it was.

Much of the grassroots strength of conservation that McFarland and Pinchot perceived was due to the activism of women. "One has but to attend any gathering of representative women, to learn that there is an overwhelming sentiment and a consensus of opinion in favor of preserving forests and conserving natural resources," proclaimed Lydia

Adams-Williams in her article "Conservation—Woman's Work." She pointed in particular to the work of the General Federation of Women's Clubs (GFWC), which "for several years has made a specialty of work for preserving the forests upon which the proper conservation of all other natural resources depends." Established on a nationwide basis in 1890, the federation linked together the women's clubs found in virtually every American town. These clubs drew together middle- and upper-middle-class women who were engaged in the lives of their communities and nation for socializing, self-education, and political advocacy. With the possible exception of the Woman's Christian Temperance Union, the GFWC was the largest and most influential of the era's civic organizations.[30]

Environmental issues were among the causes most ardently pursued by the GFWC, along with temperance and questions related to child welfare. The organizing meeting of the California Federation of Women's Clubs, for example, held in 1900, was dominated by discussion of the need for forest protection and redwood preservation. The national organization adopted its first environmental resolution at its 1896 meeting, and two years later hired Mira Lloyd Dock as its forestry advocate. Dock worked closely with Gifford Pinchot and Horace McFarland on forestry and other conservation issues through the 1910s. In 1909, she and other Pennsylvania Club women played key roles in securing the establishment of the state's department of forestry. The same circles advocated for street beautification and parks programs in Pennsylvania cities.[31]

Male conservation leaders often recognized and valued the role of female conservationists. "The State of Pennsylvania never would have had that [forestry] Department if it had not been for the organized efforts of the women of Pennsylvania," opined the journal of the American Forestry Association (AFA) in 1909: "On the morning the bill for this matter was under consideration, every desk in the House of Representatives and the State Senate was flooded with petitions from the women and their husbands. . . . The women of the state made it impossible to kill it." The AFA welcomed women as members, encouraged their attendance at national meetings, and in 1906 began printing updates about state forestry committees of the GFWC and even poems by female ac-

An editorial cartoon reflecting the strong affinities between female Progressives and urban conservation. Women's suffrage transforms the smoky, dark, and entirely artificial city on the left to a verdant and sunny cityscape with playgrounds, trees, and parks. (Life, *October 16, 1913, 646; courtesy Adam Rome)*

tivists in its journal. Gifford Pinchot and Theodore Roosevelt similarly viewed female environmental activism as an asset to their own push for conservation. Roosevelt made sure that Denver's Sarah S. Platt, then the president of the GFWC, addressed the First Governors' Conference on Conservation in 1908. In *The Fight for Conservation,* Pinchot praised the work that "the National Society of the Daughters of the American Revolution and other organizations of women have taken in appointing conservation committees." He was particularly impressed by the forestry campaigns of Pennsylvania and California women.[32]

Female conservationists played a particularly decisive role in bird preservation campaigns, which, along with forestry measures, were some of the earliest victories for conservationists. Harriet Lawrence Hemenway and Minna B. Hall founded the Massachusetts Audubon Society in 1896 in order to "further the protection of our native birds." By 1905 there were nineteen state chapters, which organized the National Association of Audubon Societies in 1905. Women were the lifeblood of state Audubon societies, which generally worked closely with state branches of the GFWC. More than three-quarters of club members and half of its officers were women; in many cases, women asked a prominent male leader to serve as chapter or state president but did most of the work themselves. Audubon Society chapters played critical roles in the passage of the Lacey Act of 1900, in the establishment of numerous federal bird preserves in the 1900s, in a 1913 tariff measure that forbade the import of wild bird feathers, and in a sustained campaign against the popular style of wearing bird feathers and heads on women's hats.[33]

Conservationists such as Mira Lloyd Dock and the Audubon leaders were not merely women who happened to be politically involved, or political activists who happened to be women. Dock's comment that "what we need here in the United States is better housekeeping out of doors" pithily captured the extent to which they understood their political engagements as extensions of what they thought of as the proper role of women. They viewed this role capaciously, as requiring not only dutiful service to husbands and children within the household, but also robust action in the public sphere—precisely why almost all were advocates of women's suffrage. Lydia Adams-Williams developed this idea in her article "Conservation—Woman's Work." She observed: "Man has always been the maker of money, while to woman has fallen the province of being the saver of money. When the necessity of economy is felt in the home, woman bravely meets the emergency, and plans for and effects the necessary saving." The new conditions of her time—"the great national crisis which now confronts us"—called for "the necessity for economizing and preserving our fast disappearing resources for ourselves and our children." In this duty, "woman is found the willing and ready partner to carry on the work."[34]

The role of women as teachers of their children, some believed, gave them a special role to play in fostering the culture of conservation. The Audubon Societies were particularly vigorous in this regard. Female Audubon club members established traveling libraries on birds and the need to protect them; they gave school lectures in the hopes that children who answered the door when a woman with a bird on her hat called would say, "Mama, there's a woman with a dead body on her hat who wants to see you." Adams-Williams placed this kind of work at the heart of women's role in conservation and in the success of conservation: "Far-reaching results may be accomplished speedily by women educating the men of their families. Then by inculcating in their children the precepts of economy, and then impressing them with the patriotic duty of elevating the Nation to the highest plane of civilization, the entire sentiment of the Nation may be changed by the motherhood of the country in a single generation, and this people converted from the most wasteful and extravagant in the world to the most prudent and conservative."[35]

Lydia Adams-Williams's male counterparts were not prone to lengthy self-reflections about the ways that notions of manhood structured their conservation politics. Men were supposed to be leaders, active in the public realm, and concerned with the fate of the nation, so the simple fact of the public prominence of men such as Pinchot or McFarland required no explanation or exegesis. Nevertheless, the statements and actions of male conservationists often reflected their particular understandings of masculinity. Whereas female activists pointed to the industrial scale of economic production as proof that they needed to enter the public sphere to protect their children and communities, men could point to how the same economy threatened the classic masculine virtues of physical strength, fortitude, and independence. "In a perfectly peaceful and commercial civilization such as ours," wrote Theodore Roosevelt in the pages of *Harper's Weekly* in 1893, "there is always a danger of laying too little stress upon the more virile virtues—upon the virtues which go to make up a race of statesmen and soldiers, of pioneers and explorers." Since these virtues were "fostered by vigorous, manly, out-of-door sports, such as mountaineering, big-game hunting, riding, [and] shooting," conservation could help preserve a robust American manhood. A decade later, as president, Roosevelt helped ensure that it would. Manliness was a major theme in his public advocacy for conservation, as in his call for "every believer in manliness . . . every lover of nature, every man who appreciates the majesty and beauty of the wilderness and of wild life," to support the protection of the nation's remaining wild places.[36]

Roosevelt's focus on a strenuous masculinity was an important strain in wilderness and large-game protection efforts, but it was far from universal among male conservationists. Early Boy Scout practices, for example, incorporated a similar relish for the return to frontier conditions, but also critiqued the destructiveness and impulsiveness of masculine frontier culture. Sport hunting magazines such as *Field and Stream* and *Outdoor Life,* whose precocious advocacy of bird and game conservation dated to the 1870s, featured female hunters and writers in their columns, articles, advertisements, and cartoons. Perhaps most remarkably, some general-interest articles, such as Ruth Pepple's regular column on trapshooting in *Outdoor Life,* were written by women. As the historian Andrea Smalley concludes, the prominence of women in sporting magazines helped their editors present readers "with an updated and upgraded image of hunting," consistent with their efforts to dissociate recreational hunting "from subsistence hunting, market hunting, and unproductive indolence." As this gender inclusiveness suggests, masculinity was not an important aspect of the political program or rhetoric of most male conservationists, who worked closely with women and voiced sentimental as well as utilitarian arguments for protecting nature. It was the flexibility of conservation—its ability to embody and speak to different notions of manhood and womanhood—that allowed women and men with a wide range of gender politics to find a place for themselves within it.[37]

Perhaps the most significant distinction between male and female conservationists was their very different relationship with scientific professions. Engineers, foresters, and range scientists provided critical expertise and organizational support for conservation. The major national engineering societies, for example—the American Society of Civil Engineers, the American Society of Mechanical Engineers, the American Institute of Electrical Engineers, and the American Institute of Mining Engineers—embraced the material side of conservation, publicizing conservation efforts and defending the federal conservation measures of the Roosevelt administration. In so doing, they joined professional foresters, whose advocacy of the long-term management and scientific analysis of timber resources had made them early proponents of federal conservation. W. J. McGee captured the connections between scientific investigation and the materialist strain of conservation in his comment that "the course of nature has come to be investigated in order that it may be redirected along lines contributing to human welfare."[38]

It went without saying that those doing this investigation were men. Excluded from most colleges, and even more so from professional and graduate programs, women had little access to scientific and technical professions. (The ranks of those who entered such professions included the industrial chemist Ellen Swallow Richards, the nature-study leader Anna Botsford Comstock, and the toxicologist Alice Hamilton, whom Harvard offered a position with the understanding that she would not use the faculty club, was not entitled to football tickets, and would not participate in the commencement procession.) Women and men both found places within an organized conservation movement, but they were usually very different places.[39]

Conservation drew strength from female activism and male scientific expertise alike, but was much less open to those who were not white. When it came to matters of race, the Progressive era was hardly "progressive" at all by modern lights. Indeed, in many respects it was the apogee of white supremacy. The imposition of Jim Crow segregation in the South deprived African Americans of many of the gains that they had made after emancipation, and northern and western black populations were isolated and too small to wield the cultural and political power that they would later, after substantial outmigration from the former Confederacy. Indian peoples were stripped of much of the land they had secured in nineteenth-century treaties, many of their tribal governments were abolished, and their children were subjected to intense forced acculturation in boarding schools and on reservations. Chinese exclusion and alien land laws—enthusiastically backed by voices on the left such as Henry George as well as by conservatives—placed sharp limits on immigration from Asia and on immigrants' freedom after they arrived. People of Mexican descent encountered new levels of economic exploitation, disfranchisement, and racial ostracism. Scientific racism— the belief that evolution had created discrete and biologically different races of humanity—provided a powerful intellectual justification for these stark hierarchies. "Democratic theories of government in their modern form," noted the conservationist and racial theorist Madison Grant in 1916, a few years before Congress essentially codified his racial views in new immigration laws, "are based on dogmas of equality formulated some hundred and fifty years ago and rest upon the assumption that environment and not heredity is the controlling factor in human development." Since this was mistaken, Grant could only dismiss as naïve the "altruistic ideals . . . and the maudlin sentimentalism that has made America an asylum for the oppressed."[40]

White Progressives were hardly free of this scientific racism; indeed, some were among its leading champions. White Progressives viewed their racism not as the atavism of inherited prejudice, but as a reflection of their own modernity and enlightenment. For Henry George, halting "the threatening wave of Asiatic immigration" was a critical part of the fight against land monopoly, since Chinese laborers were indispensable for the "great landlords of our Pacific slope." The efforts at rural revitalization deeply informed by George's critiques, such as reclamation and the Country Life Commission, similarly validated agrarian whiteness. Moreover, many Progressives believed that science had clear lessons to impart in racial matters, as in forest management or currency policy. As the historian David Southern puts it, "At college progressives not only read exposés of capitalistic barons and attacks on laissez-faire economics by muckraking journalists, they also read racist tracts that drew on the latest anthropology, biology, psychology, sociology, eugenics, and medical science." The Progressives' embrace of state power, moreover, made them amenable to systematic rather than ad hoc solutions to racial questions. Systematized, legalized, openly enforced Jim Crow and alien land laws could thus appeal to them as being more efficient and satisfactory than informal private discrimination. Racism also helps explain the support of some—though by no means all—Progressives for U.S. imperialism. It was entirely proper, these Progressives thought, for white Americans to rule over their racial inferiors. As the staunchly Progressive senator Albert Beveridge forthrightly stated, "The rule of liberty . . . applies only to those who are capable of self-government."[41]

Even those Progressives for whom white supremacy was not particularly important could easily accept racial oppression as an unalterable feature of American life. Richard Ely, for example, passionately argued for the need to ensure economic security, physical safety, and dignity for industrial workers. In contrast, "however hopeful one may be with respect to the future of the American negro," he wrote in *The Foundations of National Prosperity*, "probably his wisest friends would say that in the vast majority of cases good tenancy is the best thing for him at the present time."[42]

Conservation was no exception to this general pattern. It was easy and all too common for white conservationists to assume that their enlightened attitude toward nature reflected their own cultural and racial superiority. The prominent nature study proponent and Audubon leader Mabel Osgood Wright, for example, lumped "the newly arrived foreign element" with cats as "the worst enemies of birds." Nature educators, she warned, needed to beware of "races with instincts concerning what are called lower animals, quite beyond the moral comprehension of the animal-loving Anglo Saxon." The appreciation of a wilder and more sublime nature could also be thought of as a virtue confined to native-born whites. "The Grand Cañon of the Colorado is becoming so renowned for its wonderful and extensive natural gorge scenery and for its open clean pine woods," commented the manager of the Grand Canyon forest, "that it should be preserved for the everlasting pleasure and instruction of our intelligent citizens." The presumed inability of Indians to appreciate this landscape was a justification, he argued, for their removal from the forest. If racial and ethnic inferiors did not appreciate nature, then it went without saying that they would not be included in such conservation organizations as Audubon Societies or Sierra Club chapters, which, like virtually all civic associations not organized by minority groups, were white-only.[43]

In a different sense, however, neither conservation nor Progressivism was white-only. Key Indian, Mexican American, and African American leaders saw much to like in Progressivism. They established organizations such as the National Association for the Advancement of Colored People (NAACP) and the Society of American Indians (both founded in 1911), which shared the ethos of Progressive reform. Progressivism fit comfortably with their sense of themselves as enlightened and modern, categories that they believed did yet not encompass most of their own peoples. The Progressive advocacy of economic security and dignity—above and beyond formal political rights such as the vote —spoke to the condition of populations that were as economically exploited as they were politically disenfranchised. And the emphases on a vigorous national state and equality before the law struck civil rights advocates as potentially powerful tools against Jim Crow.[44]

Similarly, even though white conservationists excluded others, marginalized racial groups could see the appeal of conservationist sensibilities and policies. Some African Americans enthusiastically adopted conservation. The National Association of Colored Women, an organization of black women's clubs founded in 1895 as a counterpart to the white-only General Federation of Women's Clubs, sponsored a forestry division through the 1910s. The *Chicago Defender,* the nation's most influential and widely read black newspaper, covered major developments in conservation nationally, paying particular attention to the ways that Chicagoans could avail themselves of parks. The *Defender*'s health columnist, A. Wilberforce Williams, touted the health benefits of outdoor recreation and provided practical camping advice to his readers. Williams consistently articulated the conservationist call for accessible parks, invoking the familiar contrast between the urban and natural. "There is an ever increasing demand for us to get out, and away from the city—to get close to nature," he wrote in 1914, "to commune with the running brooks, trees, and singing birds, and all growing vegetation—to get far away from the heat, the dust, the hurry, the bustling marts, and streets of the overcrowded, jostling municipality and find some cool, shady spot to camp where one may find rest for mind and body with nature's purest food, water, and air."[45]

The *Defender* also had advice for those without the time or money for the excursions that Williams advocated. Ten cents, the paper told its readers, was enough for a trolley car "that will take you far beyond the city limits." Just the better part of a day "spent under sun and sky" would ensure that "you sleep good at night and have pleasant recollections of . . . close communication with birds and trees and flowers." These kinds of trips were particularly important for children, since "a day amid such surroundings is worth a whole week in school in the new and instructive lessons they will get from the greatest of all teachers, nature." Even if leaving the city for just a brief time was impossible, Chicagoans still had their urban parks, "splendid breathing spaces and . . . beautiful bits of God's country brought right into the city for the benefit of those who dwell in sections where air, sun, and elbow room are hard to get."[46]

Leaders of the Tuskegee Institute, an Alabama normal school and college that was the most important black educational and intellectual institution of the early twentieth century, embraced some of the agrarian aspects of conservation. Its founder and director, Booker T. Washington, once bragged to Gifford Pinchot that a speech titled "A Plea for the Preservation of American Forests" had won a commencement contest. Washington made nature study an important feature of the institute's curriculum, along with trigonometry, basic engineering, and vocational instruction. Nature study's emphasis on using students' immediate surroundings to awaken curiosity and to introduce abstract principles of science fit well with Washington's general pragmatic educational philosophy. As he put it in a description of tramping across a stream, "Beside the delight of wading through the water, and of being out in the pure bracing air," students "would learn by this method more about these natural divisions of the earth in five minutes than they could learn in an hour in books." Moreover, knowledge of the local environment could serve Washington's overriding goal of black economic independence. Although the southern landscape abounded with "pigs, chickens, ducks, geese, berries, peaches, plums, [and] nuts," he despaired at the ubiquitous consumption of "salt pork from Chicago" and "canned chicken and tomatoes from Omaha"— all purchased with cash hard won in a white-dominated economy.[47]

Tuskegee's most famous faculty member, the agronomist George Washington Carver, similarly linked aspects of conservation to the project of black uplift. Trained at Iowa Agricultural College (later Iowa State University) at a time when agricultural science was holistic and ecological in approach, Carver once declared, "My work is that of Conservation." For him, the plight of black farmers was environmental as well as social. He pointed to the "erosion and devastation wrought by the forest fires and the woodman's axe" as proof of the need for conservation. His lectures included coverage of major developments in the national conservation movement, and he remained in active touch with his former professor James Wilson, who became secretary of agriculture in the Roosevelt and Taft administrations. A member of the editorial board of the *Nature-Study Review,* Carver tried to impress upon southern farmers the importance of "organic unity" as seen in the "mutual relation" of the animal, vegetable, and mineral kingdoms. In the words of the historian Mark Hersey, Carver "waged a campaign aimed at persuading" black farmers "that they could defend themselves against the economic and political vicissitudes they faced as a result of their race by turning to the natural environment." The overwhelming majority of white conservationists may have cared little for the struggles of African Americans, but some African Americans saw the appeal of conservation.[48]

Just as the breadth of conservation's political and social program gave women and men, experts and laypeople, whites and blacks, ways that they could support it, so too could people with diverse economic and class ideologies see some value in conservation. Progressives' belief that expanded state power could address problems of industrial capitalism meant that they had an easier time seeing conservation as consistent with their larger political framework than did conservatives or radicals. Nevertheless, both those who embraced America's economic order most fervently and those who rejected it with equal passion could also articulate visions of conservation consistent with their own economic interests and ideological affinities.

Conservationist ranks included some of the Americans who most ardently championed the nation's explosive economic transformation. Many municipal business organizations, often the champions of weak regulation and key sources of opposition to labor unions, saw clear ben-

George Washington Carver, 1906. Carver, a Tuskegee Institute agronomist, viewed conservation as one way for African American farmers to secure their economic independence. *(Frances Benjamin Johnston, photographer; Booker T. Washington Collection, Prints and Photographs Division, Library of Congress)*

efits in the material aspects of conservation. A statement issued by the Minneapolis and St. Paul Commercial Club in 1904 on behalf of federal forest reserves was typical in this regard. Urging "the co-operation of all Commercial Organizations and all thoughtful citizens," the declaration argued that the preservation of forests was a pressing economic matter for the states of the Mississippi Valley, "whose commerce this great river fosters and whose acres it waters and fertilizes," because the reserves "tend to preserve and protect [the Mississippi's] source." Business groups such as the Commercial Clubs could in some circumstances become adamant opponents of state conservation, particularly in the West, where many became convinced that the high level of federal landownership was an impediment to economic development. But in others they were among the most energetic and influential conservationists. In Los Angeles, for example, leading orchardists and real estate developers had urged forest protection even before the establishment in the early 1890s of a federal system of forest reserves. In 1899 the Los Angeles Chamber of Commerce organized the Forest and Water Society, and in subsequent years many of the managers of the Angeles and San Bernardino National Forests were selected from members of regional business associations, who also provided key political support for continued state and federal appropriations for the new conservation bureaucracies. "Nowhere in the United States," an appreciative Gifford Pinchot told the elite Los Angeles City Club in 1909, "has the Forest Service received such hearty co-operation as in Southern California."[49]

Although monopoly was one of the great targets of Progressive ire, there was a way for it to be defended on conservationist grounds. J. B. White of Kansas City struck this note in his address to the Conservation Congress of 1910. The "successful practical application" of conservation, he argued, "often depends very much as to ownership." Concentrated ownership could easily result in "greater possibilities for conservation." White contrasted the "country butcher and his fifty percent waste with the million dollar packing house, which has no waste." He urged delegates to temper their antimonopolistic assumptions, reassuring them that "it is not the fault of conservation that there are extremes in combinations, resulting in trusts or monopolies." In the end, monopolies "are practicing conservation in the extreme, in saving of raw material by greater utilization, and by the discovery of new uses for by-products, which find a place in therapeutics, in the arts, and in vaseline, paints, dyes and a hundred other valuable chemical products."[50]

Some railroad company owners became enthusiastic about particular conservation measures, for similar reasons. They quickly realized that spectacular places such as Yellowstone, Yosemite, and the Grand Canyon would draw more tourists—and thus more passengers and freight for their lines—if they were preserved and managed by the government rather than turned over to private hands. For just such reasons, the Northern Pacific magnate Jay Cooke played a key role in securing Yellowstone's designation as a national park in 1872. James J. Hill, known as the "Empire Builder" for the power of his Great Northern Railway, was an ardent proponent of national forests and parks. He considered himself a major figure in the development of conservation thought (though he was likely the only person to do so). Hill supported vigorous state preservation of such key resources as soil and timber because he saw their waste as part of a general lack of national efficiency, also manifest in what he thought was the laziness of the workforce and the low working hours of Americans. He deemed the tight money and credit policies so important to the ideology of corporate leaders "the conservation of capital" and urged "friends of conservation" to "take steps everywhere to give to this indispensable possession the same protection from the spoiler that they are trying to give to the soil, the forest, the water power, and deposits of mineral wealth." In the 1910s, such pronouncements lead the advocates of a national park system—Horace McFarland and his circles chief among them—to solicit railroad companies for financial and political support for their positions. There was an even more compelling economic case for reclamation, since it brought new lands into commercial agricultural production, and thus new customers for railroads.[51]

Similar motives prompted some conservative elites to back urban conservation in their own cities. Whereas Progressives supported urban park spaces out of the belief that an entirely commercial and artificial landscape threatened the well-being of the urban masses, conservative political factions too could see value in well-developed park systems. In particular, they saw that urban conservation could provide cities with a competitive advantage in attracting new residents, particularly those with capital, and thus in boosting property values. The midwestern railroad developer Alpheus Stickney made this a central appeal in his pitch for a naturalistic and extensive park system in St. Paul, Minnesota, in the early 1910s. Warning of the dangers of attracting poor migrants rather than "that self-respecting class . . . who have been accustomed to breathe pure air and are not unacquainted with sunshine," he warned St. Paul's citizens that other cities were competing for such migrants "by building beautiful boulevards and parks, to make [themselves] more beautiful and livable."[52]

Los Angeles had similar wealthy and conservative conservationists. Leaders of the Merchants and Manufacturers' Association (MMA) offered key support for extensive city parks. Joseph Mesmer, a longtime leader of the MMA who played a key role in securing water for the city from federal reclamation projects, served for a term as park commissioner and became an apostle for widening streets and lining them with trees. Around 1910 he made an ambitious proposal for "improving the Los Angeles River bed," which was rapidly becoming an open sewer. Mesmer wanted to create a place where "thousands of our own people . . . can enjoy their outing and recreation in walking over beautifully laid serpentine walks amidst shady trees, beautiful shrubs, and flowers, while others enjoy the pleasures of boating, sailing and swimming," hoping that his vision would become "the crowning undertaking of his life."[53] Charles Silent, Mesmer's colleague on the MMA, became similarly active in Los Angeles conservation circles. Silent pointed to how rural conservation might benefit the city itself, anticipating "that the Owens river water supply will furnish a sufficient surplus to be used in our parks for scenic purposes so that . . . [they] can be made to gleam with miniature waterfalls, with streams, lakes and cataracts, fountains and springs with water for man, bird and beast everywhere." In the face of budget shortfalls, he used his personal funds to help underwrite a report on turning much of a major arroyo into a public park.[54]

It was easy for more impassioned conservationists to be cynical about the cooperation of wealthy and vested economic interests such as railroads. As Interior Secretary Walter Fisher remarked of railroad managers, "These men have reached that degree of enlightenment in their selfishness, that they have come to the conclusion that it is for their own best interest to have a national park bureau established." A similar point could have been made about Mesmer, Silent, and their counterparts in countless cities. Horace McFarland—who actively solicited railroad support for a parks bureau—found the environmental practices of wealthy industrialists downright hypocritical. During a trip to a bucolic retreat on Lake Ontario, he learned something unsettling about the fine summer homes he saw there: "They were almost exclusively owned by residents of a certain very wealthy and certainly very ugly American city, where iron is king. The iron manufacturers flee from the all-pervading ugliness they have created, and the money earned in complete disregard of the naturally fine scenic conditions about their own homes is used in buying scenic beauty in a foreign country!" McFarland turned this observation into an attack on laissez-faire critiques of conservation: "The most blatant economist, who sneers at the thought of public beauty, accessible by right of all, is usually much interested in private beauty of scenery, of home and of person, if accessible to him alone! Selfishly and inconsistently he recognizes in his own use the value of the natural resources he affects to despise."[55]

Just as those to the right of Fisher, McFarland, and their Progressive compatriots articulated visions of conservation consistent with their more conservative politics, so too did those on the left of the political spectrum. Socialists and labor activists often saw conservation as an unnecessary or even illegitimate use of tax dollars by elites. Minnesota labor circles, for example, condemned city park plans of the sort proposed by A. B. Stickney, and petitioned and held meetings against ballot initiatives to create parks. Similarly, in the early twentieth century, blue-collar voters in Seattle voted against proposals for independent parks boards pushed by business leaders. In general during this period, labor circles saw nature as a place for the production of wealth rather than for recreation, and thus balked at the less utilitarian aspects of conservation, including parks and game laws that seemed to them to serve the needs of sport hunters rather than those who would actually eat what they killed.[56]

Nevertheless, in certain circumstances those on the left enthusiastically embraced conservation. The Industrial Workers of the World (IWW) published a long and detailed analysis of the timber industry. The report condemned land fraud, the concentration of ownership in the industry, rampant waste, and what it prophesied would be timber famines—all on the basis of U.S. Forest Service data, approvingly and extensively cited. The IWW predicted that workers' control of the timber industry, which it sought, would serve the goals of conservation by dramatically reducing fires, waste, and fraud.[57]

Although the IWW never gained the power necessary to put its vision of worker control into practice, in some places leftists had greater opportunity to practice what they preached. In Milwaukee in the 1910s, a dynamic Socialist Party rooted in the city's German community sent

Victor Berger to the U.S. House of Representatives as the first Socialist member of that body, gained numerous aldermanic and other local positions, and won mayoral elections in 1910 and 1916. The second Socialist mayor, Daniel Hoan, who remained in office until 1940, made parks and playgrounds a top priority. This goal was a logical part of the Socialists' focus on the provision of excellent and efficient public amenities such municipally owned water and power systems, playgrounds, and schools, all of which earned them the sobriquet "sewer socialists." It was also a reflection of the conservationist philosophy of the Socialist park commissioner Charles Whitnall. Whitnall lamented the fact that urban development deprived most Milwaukeeans—especially the poor—of the regular exposure to nature that they needed for good mental and physical health. This deprivation he viewed as akin to other environmental problems, writing, "The destruction of our forests by lumbermen is no more serious than the robbing of our soil by municipalities." His solution—clearly indebted to Henry George's thought and Ebenezer Howard's proposals—was to decentralize the city as much as possible through annexations, which would allow for a less dense population, and to build an extensive system of parks where "the native landscape can not only be conserved but that [its] most distinguishing features are most useful as park areas." He put forward a large-scale plan that would have woven a connected set of parks and parkways into a larger, decentralized city, "integrating wetland protection, flood control, stream bank restoration, sanitation, environmental education, and public recreation."[58]

Socialist and radical labor circles in Los Angeles never enjoyed the kind of power their counterparts in Milwaukee wielded, but they too were smitten with aspects of conservation. Even as they battled with the Merchants and Manufacturers' Association—a struggle that would shift decisively in 1911 when two socialists pleaded guilty to bombing the offices of the virulently antilabor *Los Angeles Times*—they shared many of their opponents' ideals when it came to nature and conservation. The *Western Comrade*, California's primary socialist newspaper, frequently published articles extolling the healing power of wild nature. In her poem "Mother Earth," for example, Ruth Lea Stevens offered the familiar contrast between the artificial, frenzied pace of urban life and

the health and authenticity of nature that drove so much of the culture
and politics of conservation:

> Mother Earth is resting, resting,
> Are you tired and weary too?
> Would you like to have the blessing
> That is now in store for you?
> Leave the City's din of battle,
> Quit its noisome strife for prize,
> Wondrous wealth for you lies waiting,
> 'Neath the azure of the skies!

But in this case the contrast was marked by Stevens's socialism; the respite to be found was not so much individual as collective, an opportunity for the people as a whole:

> Mother Earth is calling, calling,
> Will you hearken to her call?
> She but waits to give the blessing
> Held in store for one and all.
> God made land for all his children,
> Not for greedy landlords' gain!
> "Sell it not," he saith—forever!
> Oh! his words are very plain.[59]

Job Harriman, whose near victory in the mayoral election of 1911
terrified the city's economic powers, used nature as a critique of industrial
society, regularly contrasting the West's natural abundance and beauty
with the harsh lot of those who labored in its fields and factories. Harriman's focus in this regard was on the utilitarian rather than the romantic
aspects of conservation. He saw federal irrigation as a model for how a
united citizenry could use their productive powers for the interests of all.

> Now that the cities and towns and villages are built, now
> that the plains are strewn with orchards and vineyards and
> fields full of grain, now that the cities are filled with various

industries and those who have worked hardest have hun-
gered and thirsted and bowed most under over-production
and under-consumption—how natural it is, when they clasp
hands and begin to feel the power of their united might, that
they should not only conceive of and construct general irrigation systems, but that they should also harness that water
power and thus shift the burdens from the shoulders of man
to power generated by falling waters.

He illustrated his point with photos of a waterfall titled "Falling Water
to Propel Our Trains" and of a palm-lined Los Angeles street with the
caption "That Little Paradise," images and ideas that could just as easily been promulgated by Charles Silent, Joseph Mesmer, and his other
antagonists on the opposite side of Los Angeles' yawning political and
class divide.[60]

The Politics of Conservation

If Job Harriman was a Progressive, he was clearly on the movement's left
edge: social progress for him, as for other socialists, would come when
the working classes gained control over the means of production. Most
Progressives were averse to that kind of class argument, and wary of the
idea of such a wholesale transfer of economic power to the hands of the
government. Yet conservation appealed to them—and even to some who
were not Progressive in any way, shape, or form. As a term that captured
a widely shared sense of tumultuous social change, and a political program that could be embraced and tailored by women and men, African
Americans and whites, trade unionists and development-minded civic
elites, conservation attracted a broad and diverse following. Seizing the
opportunity provided by Progressive political ferment and expansion of
state power, conservationists made enormous strides in the early twentieth century. They created state agencies with considerable power, civic
organizations with a national reach, and numerous books that articulated conservation doctrines for specialists and the general public alike.
Disagreements about what exactly conservation meant, and whose interests it ought to serve, soon led to bitter splits within the movement.

Fighting over Conservation

I n 1909, inspired by the enormous progress of conservation, Gifford Pinchot and Horace McFarland saw the potential for a national organization to mobilize the ideological and demographic breadth of conservationist ranks. Just a few years later, both men concluded that such cooperation was unthinkable. "It has been a very hard wrench to lose my faith in Mr. Pinchot," McFarland wrote in early 1914 to the editor of *Outlook,* "but it is gone." He complained to numerous leading conservationists of Pinchot's "insincerity, his hedging and self-seeking." Pinchot was equally damning, telling Frederick Law Olmsted Jr. that talking with his erstwhile ally was a "waste of time."[1]

The split between Pinchot and McFarland was important in its own right, wrecking any hopes that conservationists could benefit from a vigorous, broad-based national organization that would press for material and aesthetic measures in cities, suburbs, and the countryside. But it was only one of many splits between conservationists. The demographic and ideological heterogeneity that endowed conservation with so much of its appeal and reach also pitted different kinds of conservationists against one another, fragmenting and ultimately weakening the movement. Ironically, the considerable political victories of the early twentieth century—metropolitan park systems, federal bureaucracies, and an extensive domain in the West for conservation—exacerbated this divisiveness, since conservationists had gained something worth

fighting over. The division between McFarland and Pinchot was replicated time and again as the different emphasis on the sustainable use of
natural resources and the aesthetic and spiritual value of nature that put
them at odds also divided countless other conservationists.

The question of the proper scope of conservation also proved con-
tentious: Were cities part of nature in any meaningful way? Did conservation have anything to say about the daily lives of millions of urbanites,
or the houses of their generally wealthier suburban counterparts? These
sorts of debates often heightened the social and ideological divisions
that already separated conservationists. Men and women had both
made important contributions to a shared cause, yet some men dismissed female conservationists, sometimes actively suppressing their
voices and limiting their roles. Some labor advocates and leftists embraced conservation, yet others rejected it as a distraction from their
central goal of securing economic security and workplace freedom for
working people. A widespread culture of conservation gave the movement an indispensable power that underwrote and enabled its formal
legislative achievements, yet some conservationists pointed to their supposed environmental enlightenment as proof of their superiority over
others—men over women, whites over Indians or blacks. The sense of
a unified movement sweeping the country before it that had greatly animated leading conservationists dissolved over the course of the 1910s,
leaving conservationists pitted against one another as often as unified.

The McFarland-Pinchot Rupture

McFarland and Pinchot's estrangement had many roots. In the most direct sense, it reflected a personal disagreement over specific conservation policies. Like so many of their peers, the two men split bitterly over
the proposed reservoir in Yosemite National Park, each side viewing its
position as the epitome of conservation and the other as its betrayal.
In these same years, McFarland was the leading national proponent of
the establishment of a national parks bureau, a goal that he achieved in
1916 with the creation of the National Park Service, housed in the Department of the Interior. Pinchot, in contrast, refused to support such
a measure for fear of weakening his treasured Forest Service, ultimately

giving his conditional support to a parks bill only if the park service would be placed under the Department of Agriculture (which administered the Forest Service).

These issues proved intractable and ultimately destructive to environmental reform because they reflected not simply questions of tactics or priorities, but also more fundamental disagreements about what conservation meant. McFarland wanted conservation to address a wide range of spaces, from cities to suburbs to wildlands; Pinchot emphasized the paramount importance of putting expanses of the countryside in federal hands. Pinchot and his compatriots saw the maintenance and judicious use of natural resources as the linchpin of conservation, whereas McFarland spoke for those who valued what was sometimes called "human conservation," a more encompassing set of aesthetic and social goals. McFarland was sensitive to the need for material conservation, but also emphasized its limits. "The primary function of the national forests," he wrote in 1912 in the midst of heated discussions with Pinchot, "is to supply lumber. The primary function of the national parks is to maintain in healthful efficiency the lives of the people who must use that lumber. The forests are the nation's reserve wood-lots. The parks are the nation's reserve for the maintenance of individual patriotism and federal solidarity."[2]

The question of parks policy continually brought these differences to the fore, making rivals and enemies of former allies. McFarland's advocacy of a national parks bill reflected his sense, as he put it in the *Sierra Club Bulletin,* that "national parks are but a larger development of municipal, county and state parks." What parks had in common despite the very different scale and surroundings of a city park or a Yellowstone was their shared purpose. "Everything that the limited scope of the city park can do as quick aid to the citizen, [national parks] are ready to do more thoroughly, on a greater scale," McFarland proclaimed to his readers. In accordance with this philosophy, he urged Pinchot to support the hiring "of some great landscape engineer of international reputation who should act to the national parks as the same grade of landscape engineer now acts to great park systems, such as those of Boston, Minneapolis, Kansas City, and other great centers of population." National parks were urban conservation writ large.[3]

Pinchot might have agreed with this proposition, or at least tried to meet McFarland halfway. After all, he could be quite invested in the aesthetic concerns of conservation in his private life: his revelation about the term "conservation" came to him while riding in Washington's preeminent park, and he took great care with the reforestation of his Pennsylvania family estate, Gray Towers. Moreover, Pinchot was politically savvy enough to recognize that mobilizing broad popular support for the kind of conservation policies he was fighting for in Congress and the executive branch might require him to address the more urban and aesthetic forms of the movement. Indeed, by 1909 he had grown frustrated enough with the limited willingness of the American Forestry Association to support conservation policies to form the National Conservation Association, or NCA. (This was the same period when he and McFarland thought about joining their efforts.) Pinchot and the former Harvard president Charles Eliot discussed plans for a mass-circulation magazine, *Conservation,* which could help make the NCA an effective organization with a national reach. They recognized that they would have to cover not only the federal and state policies about forests, minerals, soil exhaustion, and "regulating monopoly" that were dear to their hearts, but also "public health," which they defined to include "building laws to secure adequate light and air to city-dwellers" and the "provision of parks, playgrounds, gardens, parkways, and bathing-places to cities."[4]

But Pinchot was ultimately too committed to the centrality of material conservation to join forces with McFarland or even to acknowledge the potential political benefits of his suggestion. After taking a few weeks to "cool off," he scoffed at McFarland's suggestion that national parks be modeled after urban ones. "You seem to have confused in your mind, to a degree which I confess surprises me, the intensive management of city parks with the handling of the great stretches of wild lands contained in the National Parks." The idea of applying the same management techniques to city and national parks was "utterly absurd. . . . You have evidently been misled by the fact that the name of Park is applied to both."[5]

Some of Pinchot's scorn emerged from the acrimonious debate over damming the Hetch Hetchy Valley. A part of Yosemite National Park since its founding in 1890, the valley's expanse, some three and a half miles long by a quarter to a half mile wide, remained little known and visited at the dawn of the twentieth century. It was an impressive site to those who were aware of it, one that generally evoked comparison to the nearby and already iconic Yosemite Valley. Ringed by cliffs of granite from which numerous waterfalls cascaded, the valley floor was a gentle riot of grasses, flowers, and black oak, through which coursed the Tuolumne River. John Muir first visited in the fall of 1871; writing decades later for the *Sierra Club Bulletin,* he deemed it "a grand landscape garden, one of Nature's rarest and most precious mountain mansions" where a tall waterfall was a "silvery scarf burning with irised sun-fire in every fiber" and the yellow pines towered and swayed. Another early American visitor, the geologist Josiah Whitney, noted the "extremely narrow canon, through which the river has not sufficient room to flow at the time of the spring freshets," at the valley's outlet—precisely the attribute that made it an attractive dam site. By 1900, a number of engineers had surveyed the valley and endorsed its potential as a reservoir.[6]

The valley's splendors remained the province of its very few visitors even as the interest in it as a dam site expanded. The growth of San Francisco, the nation's largest West Coast city and Pacific port, was one impetus for securing a more reliable water supply. Equally important was the Spring Valley Water Company, the city's dominant water utility. Spring Valley was a private company, and some of the state's wealthiest men, such as the railroad magnates Collis Huntington and Leland Stanford, held large amounts of stock. Its aggressive use of eminent domain to condemn private homeowners' property, its sometimes enormous profits, and its close ties to the city's political elite made the company a lightning rod for controversy for decades. Progressives singled it out for opprobrium as a monopoly that, like the Southern Pacific Railroad, embodied the abuses of unregulated economic power. Many San Franciscans blamed it for the rapidity with which the 1906 earthquake became a fire that destroyed most of downtown.[7]

The earthquake prompted San Francisco to renew its application for reservoir rights to Hetch Hetchy, which had initially been turned down by the interior secretary in 1903 on the grounds that the site was within the bounds of Yosemite National Park and thus off limits. City

leaders secured the support of Pinchot, then serving as chief U.S. forester, who encouraged them to reapply to the new interior secretary.
Alarmed by the city's renewed efforts, Muir soon called on the publisher
Robert Underwood Johnson and Horace McFarland to help him put
together a national coalition opposing the city's request.

So what might have been a local dispute over where a city should
build a reservoir soon became a running national debate that com-
manded the attention of journalists, activists, and politicians for a decade, and of historians interested in Progressive politics and environmentalism for a century. The passion of both sides' position on the question
of the reservoir was amplified by their sense that what was at stake went
beyond Northern California and indeed defined what would become of
conservation on the national stage. The reservoir's opponents saw the
integrity of the public lands system at stake. As Muir put the matter:
"Every national park is besieged by thieves and robbers and beggars with
all sorts of plans and pleas for possession of some coveted treasure of
water, timber, pasture, rights of way, etc. . . . Thus the Yosemite Park, the
beauty glory of California and the Nation . . . has been attacked by spoil-
ers ever since it was established." If San Francisco could wrest the valley
from park protection, then no place that conservationists had set aside
could be safe. This position seemed to resonate with conservationists
across the country. Muir celebrated the fact that "thousands from near
and far came to our help,—mountaineers, nature-lovers, naturalists.
Most of our thousand [Sierra] club members wrote to the President or
Secretary protesting against the destructive reservoir scheme . . . so also
did the Oregon and Washington mountaineering clubs and the Appalachian of Boston and public-spirited citizens everywhere." Along with
Muir, McFarland played a key role in building this national network,
attempting to draw in the membership of his American Civic Association, the General Federation of Women's Clubs, and the elite Cosmos
Club of Washington, D.C. One of the most valuable recruits proved to
be the Chicago poet Harriet Monroe, who soon joined Muir and McFarland as Hetch Hetchy's most dedicated and articulate defender. In 1909,
the reservoir opponents had formed the Society for the Preservation of
National Parks to coordinate their efforts.[8]

The proponents of the Hetch Hetchy reservoir relied on conventional lobbying through San Francisco's political establishment, but they too built a national network and claimed the mantle of conservation. Damming the valley made immediate sense to many Progressives: technical expertise at the service of the state would provide a valuable natural resource that was being monopolized by corrupt private interests. So Pinchot reasoned when he urged Congress to approve the reservoir based on the idea that "the fundamental principle of the whole conservation policy is that of use, to take every part of the land and its resources and put it to that use in which it will best serve the most people." For Pinchot, this principle overrode the objections of the Spring Valley Water Company, because it was a purely private endeavor devoted to profits for its owners rather than the collective economic interest of San Francisco. The position of Muir and his cohort deserved more consideration; the "delight" of those few who went to the valley was a reason "it should be left in its natural condition," but one that for Pinchot was outweighed by the benefits of the water supply to an entire city. In the end, the "intermittent aesthetic enjoyment of less than one per cent is being balanced against the daily comfort and welfare of 99 per cent."[9]

Pinchot was far from the only conservationist with a national reputation to back the dam. Congressman William Kent from Marin County thought his defense of the proposal was perfectly consistent with his long record of support for conservation and other Progressive causes. Earlier in life, as a resident of Chicago, Kent had found himself drawn to such causes as neighborhood parks, Jane Addams's settlement house, and the replacement of private utility monopolies by municipal operations. He entered national politics after moving to California, where he was elected to the U.S. House for three terms, during which he backed such measures as the protection of Lake Tahoe from a disruptive private power plan and the establishment of additional national parks. He and his wife purchased a grove of redwoods north of San Francisco, which they then donated to the federal government with the provision that it be preserved as a park named after John Muir. But other human needs, particularly equitable economic development, were also fundamental to his vision of conservation. As he said in congressional testimony in support of the Hetch Hetchy dam: "I am rather inclined to resent the criticism that we who stand for this bill are opposed to conservation. . . .

When an opportunity comes to give to a great community upward to 200,000 horsepower upon which not a cent of private profit shall ever be made; when it comes to the question of benefiting upward of a million people, then I believe that conservation demands that I do my duty and try to help rather than to hinder such a worthy project."[10]

Kent was prescient in seeing the question of electrical power as being as important as the water itself. He added a provision to the authorizing legislation stipulating that hydroelectric power generated by the dam had to remain in control of the city rather than a private firm. This was a clear curb on Pacific Gas and Electric, the state's largest utility and, like the Southern Pacific Railroad and the Spring Valley Water Company, a bête noire of Golden State Progressives. Years later, Frederick Law Olmsted Jr. acknowledged the importance of this provision. "There *were* other sources of water available to San Francisco, but not such as would provide *also* a large amount of hydro-electric power, useful as a club in dealing with the Pacific Gas and Electric. . . . I suspect that the western Progressives who were so strong for it were much influenced by their attitude on Public vs. Privately-owned Utilities."[11]

Yet Kent's indispensable support for the dam did not prevent him from backing more romantic conservationist measures at the same time: he spearheaded the establishment of Muir Woods and became a founding member of the Save-the-Redwoods League. In the next few years, he also worked closely with McFarland in the creation of the National Park Service, serving as the lead House sponsor for the bill that created that conservation bureaucracy.[12]

Kent's ability to work with opponents of the Hetch Hetchy reservoir proved to be the exception rather than the rule. It was not just each side's passion for its cause that made the debate acrimonious, but also the frequent dismissal of the other's motives. Muir characterized the architects of the reservoir as "the few cunning drivers of the damming scheme, working in darkness like moles in a low-lying meadow," who hoped that "comparatively private gain may be made out of universal public loss" and epitomized "these ravaging money-mad days." His antagonists were equally dismissive. Marsden Manson, a city engineer, first joined the Sierra Club in 1895, three years after its founding, and had published in its magazine, but he was contemptuous and unwilling to acknowledge the conservation bona fides of Muir's supporters, whom he dismissed as "the so-called nature-loving societies . . . composed largely of short-haired women and long-haired men." His later description of them as "mistaken zealots" under the control of "grasping interests" (a thinly veiled reference to the Spring Valley Water Company) left even less space for honorable disagreement.[13]

Manson's "mistaken zealots" had enough credibility to hold up approval of the reservoir until 1913, when Congress granted the city the right to flood the valley. The victors got their reservoir, but in the process they also deeply damaged the conservation movement. The Sierra Club divided between the majority that sided with Muir and the minority with Manson. Warren Olney's experiences suggest the intense bitterness of the split. A great admirer of Muir and the Hetch Hetchy Valley itself, Olney had helped organize the club in 1892, hosting the meeting in which the founders drew up the articles of incorporation. His commitment to the development of the Bay Area—he served as Oakland's mayor from 1903 to 1905—led him to support the reservoir. What his daughter recalled as "twenty years of pioneering service and close friendship" was left in shambles, and "the Hetch Hetchy project was never afterward a permissible topic of conversation in our household." John Muir's death in 1914 led many to consider him a martyr for Hetch Hetchy, though his health had suffered for years beforehand.[14]

The split within the Sierra Club reverberated throughout the nation's conservation circles. Fearing that they would seize the opportunity to make the case for their position on Hetch Hetchy, Pinchot declined to invite Muir and Robert Underwood Johnson to the Governors' Conference on Conservation of Natural Resources in 1908, the first high-profile national gathering on the subject. But he did invite McFarland, who spoke strongly in favor of keeping the valley unaltered. And his exclusion of the older foresters Bernhard Fernow and Charles Sargent seemed motivated more by personal animus than a split over Hetch Hetchy or any other particular issue. For several years, McFarland and Pinchot tried to maintain collegial relations, even as they argued with each other both directly and publicly over the disputed valley. In early 1913, McFarland expressed his hope that he and Pinchot could work together on matters of mutual agreement, even as the executive director of the American Civic Association cautioned McFarland: "[Pinchot's] attitude has cost him scores of friends who have been alienated from him and his Conservation policies. You are still a Conservationist, but there are others in the west who are so bitter over H-H that they can see no good side to Mr. P. That's unfortunate for a good cause."[15]

The City Versus the Country

Because the Hetch Hetchy fight was principally a struggle between conservationists, some of the core issues that it raised were the closely related questions of whose interests and what places conservationists ought to prioritize. How should the needs of the country's swelling cities, which, despite their sometimes horrifying majesty, still depended on faraway forests and waters, be balanced against the splendors of the remote and wild? Taken as a whole, conservation offered specific interventions into urban, suburban, and wild landscapes. Cities were to be supplied with water and adorned with substantial parks designed to emulate their region's natural environment; neighborhoods and suburbs with substantial home lots were to be planted similarly. Domestic architecture should blend in with naturalistic plantings. The countryside was to be managed for material ends—to preserve and even increase the ability of the land to provide timber, water, and agricultural fertility into the future—as well as spiritual ones, particularly the protection of iconic places with the power to awe.

Some conservationists embraced what might be called the full spectrum of conservationist landscapes. Horace McFarland, Dana Bartlett, Mira Lloyd Dock, and Charles Francis Saunders embodied this breadth. Each could stand in reverence before a soaring mountain or plunging waterfall, resolute that the American people should use their government to protect such places from despoliation. And they similarly resolved that urbanites, soon to be a majority of the population, needed natural places of respite close at home, and that a wholly private economy was no more able to provide them than it would still its hand in the face of pristine natural splendor. Bartlett's *The Better City* (1907) advocated the creation of parks, greenways, and other public spaces in Los Angeles, as well as easy and affordable access to mountain and beach retreats nearby. Four years later, in *The Better Country,* he extended his reasoning from the municipal to the national government and from the metropolitan environment to the nation's forests and waterways. The campaigns of McFarland and Dock for national parks, state forests, and city parks put these principles into action.

Nevertheless, the breadth of the conservation movement did not mean that all its advocates were equally committed to the landscapes of city, suburb, and countryside. Most conservationists cared deeply about some landscapes and much less—or not at all—about others. These differing priorities came to the fore again and again in the 1910s, helping fracture a previously more or less cooperative politics of conservation.

Most conservationists viewed the countryside as the locus of their efforts. On this count, despite their bitter split over Hetch Hetchy, Muir and Pinchot stood united, and separate from conservationists invested in the aesthetics of cities and their residents' quality of life. For both men, as for so many of their Romantic and materialist followers, cities embodied artificiality. Since they were not a part of nature, conservation had nothing to say about their design or about the daily life of their residents. For Muir, cities made people "nerve-shaken" and "over-civilized," subjecting them to the "stupefying effects of the vice of over-industry and the deadly apathy of luxury." Nature could be found only beyond urban confines, so it was there that conservation should act, whether to preserve such transcendent refuges as the High Sierra and Yellowstone, or to ensure that there was enough water, timber, coal and other resources for future generations to use equitably. Neither man paid any real attention to urban conservation. Muir did acknowledge the "growing interest" in "the half-wild parks and gardens of towns" in his list of examples of how Americans at the dawn of the century were "trying as best they can to mix and enrich their own little ongoings with those of Nature." And he did put McFarland on the board of the Sierra Club. Yet he had no concern for the kind of home-ground conservation practiced so prominently by his close friend Jeanne Carr. His own farming and orcharding was purely a business proposition. Muir inherited his bountiful orchards from his father-in-law, John Strentzel, but did not claim Strentzel's Arcadian vision of horticulture. Whereas Strentzel was a Grange leader who pushed for irrigation and forestry programs in the

Alhambra Valley, Muir never published a word about the place that provided his home and wealth for twenty-five years. Instead, Muir's heart was always called to the wild and untamed. Under his leadership the Sierra Club and its publications barely noted urban environmental matters. Pinchot similarly cared little for urban conservation. Even when he seemed to consider close cooperation with McFarland's American Civic Association, he demonstrated no enthusiasm for city parks or urban conservation of any sort.[16]

A deep strain of antiurbanism also marked many of those conservationists who valued the less sublime nature to be found closer to home. Essayist Dallas Lore Sharp owed his wide acclaim to his loving evocation of the partly agricultural, partly agrarian landscape of outer-edge suburbs, whose extent was greatly expanded by metropolitan commuter rail networks. Sharp made himself the bard of the commuting life in these early suburbs. Suburban life, in his presentation, offered both meaningful communion with nature and the prosperity, stimulation, and social engagement made possible by urban professional life. In *The Face of the Fields,* he wrote of the kaleidoscopic changes of "every passing wind, every shifting cloud, every calling bird, every baying hound, every shape, shadow, fragrance, sound, and tremor," which could allow his readers to immerse themselves in the totality of life's connections "if we will but see what pushes the falling leaves off, what lies in slumber under the covers of the snow; if we will but feel the strength of the north wind and the fierce joy of the fox and hound." Although Sharp is not as well remembered today as John Muir or even the tamer John Burroughs, his sensibility and the grace he expressed it with shaped later naturalists and conservationists. In the mid-1920s, a young Rachel Carson, then a college student, encountered Sharp's essays, which, she wrote, "have about them the tang and freshness of a sea breeze, the limpid beauty of a mountain pool." Carson's classic *Silent Spring,* published decades later, in 1962, bore the mark of Sharp by invoking the beauty and harmony of suburban nature in order to underscore the horror of toxic pollution that wreaked havoc in such places.[17]

Cities did have a place in Sharp's vision, but one apart from nature. The beauty of suburban life was that one could constantly witness this larger order even while commuting regularly to a professional job in the city, which functioned as "a head to the body, the nervous centre where the multitudinous sensations are organized and directed, where the multitudinous and interrelated interests of the round world are directed." But suburbs were for living, as he put it pointedly earlier in the same essay: the commuter "knows the dark gray city . . . he feels and hears the throbbing heart of man all the day long; and when evening comes he hurries away to the open country, where he can hear the heart of Nature beat, where he can listen a little to the beating of his own."[18]

Some of Sharp's essays suggested that urbanites might be able to hear the "heart of Nature beat," perhaps by witnessing a squirrel's resourceful preparations for winter or by growing up on the same street as a maple rising from concrete. But ultimately, cities were lost to nature. "A city is a sore on the face of Nature," he wrote in 1908, "not a dangerous ugly sore, necessarily, if one can get out of it often enough and far enough, but a sore nevertheless, that Nature will have nothing kindly to do with." While he presented the suburbanite's engagement with nature as sophisticated and modern, Sharp disdained the primitiveness that he saw, paradoxically, coiled in the heart of contemporary city living. "Flats, tenements, 'chambers,' 'apartments,'" he asked, "what are they but public buildings, just as inns and hospitals and baths are . . . and what are they but unmistakable signs of a reversion to earlier tribal conditions, when not only the cave was shared in common, but the wife and the children and the day's kill?" Sharp's version of conservation culture had only this to say to city dwellers: get out if you can.[19]

Urban-oriented conservationists such as Dana Bartlett and Mira Lloyd Dock shared some of the antiurbanism that animated Sharp and countless others, in the sense that they wanted their cities to be less city-like. Bartlett, for example, forthrightly described his plans for Los Angeles as part of "the movement to ruralize the city, by adorning it with trees and parks and liberal lawns." Yet Bartlett and his compatriots differed from Sharp's brand of conservation in two regards. First, they saw urban landscapes as redeemable. Bartlett acknowledged that "the crowded tenement, the rookery, a city's ill-kept streets and yards are not incentives to higher living," but insisted that "the fairer the city, the nearer to Nature's heart the people are brought; the more easily they are governed; there is less crime and more of the normal, spiritual, helpful life which is the product of the ripest civilization." Second, conservationists whose visions encompassed cities held strikingly different opinions about private property and communal life than did those who thought cities and conservation had nothing to do with each other. Sharp valued his suburbs not only for the exposure they provided to nature, but also because they were landscapes of private property and the nuclear family—unlike cities, where "the rented house is in the end a tragedy, as the willfull renter and his homeless family is a calamity, a disgrace, a national menace," adding, "Drinking and renting are vicious habits." Bartlett, in contrast, typified urban conservationists in consistently pointing to the dangers of concentrated economic power; "swollen fortunes," he wrote, "are a menace to the individual and the nation." The corollary of this could be found in common property, which could embody the public good, as it had in England before the commons were wrested from the populace by the aristocracy, and as it might again be in the United States and across the world with the "growing paternalism of the government."[20]

Fragmentation

Philosophical differences over the proper landscapes of conservation were not the only divisions that weakened the movement during the 1910s. Although much of conservation's strength came from its ability to attract supporters from across the divides of gender, class politics, and sometimes even race and ethnicity, it did not dissolve these divides. Indeed, disputes among conservationists often reflected these deeper social divisions.

Many male conservationists reconsidered their acceptance of women as leaders and activists. The shifting stance of the American Forestry Association (AFA) embodied the retreat from inclusiveness. For a few years starting in 1906, the association's leadership encouraged the participation of women in its conferences. It regularly printed their speeches and poems in its journal, *Forestry and Irrigation,* and solicited reports from the forestry committees of the General Federation of Women's Clubs (GFWC). This was a part of the effort by professional foresters, who had been a critical source of conservation policy and institution building, to deepen their influence by widening their appeal to a mass audience. At

Pinchot's behest, in 1908 the association changed the name of its journal to *Conservation* to reflect this broadened approach.

By early in the decade after 1910, however, foresters were souring on this initiative. Female support and activism were useful, but women were prone to making arguments on grounds that jeopardized professional scientists' reputation for rationality and hardheadedness. A editorial in *Conservation,* "The Women's Clubs and the Forests," in 1910 expressed this concern. The editors began with an acknowledgment of the political influence of women—"the support of the women of America is a powerful aid to any cause"—and the particular role of the GFWC with "the forestry and conservation movements." But they cautioned that "much harm has been done in the course of the forestry movement, and the same is true of all branches of conservation, by immature thought arising from insufficient knowledge." Indeed, female conservationists' ignorance threatened the movement as a whole: "The women's clubs sometimes undertake too much and gain only that little knowledge which is a dangerous thing, on subjects they take up. This produces mental dissipation in the individual which is unfortunate, but when it is applied to the advancement of a great public cause resting on a scientific foundation, it really becomes serious." The solution was for women to defer to the scientific expertise offered by male leaders of such organizations as the American Forestry Association. The editorial did have some advice on how women could improve themselves: "Study these forest and conservation questions so that you can give sound reasons for the faith that is in you." Following this advice would demonstrate that "under wise leadership," women could be effective advocates for conservation.[21]

Perhaps club women were not amenable to the foresters' patronizing advice or were otherwise unwilling to submit to "wise leadership." In any event, the leaders of the AFA soon decided that women were more trouble than they were worth. Within a few years, the journal had ceased publishing updates on forestry work by the GFWC, or indeed any female speech or writing. It also changed its name from *Conservation* to *American Forestry* and replaced much of its coverage of federal policy debates with an emphasis on state and private forestry management practices. In this case, the exclusion of women was part of a narrowing of conservation to a more technical, applied approach that shied from engaging not only aesthetic and urban questions, but also the concerns about monopoly and unchecked economic power that continued to animate Pinchot and his circles.[22]

The American Forestry Association was not alone in its retreat. The Fifth National Conservation Congress, held in Washington, D.C., in 1913, ostensibly had a GFWC leader as vice president, but she did not speak and was not even represented in the photographs of attendees and speakers later published by the organization. No GFWC or DAR speakers were heard from. The only female speaker offered a brief presentation on safety in lumber camps. The infant profession of city planning followed a trajectory similar to that of the Conservation Congress and the AFA. Women helped organize the first National Conference on City Planning, held in 1909, drawing on the important roles they had played in lobbying for city parks, sanitary municipal water supplies, and early restrictions on pollution. They were soon entirely pushed out of national meetings by male city planners, who stressed the "vigorous, virile, sane" basis of their approach in contrast with the "effeminate and sentimental" approach of "tying tidies on telephone poles and putting doilies on cross-walks."[23]

Gifford Pinchot also became more cautious about the influence of women in conservation over the course of the 1910s. In the years before 1910, when he was most intent on broadening the public appeal of conservation, he repeatedly praised and encouraged female conservationists. In 1907, he hired the Colorado conservationist Enos Mills, whose numerous addresses to GFWC meetings had earned him the affection and respect of club women, as a forestry agent charged with traveling the nation to rally support for the Roosevelt administration's conservation agenda. Mills's preferred audience remained women's groups. But Pinchot, like his colleagues in the AFA and National Conference on City Planning, soon backpedaled. A frustrated Mrs. Draper, as she identified herself, the chairwoman of the Daughters of the American Revolution's Conservation Commission, wrote to Pinchot in 1909 that she had followed his request that DAR conservation commission members write to the (male) leaders of Pinchot's National Conservation Association to offer their services. Draper and her compatriots across the country had done so, but nobody had accepted their offer. Whether Pinchot bothered to reply is unclear, but his dismissal of Enos Mills as a lecturer for the Forest Service that year effectively canceled his outreach program to club leaders and other women activists.[24]

Unlike the AFA's leaders, Pinchot never explained his retreat from empowering female conservationists. He did share the forestry organization's privileging of hardheaded rationality over women's more emotional and aesthetic appeals. Writing a retrospective of his career decades later, he credited his advocacy of scientific forestry with convincing the public and policy makers of the need for rational timber management and harvesting—in sharp contrast with the "sentimental horror" of "denudatics" who entirely opposed cutting trees on public lands. In the early 1910s, he drew similar contrasts between the ephemeral aesthetic value of the Hetch Hetchy Valley and the concrete economic benefits of damming it. It may be that the deep opposition of most active female conservationists to the reservoir that he so ardently championed impressed upon him the downside of an active female role. The national GFWC, the California Federation of Women's Clubs, and numerous other state federations approved resolutions against the use of the valley as a reservoir. By 1910, some 150 women's clubs were actively fighting to protect Hetch Hetchy. Harriet Monroe, in the historian Robert Righter's estimation, was second only to John Muir in efficacy and prominence as an opponent to the reservoir scheme. Women were so significant within the opposition to San Francisco's plans that one city paper lampooned John Muir as a woman, sporting a dress, apron, and bonnet, trying desperately to sweep back a torrent labeled "Hetch Hetchy Project" with a broom labeled "Sierra Club."[25]

On the other hand, Pinchot never became a reactionary on gender questions in general. He wrote the women's suffrage plank in the Progressive Party's platform for 1912. His wife, Cornelia Pinchot, was a vigorous advocate for her husband's electoral campaigns. This openness to feminism earned Pinchot the deep and abiding loyalty of many Progressive women, who provided key electoral and campaign support when he won Pennsylvania's governorship in 1922, the first Pennsylvania gubernatorial election in which women could vote. As governor, he filled seventy-nine administrative positions with female appointees, in-

Sweeping Back the Flood

The *San Francisco Call* paid ironic tribute to the role of women in opposing the Hetch Hetchy reservoir by feminizing John Muir in this cartoon from the 1910s. (San Francisco Call; *courtesy Adam Rome*)

cluding the first female cabinet member. Nor did Pinchot retreat into an entirely technical and private vision of efficiency, as did the American Forestry Association. Instead, his work on conservation, labor relations, workplace safety, and public utilities continued to address questions of monopoly and the undemocratic effects of concentrated economic power. In the years ahead, he even championed conservation measures particularly close to the hearts of women, such as the creation in 1923 of Pennsylvania's Sanitary Water Board, which his biographer Char Miller describes as "arguably the first state-level anti-pollution agency in the country."[26]

Nevertheless, Pinchot's retreat from female activists in the early 1910s cost him and the larger conservation movement dearly. The rebuff was part of his unwillingness to maintain active coalitions with other ardent conservationists he disagreed with. This animosity and alienation deprived McFarland, Dock, and thousands of GFWC activists of the power and leadership on the national stage of the single most politically influential and well-connected conservationist. McFarland courted Pinchot for good reason: he was indispensable. But in winning numerous battles with other conservationists, as in the fight over Hetch Hetchy, Pinchot lost the war for a continued vigorous national conservation movement.

Pinchot's National Conservation Association (NCA) was a case in point. Although it marshaled political pressure for the protection of public lands against encroachment by mining and timber interests, in most respects it was a pale shadow of his original vision for it. The NCA recruited hundreds rather than tens of thousands of members; its operations were funded by Pinchot and a handful of his most trusted comrades; its national magazine survived only a few months; and the state chapters that it set up quickly withered or disbanded out of frustration with the lack of communication from national officers and their exclusive focus on federal policy making. The organization limped into the 1920s, by which point Pinchot was often providing the entirety of its budget, and he and his brother Amos were sometimes the only board members present at "meetings." It finally died in 1923, when Pinchot began his first term as Pennsylvania's governor.[27]

Other Progressive reforms did not founder on the shoals of internal dissension, as did conservation. Prohibition was a case in point, following a road that conservation might have taken. Antialcohol activism had deep roots in Protestant American culture, but became particularly energized by Progressivism's emphasis on moral reform, efficiency, and state power. Temperance split along one major ethnic and cultural fault line—the division between overwhelmingly native-born Protestants and heavily immigrant Catholics—but it transcended numerous others, linking together women and men, northerners and southerners, blacks and whites and Native Americans, and members of often quarrelsome Christian denominations. Its principal national organization, the Woman's Christian Temperance Union, operated with the national reach, vigor, and wide membership base that McFarland and Pinchot envisioned and might have approximated had they been able to work together. The organization benefited from the charisma and drive of its leader in the 1890s, Frances Elizabeth Willard, but survived her untimely death in 1898. This national cohesiveness paid off when a constitutional amendment banning the production, importation, transportation, and sale of nearly all alcoholic beverages passed Congress in 1917 and became the law in 1920. This success by the temperance forces suggests what a conservation movement less hampered by infighting might have achieved.[28]

Conservation Endures

Pinchot's burning of bridges, the AFA's outright purge of women, and the overall failure of conservationists to create a vigorous national organization constituted one of the major patterns of environmental politics before 1920, but they were not its only one. Some activists continued their cooperation, winning significant victories in the late 1910s and early 1920s.

The preservation of substantial tracts of old-growth redwood forests in California constituted one such victory. Close work between male and female conservationists, of exactly the sort the AFA retreated from, made this possible. California club women had long prioritized redwood protection. In 1902, at the founding convention of the California Federation of Women's Clubs, President Clara Bradley Burdette called attention to redwood groves both for "their matchless grandeur" and for their benefits to the watershed. From that point on, women's clubs, particularly in Humboldt County, worked actively to introduce and support redwood preservation efforts at both the state and the federal level. California congressman John Raker solicited and welcomed the support of club women for his unsuccessful bill in 1912 proposing a national redwoods park, and the men who in 1917 founded the Save-the-Redwoods League from the beginning drew on the support of California's female activists. Despite some disagreement over which areas should receive priority in preservation—with the principals of the league favoring a larger tract less altered by human beings, and most Northern California club women prioritizing groves that they often used for camping and picnicking—women and men worked together quite amicably. In 1921, the male councilors of the league elected three women, all club activists, to join them. Even as the league's predominantly male leadership provided the political connections and money that made possible the creation of California's Humboldt Redwoods State Park, the long campaign to protect some of the state's most iconic forests could not have been won without years of cooperation with women. To this day, the "Federation Hearthstone," an enormous fireplace built of redwood and local stone in the Arts and Crafts style, commemorates the efforts of the California Federation of Women's Clubs.[29]

The establishment of the National Park Service in 1916 resulted from similar cooperation, this time between some of the former antagonists over the Hetch Hetchy question. The push for the establishment of an agency with the purpose of managing and protecting the parks originated with the reservoir's opponents, who became convinced both that they needed a national organization to wage their battle and that the parks needed their own agency. (The Sierra Club, badly split and in any event lacking a national presence, could not serve as such a platform.) In late 1909, they formed the Society for the Preservation of National Parks, with a council that included Horace McFarland, Harriet Monroe, and members from the largest cities of the West, Midwest, and Northeast. The society continued its work after the approval of the reservoir, turning its attention to the creation of an agency to manage the national parks.[30]

The crucible of the Hetch Hetchy battle deepened the belief held by McFarland and the other principals of the society that the institutional arrangements for national parks were inadequate. This was a product both of their growing familiarity with the weaknesses of federal conservation bureaucracies and of their split with the more material conservationists led by Pinchot. McFarland was taken aback by the response to his request of the Interior Department for information about the size, funding, and management of the thirteen national parks. There was no such information, he was told, and no position charged with gathering or monitoring it. Instead, the parks were secondary concerns for agencies with other mandates. By the 1910s, about twenty monuments were administered by the Interior Department, ten by the Forest Service (part of the Department of Agriculture, entirely separate from Interior), and two by the Department of War. The interior secretary reported to Congress: "These various reservations have been created from time to time under laws which are not uniform. For administrative purposes each of the reservations is a separate and distinct unit . . . even to the extent that it is not possible under existing law to transfer a ranger from one park to another." Whatever the result of the Hetch Hetchy battle, this was bureaucratic chaos that called for some kind of order.[31]

The order that McFarland and others brought forth was embodied in the National Park Service Act of 1916, which created a single bureaucracy, the National Park Service, whose charge was to "promote and regulate the use of the Federal areas known as national parks, monuments, and reservations." The act reflected the fight over Hetch Hetchy and wider splits within conservation, in two paradoxical ways. On one hand, its language embodied the Romantic and aesthetic side of conservation: whereas the national forests were to provide lumber, grazing, and water protection, the purpose of parks (as the act read) was to "conserve the scenery and the natural and historic objects and the wild life therein and to provide for the enjoyment of the same in such manner and by such means as will leave them unimpaired for the enjoyment of future generations." The advocates of a separate parks agency understood its creation as a victory over more material conservation, since Pinchot had for years sought to bring the parks under the jurisdiction of the Forest Service—and indeed opposed the National Park Service Act on precisely those grounds. On the other hand, unity among conservationists enabled the act's passage. Key congressional Progressives such as William Kent and John Raker, both of whom had defended San Francisco's side in the Hetch Hetchy debate, supported the act with enthusiasm. And although Horace McFarland's prominence in the campaign for the bill earned him the moniker "Father of the National Park Service," female conservationists such as Harriet Monroe and Mrs. John Dickinson Sherman, the chairwoman of the Conservation Committee of the General Federation of Women's Clubs, provided indispensable lobbying and congressional testimony. This brand of conservation continued to reflect cooperation between women and men; indeed, by the end of the

1920s a majority of the membership of the Society for the Preservation of National Parks was female.[32]

McFarland and his circles saw the National Park Service Act as the embodiment of the kind of broad conservation vision they had pressed for in their courtship and eventual rupture with Pinchot and more materialist conservationists. The act and the bureaucracy it created were geared toward the management of particularly iconic and generally remote places, rather than providing for the creation and management of city, metropolitan, and wilder parks. But McFarland and others advocated for its passage by invoking the unnaturalness of the nation's urban landscape and the need for all sorts of parks as the democratic and American solution to this problem. "London has barely an acre of parks for each thousand of her people—only one tenth of the ideal American provision," he told the annual convention of the American Civic Association as it geared up to push for a federal parks bureau. In contrast, he argued in his talk, the "American service park idea . . . has its intensive development in modern playgrounds . . . of which few examples are found abroad." Industrial landscapes provided no inspiration and fostered no attachment to the nation: "Is it the smoking factory chimneys, the houses of the grimy mill towns, the malodorous wharves along our navigable rivers, the metropolitan skyscraper, or the great transcontinental steel highways . . . that inspires us as we sing our national hymn?" Parks could change this, since "into the brick and concrete heart of the city the park brings a little of the primeval outdoors, and here grows best the love of country which sees with adoration the waving stars and stripes." Only after making the case for urban parks did McFarland turn to the specific question of national parks, which he characterized as "our larger playgrounds . . . everything that the limited scope of the city park can do as quick aid to the citizen, the national parks are ready to do more thoroughly, on a greater scale."[33]

Class and Ethnicity

Conservationists thus maintained enough unity to expand the nation's park system. Despite gender tensions, in some organizations men and women still worked together; some of the partisans in the heated dispute over Hetch Hetchy transcended their differences. The class and ethnic divides within conservation proved more intractable, however, especially when it came to cities.

Urban conservationists such as Dana Bartlett and Mira Lloyd Dock linked their advocacy of city parks to wider critiques of how un-regulated capitalism failed to provide for the common good. But these parks could also appeal to those who wanted to neutralize critiques of industrial capitalism rather than embody them. Conservative urban conservationists thus supported accessible and extensive parks precisely because the outdoor experiences that they offered might help reconcile wage earners to permanently subordinate positions. The influential Chicago parks official Henry Foreman made this case in a speech given at a Chicago park on Labor Day in 1904. He opened by acknowledging that "the great problem that occupies the public mind to-day, of all days in the year, is the tremendous problem of the masses." Labor strife and uncertainty arose because people could not reconcile themselves to ine-quality: "Contrary to a usually accepted declaration, all men are *not* cre-ated equal . . . some men employ and some men are their employe[e]s." Responding to some of the grievances of the urban masses would make them more likely to accept this basic fact of life. The conditions of city life were "a cause for alarm" because they closed off access to nature for so many: "While the well-to-do, recognizing the need of pure air and change of scene for their health and contentment, are seeking country life, vastly greater numbers are leaving a natural existence to take up one that is artificial and baneful."[34]

A robust system of city and suburban parks could help ameliorate these conditions, leaving workers more satisfied with their lot. Foreman enthusiastically advocated for the annexation of the city's entire Lake Mich-igan frontage, the construction of a boulevard paralleled by strips of park along the lakefront (the future Lake Shore Drive), and aggressive measures to purchase large tracts of land on the city's periphery. Larger parks should be "left in their native state" rather than receiving "artificial park treatment." This would allow for the robust outdoor recreation workmen had been de-prived of: "Residents of our crowded districts can enjoy the pleasures of camp life there. They can have boating. They can fish. They can bathe and swim. They can pick and eat the nuts and wild fruits. They can gather the flowers of the field and forest. They can see and hear the birds and other forms of wild animal life. They can be close to the heart of nature. They can find rest from their toil, and refreshment for work to come."[35]

Conservationists who shared Foreman's ethnic and class perspectives were not always pleased with the actual uses of urban parks. Henrietta Keith's ode to the parks of Minneapolis suggested how the public spaces created by urban conservation became battlegrounds in struggles over ethnicity instead of instruments of social control. Writing in her lyrical book *Pipes o' Pan in a City Park,* Keith sounded all the classic notes of urban conservation. Urban life posed numerous challenges: "You are in the midst of the tumult and the turmoil of a great city. There is the clang of the bell and the scream of the iron wheels grinding the steel rails of an almost unbroken line of street cars. There is the rushing stream of automobiles and the roar of motor trucks." Fortunately, the city's splendid parks provided a respite that could turn the public's minds to more important matters. "A green wall of encircling trees divides [the park] from the swirling din you have just left. Long, undulating slopes of green sward slant gently down on all sides to the low brim of the winding lake, whose bright waves ripple softly on dun sands or are broken on steeper banks." The tranquility available in such places was valuable precisely because it had "no market value," conveying only "the greenness of the grass and the blueness of the sky, and the joy of being alive in a beautiful, wonderful world."[36]

Keith took great pride in Minneapolis parks, presenting them as a Progressive achievement on the magnitude of women's suffrage. But the darker tones of her later chapters kept *Pipes o' Pan* from being a triumphant story. "I hate to confess it," she wrote, "but even in Our Park there is a fly in my ointment. Fellow citizens of Czecho-Slovak, or Greek or 'Eyetalian' extraction, literally swarm over it on Sunday evenings and holidays." Instead of a quiet reverie, these visitors engaged in boisterous family celebrations. "They wheel small Slovaks, in awful red woollen caps, about in precarious go-carts; they pre-empt the benches and lie around on the grass, strewing it with remains of Frankforters, doughnuts and greasy paper bags, in defiance of all the Park Board's rules and regulations, conspicuously posted." Keith was further enraged by what she saw as their lack of due appreciation for the propertied classes, whose stability and wealth underwrote the creation and maintenance of the park. "And do THEY pay any of the taxes for acquiring and maintaining this beauty spot?" she rhetorically asked. "They do not. That is the despised 'employer's' business." The destructiveness and class animosity of the lower orders nearly destroyed Keith's love for her beloved green space. As one of those "who made the park and pay for it," she pronounced herself unable to "be humbly content with such crumbs of it as the great proletariat chooses to leave for us." Because of their uncouth intrusions, she was "desolated, because all the dryads and 'wee folk' are frightened away, and the oaks and elms can scarce be persuaded to utter a word."[37]

By the end of her book, Keith had in a sense blocked her ears to Pan's music, which once called her so strongly: "No more is the sweet Heart of the City a walled garden, secluded and still; it is a picnic ground for the great unwashed." The thought that the unwashed might no longer be content with their place seized her imagination. "Our bandits have taken Robin Hood for a prototype and are imitating his 'readjustments of the distribution of property,'" she noted darkly. "Between the bandits and the Labor Unions, there will be little property to readjust—if they keep on." The park that once embodied the promise of American democracy had become the stage for its excesses.[38]

Keith was not alone in her retreat from urban conservation in the face of ethnic and class tensions in public spaces. In Los Angeles, for example, between 1910 and 1920 a key segment of Progressives neglected and ultimately abandoned their enthusiasm for urban environmental reform. This turn is particularly striking in light of the fact that the vigorous Progressive movement in Los Angeles exercised enormous power over local government and added important voices to the national conversation about conservation. Despite the resolutely antilabor stance of its business elite and many of its Progressives, Los Angeles taxed and spent more heavily than most cities in the 1910s and 1920s. Progressives were remarkably successful in boosting the power of city government as well as in the strategic use of federal agencies such as the Forest Service and the Bureau of Reclamation. Property taxes were among the highest in the country, and the city's Department of Water and Power, exalted by Progressives as the enlightened alternative to corrupt and monopolistic private utilities, was the largest such department in the country.

The City of Angels pioneered zoning ordinances and organized the first municipal playground department.[39] Despite its later reputation as the epitome of unplanned sprawl and environmental profligacy, in this period Los Angeles embodied the successes of Progressive municipal and environmental politics.

Perhaps the vigor of Progressivism in Los Angeles helps account for the sharp decline in fortunes of its urban conservationists. Progressive victories and sharp class conflict forced the movement's leaders to make hard choices. As early as 1910, the debt load from the city's water system was so crushing that other municipal departments had to minimize expenses. With the city government running near its maximum bonding capacity of 3 percent of assessed value of property to pay for water and power systems, money for anything else was scarce. Park commissioners Joseph Silent and James Lippincott paid for studies of possible parks out of their own pockets. The commission turned down dozens of detailed requests for more parks made by neighborhood associations, pleading lack of funds. The commission was not able to secure a general, citywide assessment for new parks, forcing specific neighborhoods to tax themselves more heavily if they wanted parks. Residents of wealthier areas, who could afford to buy or create environmentally appealing private homes and lots, felt no pressing need to do so, and poorer districts often felt they could not afford to. Larger visions for making the Los Angeles River an accessible green space in the heart of the city, promulgated by Dana Bartlett and Joseph Mesmer, were simply out of the question.[40]

No clear watershed moment or crisis points to a conscious decision of Progressives in Los Angeles to turn their backs on urban conservation. Yet the fact that urban public space of all sorts became a subject of controversy and even anxiety for some Progressives in the decade after 1910 played a key role. The long struggle between socialists and trade unionists against the insistence on the open shop by the city's major employers led many Progressives, unwilling to countenance socialism or any trade unionism, to join the drive against public assembly and speech led by the city's major employers. This campaign included restrictions on assembly in parks (favored meeting grounds of the city's socialists), to which the Park Commission members readily agreed, and the banning of all political gatherings or speeches in order to keep unionists out. The city's business leadership won this battle, making Los Angeles a citadel of the open shop, a place where Upton Sinclair would be arrested for reading the Bill of Rights to striking dockworkers.[41]

The culture of conservation came to similarly reaffirm class hierarchies. A widely shared valuing of outdoor recreation, nature study, nature writing, domestic architecture, and appropriate landscape architecture bolstered the politics of conservation. This culture brought together a wide range of conservationists and helped their appeals fall on receptive ears. But it could also be a vehicle for the expression of class and ethnic superiority, in ways that narrowed the appeal and power of conservation.

A loving, detailed description of plants and animals typified the era's prolific nature writing, providing a powerful emotional and psychic underpinning for the formal politics of conservation. It was all too easy for some nature writers to see in the patterns of nature a hierarchical template for society. Marjorie Benton Cooke's novel *The Girl Who Lived in the Woods* (1910) was a good example. In Cooke's account, the woods outside Chicago were a welcome respite from the stressful grind of city life. Those who retreated there could find physical health, renewed marital and familial intimacy, and an appreciation for the rhythms of nature that would enable them to transcend the petty demands of their social and business lives. The violent class conflict of the city is the offstage thunder that gives the book's plot much of its tension. Cecilia Carné, the protagonist, has fled the oppression of the industrial workforce for the charms of the woods, but remains haunted by the wreckage she left behind. In a heated discussion with the much wealthier friends she makes in the woods, she invokes "great lives that are cramped and hideous for lack of decencies that every human creature is entitled to . . . children born in want and doomed at birth to death and worse," and "men fighting like tigers for food and a roof for those they love."[42]

Despite this acknowledgment that exploitation and violence could characterize labor relations, the central development of the plot is Cecilia's abandonment of her radicalism and the replacement of it with an appreciation for nature as the model of a social order that is deeply hierarchical but nonetheless harmonious and good. Cecilia realizes that she is growing out of her youthful radicalism when she invites her anarchist and socialist friends from the city out to the woods, hoping that they could "share with her the quiet and loveliness of the country" and "find something of the peace that had come to her." But "there was no cessation in the hubbub and chatter" when they saw the view of Lake Michigan through the woods that had so stunned Cecilia. Cecilia opens herself up to friendship with the wealthy Barrett family, and to love and, ultimately, marriage to a judge nearly twice her age. The most explicit use of natural hierarchies as a basis for the social order comes from the mouth of Richard Barrett, responding to his young son's question whether pumpkins like to be eaten: "The pumpkin is educated up to a point where its only object is to be pie. And there is a lesson for all of us,—if we would just submit to being pies, instead of trying to be some fancy kind of dessert, when Nature meant us for plain pumpkins."[43]

In Cooke's novel, an appreciation for nature served as the marker of those mature and responsible enough to reject class radicalism. The culture of sport hunting, tightly linked with some of the earliest and most successful conservation measures, lent itself to class and ethno-racial chauvinism. The hunting ethic propagated influentially by such publications as *Outdoor Life* and *Field and Stream* was premised on sharp distinctions between hunting for recreation and hunting for subsistence or the market. But the articulate and influential spokesmen for hunting as sport went further, consistently drawing sharp distinctions between the different classes of hunters. Refined hunting—observing and supporting regulations about season and bag limits, avoiding unnecessary cruelty as well as netting, lights, and other ways of taking prey that minimized the hunter's skills—was for refined people. The *Forest and Stream* editor Charles Hallock was typical in his forthright description of his readers as coming from the "upper and authoritative classes," in contrast with the "unclean creatures" who made up the "great mass of those who shoot—the small farmers, bushrangers, frontiersmen, (to say nothing of the negroes of the South, who all use guns)." Hunting properly was not only the right thing to do in principle, but indoctrination into its techniques, as a *Forest and Stream* editorial put it, would "secure the survival of the fittest intellectually and morally" over the "Sclav [*sic*] and Latin races," with the added benefit of preparing real Americans for "sectional wars or class wars at home." Critics of sport hunting pointed out that recreational hunters also ate their harvests and could slaughter large numbers of animals, suggesting that perhaps they were not so different from those they condemned as "pot-hunters" after all. But *Forest and Stream* dismissed the need to be "scrutinized by the inferior," whose charges needlessly set "class against class." This harsh rejection of "inferiors" deeply colored the way that conservation bureaucracies administered game laws.[44]

A similar class and ethnic sensibility marked other aspects of the culture of conservation. Audubon clubs and Boy Scout troops were among the most active propagators of an ethical sensibility toward nature, encouraging their members to practice conservation and preach its virtues to others. This environmental responsibility could distinguish them from the primitive and destructive lower orders of society. The archetypal woman who continued to wear a bird hat, as depicted in one Audubon publication, was a "'real loidy' who . . . with hat cocked over one eye . . . haunts the cheaper shops, lunch[es] on beer . . . rides a man's wheel, chews gum, and expectorates with seeming relish." The contrast being drawn in this article was with the proper femininity of club members. Scouting publications painted similar distinctions on ethnoracial lines, encouraging young men to embrace conservation consciousness as evidence of their social superiority. Wanton destruction of nature, such as setting wildfires, pronounced the 1914 edition of the *Handbook for Boys,* could be excused on the part of Indians—"They were uncivilized and thought only of their own immediate needs"—but among "white people such useless waste . . . is criminal—uncivilized." In the 1919 edition of the handbook, written in the midst of World War I, William T. Hornaday sketched a sharper and more militarist contrast. Conservation was a battle pitting an "Army of Destruction" made up of millions of "short-sighted, selfish, and cruel members of the American nation" against a much smaller "Army of Defence," for whom "the protection of wild life and forests is a matter of duty, a 'white man's burden' that cannot be ignored." Hornaday, like so many others, married environmental virtue and white supremacy.[45]

Success and Fragmentation

William Hornaday's strident tone was the product of the xenophobia and antiradicalism spawned by World War I and of the divisions within conservation that had repeatedly surfaced in the previous decade. These schisms clearly weakened the conservationist goal of using state power and cultural revitalization to foster a less destructive relationship between people and the rest of nature. Yet they were also an ironic testimony to the power of conservation, for it was conservation's substantial achievements in the early twentieth century that brought many of these divisions to the fore. Should national forests be managed exclusively for timber production and watershed benefits, or could they also provide the opportunity for rugged physical exertion and solitude that city life precluded? If impounding water between the steep walls of a Sierra Nevada valley would eliminate its serene majesty, was the blow that the new public water supply struck against a predatory monopoly worth it? Should the attention of women's clubs and other rank-and-file conservationists be spent on their own cities and surroundings, or enlisted to protect iconic places like Yellowstone and Hetch Hetchy, which were remote to most? Ought conservationists always be hostile to monopoly, or could concentrated industries sometimes use nature more sustainably and productively? Was it a problem if laborers used the resources of parks for their sustenance, or used them to stage ethnic gatherings? Should the culture of conservation provide an outlet for a primal masculinity not usually tapped by modern life, or should it reflect the liberation of women from outdated strictures? Conservationists could fight about these kinds of questions because they had succeeded in establishing an extensive public lands system, bureaucracies such as the Forest Service, numerous local and national organizations, and a vigorous culture of nature. These achievements meant that how conservation was defined and whose interests it served were not merely philosophical questions.

This paradoxical success and fragmentation was also at work in Progressivism as a whole. By the 1910s, Progressives had made remarkable headway in expanding the power of civic society and the federal government to address some of the leading problems of industrial life— child labor, working conditions and hours, monopolies, the safety of food and drugs, and the political influence of the new industrial wealth. Yet these accomplishments divided as much as unified them. Progressives argued with one another over such questions as immigration policy, whether ethnic diversity ought to give way to a unitary American identity, the legitimacy of labor unions, and whether large businesses should be regulated for the public good or broken up to restore a competitive and smaller-scale marketplace. When former president Theodore Roosevelt broke with William Howard Taft in 1912—in no small part because of Taft's dismissal of Gifford Pinchot—he formed the Progressive Party and ran for president as its nominee. But the Democrat Woodrow Wilson and the socialist Eugene Debs also embraced the Progressive approach of turning to the national state to protect democracy from concentrated economic power. With the more conservative Taft carrying just over a quarter of the national vote, in a contest won by Wilson, the election marked the high tide of electoral Progressivism. It also reflected its fragmentation. Progressives were further divided by the policies of the Wilson administration, particularly its military interventions in revolution-torn Mexico and its decision to insert the United States into World War I. Conservation was not the only aspect of Progressivism that found itself badly split by the end of the decade.

Fighting Against Conservation

By the 1910s, conservationists felt that they had enough power to make it worthwhile to fight over which kind of conservation would prevail. But their optimism led them to underestimate the challenges their movement faced. Allocating more control to the federal government in the name of environmental necessity provoked powerful opposition from those whose economic interests were thereby threatened, those who doubted that pressing environmental problems existed at all, and those who objected in principle to the more muscular state called into being by Progressives. Federal conservation thus became an important issue in electoral politics, particularly in the West. Moreover, because a wide range of rural Americans continued to hunt, fish, gather, log, and farm in the new parks and forests, in practice the conservation state often criminalized their ways of making a living. Local people generally sought to maintain their subsistence practices in the face of efforts by public lands bureaucracies to prevent them from doing so. While some of this resistance was conducted through formal politics, it also gave rise to widespread community-supported lawbreaking, violence against conservation officers, and arson and sabotage.

In the 1910s, conservation as an organized political movement met these challenges: it defeated opponents in state legislatures and the halls of Congress, and arrested, intimidated, and sometimes killed its plebeian antagonists. Yet these struggles left their mark on the movement. By the decade's end, conservationists, like so many Progressives who had embraced state coercion as a wartime emergency, were less tolerant of dissent, less interested in the power of cultural change and introspection, and more willing to embrace authoritarian approaches to social conflict. These shifts made conservation vulnerable to another challenge: just as people frustrated conservation on the ground, so too in a sense did nature. Forest fires, insect outbreaks, and unexpected changes in animal populations and vegetation in the following decades seemed to make a mockery of the scientific management of natural resources.

Political Backlash

Conservation became most controversial in places where it promised the greatest political and economic reshuffling. The mountain West, where the federal government owned the largest percentage of land, and where the economy was dominated by extractive industries such as mining, ranching, and timber, became the key battleground over conservation policies, a field on which the opponents of conservation cohered and formulated their arguments. Many newspaper editors, state elected officials, and development-minded business leaders watched the growth of the federal public lands domain with alarm. Concern had turned to fury by 1907, when numerous westerners focused their ire on the newly established Forest Service. The service managed an enormous area—150 million acres, or nearly twice the size of the nation of Germany—and had gained the power to charge grazing fees and to arrest violators of its regulations without securing a warrant anywhere in its vast domain. In that year, the Colorado Legislature directed its governor to convene a "Public Lands Convention" to assemble western stockmen, farmers, and elected officials to discuss and pursue grievances against the Forest Service, the Bureau of Reclamation, and the Interior Department. The gathering, held in Denver in the summer of 1907, drew hundreds of delegates and attracted sustained national press attention. Gifford Pinchot, then head of the Forest Service, felt compelled to attend in order to make his case, as did the secretary of the interior and the head of the Bureau of Reclamation. One of the key Colorado figures behind the conference,

J. Arthur Eddy, soon organized the National Public Domain League, to continue the campaign of western grievances against federal land management. In 1909, a newspaper editor in Washington state organized the Western Conservation League to advocate across the region for national forests and other federally administered lands to be put under the administration of state governments. In the following year, some western governors sympathetic to the organizations tried but failed to secure support for this goal at the second national Conservation Congress.[1]

These figures sometimes showed themselves reluctant to confront conservation directly. They recognized the rising national fortunes of the movement, which, during President Theodore Roosevelt's administration, was reaching its legislative and administrative zenith. And some conservationist measures were appealing—the ballooning federal role in creating irrigation networks under the guidance of the Bureau of Reclamation enjoyed support even from the most vociferous western critics of the Forest Service. The very name of the Western Conservation League suggested that its adherents accepted the legitimacy of conservation and argued only for a state rather than federal version. But in fact, groups like the league offered thorough repudiations of the premises behind most conservation policies. They rejected outright the idea that industrialization threatened to exhaust irreplaceable natural resources. For them, the idea was simple alarmism and bred worse consequences than the supposed crisis that it invoked. "If the time ever comes in the history of the world when there will be such a scarcity of timber as is predicted," Colorado senator Henry Teller told the Public Lands Convention in 1907, "the ingenuity of man will find something else to take its place." The applause that greeted his remarks suggested just how widely shared this idea was among conservation skeptics. J. Arthur Eddy made this point the centerpiece of the National Public Domain League's pamphlet *Conservation Alarms* (1909). Eddy took aim at the chief forester in order to refute the basic principals of conservation. The pamphlet began with the derogatory poem "Little Prophet Pinchot," which accompanied a cartoon featuring the chief forester's mustachioed visage conjuring up images of goblins labeled "coal famine," "lumber famine," and the like for three wide-eyed children.

An editorial cartoon from 1909, reproduced by western opponents of the expansion of the National Forest System, spoofed Gifford Pinchot as a spinner of tall tales of environmental destruction meant to frighten gullible children. (J. Arthur Eddy, *Conservation Alarms [1909]; courtesy Denver Public Library*)

An' little Baron Pinchot says afore the coal's all gon',
An' the lumber stuff is 'member'd only as a jag 'ats on,
'Fore the landscape has all glided in erosion to the sea;
An' the iron ore's all bucketed, an' mines not worth a D;
You'd better heed your Gifford, who can see most anything.[2]

Even those who did not reject the conservationist diagnosis outright were skeptical of the cure, questioning the wisdom of the expanded powers of the federal government that conservationists used to implement their vision. This line of argument against conservation dated back to the initial creation of forest reserves in the 1890s, before there was a robust conservation movement. When the Grover Cleveland administration abruptly created thirteen forest reserves totaling about twelve million acres in 1897, numerous western newspapers and elected officials denounced the move as contrary to representative government. The creation of federally administered forest reserves, complained one western representative, treated the affected states "as though we were mere provinces and not sovereign states of this great Union." The more aggressive measures of the Progressive conservationists—particularly the establishment of a regular forestry bureau with increased oversight over timber harvesting and grazing, and the move to establish a national park system—breathed new life into this critique of conservation. Speaker after speaker at the Denver gathering invoked the strict interpretation of the Constitution that bolstered so many arguments against the Progressive state. They asserted over and over again that the federal government had no authority to hold lands in the form of national forests or parks.[3]

Since the national forests and other conservation measures placed vast tracts outside the market economy and the sovereignty of elected state governments, conservation foes concluded that they constituted a usurpation of American democracy. The Montana politician Thomas Walsh portrayed the administrators of forest reserves as petty autocrats: "It is by the favor of these officials that a man in the stock business and depending upon the public lands for range, remains at it. The entire future of his business is placed absolutely in the keeping of the officer charged with the administration of the proposed law and to no small extent in that of his subordinates in the field. The man at the top is clothed with an autocratic authority a Czar might envy. My business may flourish nurtured in the sunshine of his smiles, or he may put forth his hand and crush it." The bureaucratic leviathan created by such agencies as the Forest Service had "become a menace to republican government!"[4]

Particularly in the West, Gifford Pinchot became the lightning rod for these sorts of critiques. To those who thought that state conservation was illegitimate, he was an easily recognizable symbol of the whole of the movement, not withstanding his intense disagreements with other conservationists. "Czarism" became "Pinchotism" in countless speeches and editorials. J. Arthur Eddy repeatedly castigated the chief forester. "The most 'touching' feature" of conservationist proposals," he wrote, "is that they always embrace a tax or charge, and likewise a paternal supervision over the business incident to their operation." Whereas Progressives saw this kind of regulation as the embodiment of democracy in an industrial era, Eddy and his circle saw authoritarianism. "Fate seems to have ordained by inexorable command," Eddy sarcastically noted, "that some men be born to rule, and what other manner of man could have discovered and have developed within the very heart center of the world's great Republic, an imperial sphere to serve his destiny? Of a truth Gifford Pinchot possesses to the full degree the true imperialistic temperament!"[5]

Yet the ideology of anti-conservation was not confined to the regions most affected by the rise of the conservation state. Many of the congressional foes of the Forest Service were drawn from what a strongly pro-conservation author described in 1920 as the "anti-administration wing of the Republican party which grew up in the latter years of Roosevelt's administration." These Republicans and conservative Democrats in Congress frequently invoked wider arguments against the Progressive state when specific conservation issues came to the fore. In congressional hearings about appropriations for the forestry bureau, for example, some representatives casually referred to district foresters as "carpetbaggers," seeking to associate the forest service with perceived abuses of federal power during Reconstruction. Others went further: a South Carolina congressman warned that a robust forest service was an example of a "movement to-day to substitute the will of men rather than rules of law," a push that was particularly disturbing because "it is participated in by the rich, the strong, and the powerful." Along with the anarchists threatening "mobocracy," this demand "for a bureaucracy . . . would destroy our government of law." Texas representative Martin Dies invoked the "ultraradicalism of the country at this particular time" to support his motion to strike funding for the national forests. Arguing that "there have been no new lessons in free government since the Constitution was written," he saw Theodore Roosevelt's development of such agencies as the Forest Service as proof that the president was in league with the populist Democrat William Jennings Bryan and Wisconsin

Socialist Victor Berger, "a trio of the foremost enemies of free government in America to-day." Dies was an extreme though hardly singular case. But he found many allies in his insistence that conservation was a tainted part of the larger course of Progressivism.[6]

The entanglement of conservation with Progressivism as a whole explains the sharp differences in the histories invoked by conservationists and their foes. Conservationists asserted that resources were scarce and endangered and that what remained would be monopolized, and these claims justified the creation and perpetual management of federal forest reserves as well as other measures of state conservation. Whatever their disagreements on the proper scope and priorities of conservation, such figures as Gifford Pinchot and Horace McFarland agreed that they lived in an era that required new measures to meet the unprecedented challenges of resource scarcity and artificiality. Those who opposed these measures told a very different story about the nation's history. "I belong to the generation which has seen the birth of the electric transformer, the internal-combustion engine, the navigation of the air, and the commercial use of aluminum," pronounced the journalist George L. Knapp, "and I quite decline to worry about what may happen 'when the world busts through.'" Knapp not only denied that there were meaningful environmental crises, but also called his readers' attention to the dim view that conservationists took of American history. "For all these evils" in conservationist accounts, "the remedy is 'conservation.'" "The 'Government,' that potent 'conjuh word' of civic atavists and political theologians, must stint its nature and proper tasks to engage in the regulation of this, that, or the other industry, to 'conserve' our resources."[7]

The more sensible view of U.S. history, those opposed to conservation insisted, was one of triumph—a climb to prosperity, power, and greatness that should be continued rather than rejected. Knapp made this argument most explicitly near the end of his piece:

> The pine woods of Michigan have vanished to make the homes
> of Kansas; the coal and iron which we have failed—thank
> heaven—to "conserve" have carried meat and wheat to the

hungry hives of men and gladdened life with an abundance which no previous age could know.

We have turned forests into villages, mines into ships and skyscrapers, scenery into work. Our success in doing the things already accomplished has been exactly proportioned to our freedom from governmental "guidance," and I know no reason to believe that a different formula will hold good in the tasks that lie before.[8]

Others waxed even more rhapsodic about the course of national development. Montana senator Thomas Walsh's vision was especially triumphalist: "Within the last fifty years the most marvelous development known to this world's history has occurred in the public land states of this Union. . . . In every section and in every state, this remarkable development has not only been a benediction to the participants, but has become the marvel of the whole civilized world."[9]

The politics of conservation did not hew to a single clear line, whether of party, region, or even ideology. In Congress and state legislatures, Progressive Republicans and Democrats made common cause to pass conservation measures, while conservatives of both parties looked askance on their efforts. Western anti-conservationists' loud cries of being spokesmen for a distinctive region subjected to the colonial rule of the East could not drown out the numerous western supporters of the federal conservation state. These supporters ensured the victories of numerous western congressional and gubernatorial candidates who ran explicitly and enthusiastically on conservation platforms. The clearest pattern was a link between a general Progressive outlook—the willingness to expand state powers to address problems created by the industrial economy—and support for conservation. But more than a few figures defied this rule of thumb. Colorado's Henry Teller, for example, established a moderately Progressive record in Congress, backing such measures as a ban on the corporate financing of elections, even as he dismissed the need for conservation. Senator William Borah of Idaho was not alone in mixing disdain of federal conservation measures into his anticentralist brand of Progressivism.[10]

Nevertheless, there was a strong electoral and ideological affinity between conservation and Progressivism as a whole. These ties help explain the sharp limits of anti-conservationist politics, even in the parts of the West where it made the most headway. Eddy and the other organizers of the National Public Domain League hoped that it would grow into a vigorous organization that could push Congress to cede control of federal lands to the states, which would in turn put them into private hands for rapid private-sector economic development. They did succeed in mobilizing western governors, attracting widespread press attention, and securing extensive financial support from Louis Hill, then the proprietor of the Great Northern Railway, which his father, James, had begun. (Hill was later an enthusiastic backer and developer of Glacier National Park, which the Great Northern serviced, so his opposition to conservation was opportunistic and piecemeal.) But Eddy and his counterparts made more noise than progress. Even at western gatherings, such as the public lands conventions held in 1909 and 1911, western conservationists made strong showings as members of stock and timber associations, state conservation organizations (including some of the few active state branches of Pinchot's National Conservation Association), and as delegates appointed directly by governors sympathetic to conservation.[11]

More fundamentally, anti-conservation never took on the aspects of a mass movement in the way that conservation did. The National Public Domain League and the similar Western Conservation League issued intermittent publications, but never built or maintained a network of chapters made up of local activists, as did Horace McFarland's American Civic Association and the conservation committees of the General Federation of Women's clubs—or for that matter, the conservative "wise use" movement of the 1990s, which advocated similar policies. Perhaps this failure was due in some measure to the fact that women played no apparent role in anti-conservation organizations, unlike their galvanizing presence in temperance politics, prowar and antiradical civic associations during World War I, and subsequent conservative mobilizations in the 1930s and 1960s.[12]

National political developments in the early 1910s proved equally inauspicious for Eddy and his compatriots. The foes of conservation cheered Gifford Pinchot's departure from the executive branch early that year, when President William Howard Taft fired him for insubordination after Pinchot charged secretary of the interior Richard Ballinger with corruption in his handling of Alaska coal lands. But the months of subsequent congressional hearings over the Pinchot-Ballinger dispute galvanized conservationists, persistently raising the issue of monopoly and the potential damage from unregulated natural resource exploitation. That November's elections brought a Democratic and Progressive Republican majority to power in Congress, halting any real possibilities of legislative success for the National Public Domain League. Ballinger resigned a few months later. His dispute with Pinchot and the warning that he issued to the next Public Lands Convention of the dangers of "bureaucratic government in America" made him a hero to conservation skeptics. But Taft replaced Ballinger with the Chicago Progressive and former head of the National Conservation Association Walter Fisher, ensuring that "Pinchotism" survived even with Pinchot out of office and fomenting a Progressive Republican revolt against the Taft administration.[13]

That revolt resulted in the formation of the Progressive Party, which nominated former president Theodore Roosevelt for the presidency in the 1912 election. Declaring the "first task of the statesmanship of the day" to be "to dissolve the unholy alliance between corrupt business and corrupt politics," the Progressive platform included a strong conservation plank written by Pinchot, alongside support for minimum-wage legislation, an eight-hour workday, social insurance, the direct election of U.S. senators, women's suffrage, and aggressive regulation of corporations. In its second paragraph, the platform explicitly rejected the constitutional fundamentalism advocated by those opposed to conservation and other Progressive measures, declaring: "The people are the masters of their Constitution, to fulfill its purposes and to safeguard it from those who, by perversion of its intent, would convert it into an instrument of injustice. In accordance with the needs of each generation the people must use their sovereign powers to establish and maintain equal opportunity and industrial justice, to secure which this Government was founded and without which no republic can endure." The platform's conservation measure was an explicit rebuttal of the critics of federal lands: "We believe that the remaining forests, coal and oil lands, water powers and other natural resources still in State or National control (except agricultural lands) are more likely to be wisely conserved and utilized for the general welfare if held in the public hands."[14]

Eugene V. Debs, the Socialist candidate in the 1912 presidential election, ran on a platform that similarly advocated "further conservation and development of natural resources for the use and benefit of all the people" as part of the collective ownership of most economic assets. Although both insurgent parties focused on resource rather than aesthetic or romantic conservation, the Socialist platform did reflect something of the breadth of conservation in its declaration of support for "the conservation of human resources, particularly of the lives and well-being of the workers and their families" and "the conservation of health." The Democrat Woodrow Wilson, the eventual winner of the contest, largely avoided the issue of conservation in the campaign, and once in office he showed no interest in relinquishing federal control of lands or ending an active state role in the development of timber, power, and water.

Thus, borne by the rising tide of Progressivism, conservationists fended off these serious challenges to their public lands policies. The conservation state that they had created over the previous twenty years survived, even after the Progressive wake receded at the end of the decade.[15]

In the Countryside

In the same years that the conservation state survived formal political challenge, it faced widespread dissent on the ground from people who still derived much of their sustenance directly from the land. Pinchot and Muir faced potshots in the press and legislative hearings, but forest and park rangers routinely faced actual gunfire and physical violence in the field. Whereas a concern that federal conservation would preclude future development prompted the organized anti-conservation politics led by men such as Eddy, the immediate threat to ongoing ways of life generated the more widespread and lasting but less cohesive rural conflict over conservation. Whereas anti-conservation politics typically bowed to the idols of limited government and the market economy, diverse indigenous notions of sacred landscapes and republican and radical justifications of economic independence undergirded much of the grassroots opposition. Because so many of the rural people at odds with conservation bureaucracies were Indians and unenfranchised immigrant workers, they had limited access at best to the formal mechanisms of representative democracy. So they turned to dissimulation, violence, and sabotage, in many places waging what amounted to low-intensity guerrilla warfare against conservation. Conservation emerged triumphant in this contest too, though not without producing a long legacy of bitterness and alienation across much of the country. Progressivism promised deliverance from undemocratic concentrations of economic power, but in much of the countryside was itself an undemocratic agent of dispossession.

To regulate the use of nature was to regulate people: there was no escaping this fact. The United States became the world's largest industrial economy in the early twentieth century, but many Americans continued to turn to the land for some or all of their sustenance. Farming remained the most common occupation, and most family farms continued to grow crops and gardens and keep animals for their own consumption and use. Those with too little productive land to make a living by farming could still plant gardens or clear a field for hay for a dairy cow or two, either on their own property or on areas used in common. Women and children made valuable additions to their family's meals by gathering herbs and berries. Young boys often set snares or hunted for small game such as rabbits or edible birds. All family members could fish in nearby streams, rivers, or lakes. Indeed, most rural men were opportunistic hunters year-round, and in some places they would go on extended fall hunting excursions with neighbors and family. Large game such as deer, moose, or wild hog could provide a large portion of a family's diet, regardless of the hunting season. "When we run short [of food] we just go out an' get another one . . . we salted down a lot of moose and fish," remembered August Stromberg of his boyhood in early-twentieth-century Minnesota. Wood, whether from one's own land or not, could be used for building homes, fences, animal shelters, or watercraft. In colder climes, cutting firewood was a necessary—and free—ritual each fall.[16]

Some of the earth's bounty was traded for money: nature was val-

A garden near the Pioneer Mine of Ely, Minnesota, in the early 1920s reflects the extent to which laborers in even the nation's most critical industries retained connections with a subsistence economy of gardening, hunting, and gathering. Conservation sometimes curtailed this economy, provoking backlash and resentment. *(Courtesy Minnesota Historical Society)*

uable not just for subsistence but also as a storehouse whose contents could be made into commodities with the addition of human labor. Wild ginseng fetched a nice price from traders. Meat, particularly venison or moose, could be sold as well as eaten, though one had to be careful not to run afoul of the game warden. Firewood would not always sell for enough to make cutting and hauling it worth the effort, but merchants might pay a decent price for Christmas trees. Pigeons were good eating, which made game dealers willing to pay good money for fresh birds that could be iced and shipped to fine restaurants in New York or Chicago. Fur trapping could also be a source of scarce cash. Even children could run small trap lines close to home.[17]

Indians were among those who relied most heavily on the bounty of nature. By the 1880s, all previously independent Indian nations had been conquered by the United States and confined to reservations. Reservation life was supposed to make Indians self-supporting independent farmers (at a time when the nation's farmers found their economic and political power eclipsed by the industrial economy). In the meantime, annual rations of food and clothing mandated by the treaties between Indian peoples and the U.S. government were supposed to be enough to support them. Conventional agriculture, however, enjoyed at best a limited success on reservations. It was alien to the traditions of many peoples and unsuited to the soils and climate of many reservations. Moreover, many Indians rejected it outright because it was explicitly intended to destroy their culture and forcibly assimilate them into the mass of American society.

Thus, hunting, fishing, and gathering continued to be particularly critical to American Indians, whether the activities took place on reservations, their private land, or territory that they considered their own despite the federal government's claims. The Yosemite Indians, for example, derived most of their sustenance from trout, sweet clover, roots, acorns, pine nuts, fruits, and berries until park regulations pressured them into working for wages. The Blackfeet, like many Indian peoples, sought to protect their rights to live off the land even when they were forced to cede much of it to the federal government. The tribal negotiator White Calf was successful in adding language to an 1895 treaty that preserved "the right to go upon any portion of the lands [ceded in the treaty] . . . to cut and remove timber . . . to hunt upon said lands and to fish in the streams thereof, so long as . . . they remain public lands of the United States." Blackfeet leaders believed that this language protected their usufruct rights in perpetuity, even when the founding of Glacier National Park in 1910 put much of their former territory under the control of a different part of the federal government. (The National Park Service, as they found out, saw things differently.)[18]

Even Americans more fully incorporated into the industrial economy could find themselves in need of direct reliance on the nonhuman world. In small towns and the countryside, Americans deeply embedded in the market economy could find a safety net in nearby fields, forests, lakes, and streams. If drought or a collapse in grain prices ruined a year's harvest of wheat, or if a slowdown or strike led to unemployment, hunting or trapping could keep food on the table. Many parks experienced sharp rises in poaching arrests during recessions; in Yellowstone, for instance, they quintupled during the 1907 slowdown.[19]

Subsistence was important even for the workforces of some of the most modern and advanced industries. In Minnesota's Iron Range, for example, large mining companies produced much of the ore necessary for the nation's industrial growth, but at the same time their employees found the woods an indispensable resource during frequent strikes, lockouts, and slowdowns. Indeed, the importance of the woods was one of the few things that both sides in the region's bloody labor battles could agree upon. "The readers of the red-flag outfit have taken off their best clothes and have gone to the woods," vented the pro-business editor of the *Miner* in the aftermath of a violent 1907 strike, "in all probability to use some of the dynamite in blasting fish to fill their aching voids." The labor radical Andy Johnson was on the other side of the conflict, but remembered the same dynamic: "Those old time pioneers who came here before and after the turn of the century . . . many of them settled out here in the woods because they were blackballed . . . because of their political activity on behalf of the working class."[20]

The new park and forest bureaucracies moved decisively to curtail and even ban such practices. Hunting, timber gathering, trapping, and other activities were outlawed from many areas altogether, and subjected to strict regulation and stiff fees in others. For some nearby residents, such restrictions did not necessarily mean much change in the fabric of daily life. State game laws establishing regular hunting seasons and banning unsporting though efficient means of taking game—typically, fishing with nets, spears, or explosives, and hunting with dogs or lights—had long since been in place. And new regulations and managers did not always mean more effective or stringent enforcement.

For other Americans, however, federal conservation fell like a thunderbolt. In the fall of 1898, for example, Havasupai Indians began leaving their village in Havasu Canyon, an offshoot of the Grand Canyon, in order to hunt game and gather plants, as they had for as long as they could remember. The supervisor of the surrounding forest reserve was outraged, fearing that their presence would mar the scenic beauty of what was rapidly becoming a major tourist attraction. He ordered them to return to their village and cease hunting and gathering on what was now government land. Since the forest entirely surrounded the Havasupai reservation, it had effectively become impossible for them to live off the land. They would have to think of some way to replace the firewood and meat that they had always relied upon. "We got no meat. My family hungry," one Havasupai matter-of-factly informed his captor when arrested for poaching.[21]

Others all across the United States shared the Havasupais' complaints. The Blackfeet had larger hunting grounds still available to them, but faced similar obstacles if they crossed the line into the part of their traditional domain that became Glacier National Park in 1910. Other instances of dispossession in the name of conservation were slow-moving, grinding affairs rather than singular moments of clarity. The Yosemite Indians, for example, were among those most subject to the rule of conservation bureaucracies, since they lived smack in the middle of the park, but they remained as residents for most of the twentieth century. Even after park regulations made the Yosemite's traditional subsistence practices impossible to continue, they managed to earn cash by working as guides, in hotels, as drivers of sightseeing wagons, and as maids and domestics. They lived in an environmental version of a company town, since park officials controlled nearly every aspect of their lives, including deciding who would remain in the valley. Officials punished theft and drunkenness with expulsion and tried to remove Indian residences from the view of campers and hotel customers. In the late 1920s, Superintendent Charles Thompson wanted to remove the Yosemite entirely, arguing that "they should have long since been banished from the Park" and that their ejection "would ease administration slightly; would eliminate the eyesore of the Indian village"; and "would remove the final influence operating against a *pure status* for Yosemite." Even the Indians would be benefit, since removal would "tend to break them up as a racial unit and, in time, to diffuse their blood with the great American mass."[22]

Thompson was too fearful of a backlash by the Yosemite and their allies to follow his urges. Instead, he opted to build a new Indian village, intended to be more "traditional" looking, farther away from the most heavily visited portions of the valley. The National Park Service took the opportunity to inform the Indians that their continued presence was a "privilege dependent upon proper deportment" and that anybody who "did not want to work reasonably steady, cannot get along with his neighbors, or in any way prove[s] to be a poor member of the Village . . . would have to go away and give up his house." The service allowed about fifty people, including the most skilled craftsmen and cooperative employees, to move into the new village, but banned some ordinary laborers and those who had clashed with the park's management. After World War II, housing was restricted to permanent government employees and their immediate families. As the Yosemite retired or were dismissed, they were forced to pack up their belongings and leave the valley. The last resident, Jay Johnson, retired from the National Park Service and moved to Mariposa, California, in December 1996.[23]

Indians were not the only ones affected. By 1907, Hispanic villagers in northern New Mexico found themselves charged money (of which they had very little) by the U.S. Forest Service to run their cattle and gather firewood on land that had belonged to their villages for generations and that had supposedly been guaranteed to them by treaty with Mexico in 1848 at the conclusion of the Mexican War. More than a fifth of northern New Mexico's national forests were carved from what had been Spanish and Mexican land grants initially upheld by U.S. courts, with even more acreage coming from lands that the villages claimed had been part of their grants. In the same year, miners in the small towns of northeastern Minnesota dodged aggressive game wardens when they went out to hunt, and faced arrest for timber trespass if they gathered abundant wood from the forests around them. White settlers around Yellowstone National Park faced similar sanctions for gathering wood and hunting in the park, outside any regular judicial process, since the army ran the park from 1886 to 1918. In other places, the offense was as much spiritual as material. In 1906, residents of Taos Pueblo in northern New Mexico were enraged to find that the government had placed Blue Lake, high in the Sangre de Cristo Mountains above their village, into the national forest system. One of the holiest sites in their religion and the destination of an annual pilgrimage, the lake was now open to all tourists who wanted to enjoy its cool waters.[24]

Even when the changes brought by conservation were not as dramatic as they were for Taos Indians, the stakes in these disputes were quite high. At a time when bitter strikes were fought for a daily wage of $3, Minnesota's fines for possession of untagged venison ran around $25 plus court costs, hunting deer out of season was $100, and even netting fish was $10. When wardens sold confiscated goods, as they commonly did, moose meat and venison could fetch almost $20 per animal, mink fur $5, and more common furs $1 or $2. In Pennsylvania, the Italian immigrants who so often found themselves under the eye of the game warden generally earned under $2 a day in the early twentieth century. They could be fined $25 for carrying a gun "in the fields or in the forests or on the waters of this Commonwealth" without a license (which itself cost $10), and another $10 for any nongame bird in their possession. An additional $25 was added to the base fine if the illegal hunting took place on a Sunday. In 1905 the secretary of the state's Game Commission reported that an arrest of a poacher "seldom results in a penalty of less than $60 or $70 with [court] costs, sometimes very much more than this amount." The average fine was thus well over a month's wages. Not only were these fines and proceeds a significant blow to hunters, but the destruction, confiscation, or selling of canoes, traps, and guns also deprived rural Americans of equipment necessary to engage in common subsistence activities.[25]

Wardens and park and forest rangers must have enjoyed at least some success in enforcing these regulations, or they presumably would not have been the targets of violence and even assassination, as often as they were. Serving as a conservation officer was dangerous work; as Abbot Kinney observed in 1900, "Feuds, fires, and assassinations curse our entire western mountain area of public lands." Places where local communities were tight-knit and resilient enough to press their resource claims were particularly violent. The Blackfeet, for example, never stopped insisting on their right to travel and hunt in what is now Glacier National Park. Relations between the park agents and Indians were described as "a near state of war ... with Blackfeet and rangers prepared to shoot and be shot upon at any given time." In New York's Adirondack Mountains, where numerous private parks banned hunting, fishing, and foraging outright, a local man shot estate owner Orlando Dexter in 1903. Other locals subsequently sent notes to state Forest Commission members warning that "somebody else is liable to be shot in the back," cut fences, routinely shot at the guards of private estates, and set some tracts on fire. Little wonder, then, that wealthy Adirondack landowners, generally New York City elites, began traveling with bodyguards. Hispanic villagers of northern New Mexico similarly directed their animosity at rangers, occasionally shooting at them, beating them, cutting their fences, and defacing or destroying the camps and signs they erected. All rangers were instructed to travel in pairs, never to leave their homes unarmed, and to sleep well away from their campfires so as to avoid ambush.[26]

The resort to sabotage and violence reflected not only anger at conservation but also the political disenfranchisement of so many of the disaffected. To be sure, some of these rural people supported elected officials crusading against the conservation state. Local newspapers around large parks and forests could be vociferous in advancing the rhetoric of congressional anti-conservation crusaders, as in the widespread condemnation of Yellowstone superintendent Captain George Anderson as the "Czar of Wonderland" in the regional press. But the printed marketplace of ideas and the ballot box were not available to Indians, southern African Americans, and most immigrants. So their violence was anti-conservation politics by other means.

In later years, political openings allowed for more direct expression of dissent. In northern Minnesota, the advent of citizenship for Finnish and Slovene immigrants had made it difficult to secure jury convictions for game law violations by the 1920s, and their influence on local government complicated the previously seamless relationship between mining employers and conservation enforcement. John Muir articulated an assumption shared by many Americans when he said of Indians that "most of them are dead or civilized into useless innocence," but Indian peoples pursued numerous avenues to maintain their access to places taken by state conservation. The Taos lobbied before a special Pueblo Lands Board in the 1920s for the return of Blue Lake, and again in Congress in the 1930s, though it was not until 1970 that they were successful. In the 1930s, when the New Deal allowed for the formation of tribal governments even when they had been destroyed, the Blackfeet became one of the first Indian groups to do so, soon filing lawsuits and petitions over Glacier National Park. "Negative opinions of the park service," the historian Mark Spence concludes, "had become a central aspect of tribal policy and a fundamental expression of Blackfeet national identity."[27]

The fact that those most alienated by the conservation state had their own conservation ethos, their own ideas about nature and what constituted acceptable and unacceptable uses of it, lends a tragic aspect to the disputes over conservation. Plebeian attitudes are of course hard to recover: such people generally did not write books and were more preoccupied with avoiding law enforcement officials than with leaving a cohesive record of their thoughts and actions. Oral histories, court transcripts, and diaries, however, suggest that many rural folk saw the natural world as a deeply human place, one bound up in the fabric of their daily lives. When describing the lakes and forests around them, residents of the Iron Range, for example, were more likely to orient themselves by referring to nearby homesteads, familiar trapping grounds, and places where important events in their own lives had occurred than by reference to the natural landmarks that wilderness advocates and outdoor enthusiasts used to navigate the same territory.[28]

Indian peoples, particularly those who remained in their ancestral homelands, likewise attached deep social significance to particular places. This was not only a matter of remembering special locations as favorite hunting grounds or sheltered campsites, but also of believing them to be spiritually important. Blackfeet, for example, considered the mountains of what became Glacier National Park to be part of Mistakis, the Backbone of the World. Some of their most powerful spirits resided there, and they believed that their ancestors had received tobacco and horses at several of the lakes nestled high in the mountains.[29] Similarly, the Pueblo peoples of New Mexico held that they emerged into the present world from a lake. Regular retreats to perform ceremonies and rituals near special lakes in the mountains around their towns thus kept them spiritually connected to the power of the lake of their emergence. Even the less powerful landscapes closer to home were—and still are—sacralized places. Countless Indian peoples also engaged in ritual journeys and hunts to mark critical times of passage in life, such as entering adulthood. Indian identity was thus deeply entwined with the landscape.[30]

Like all humans, country people could treat these landscapes recklessly and even self-destructively. A farmer might give in to the temptation to plow a steep hillside, whether pushed by falling grain prices or enticed by what a larger harvest might buy from the Sears catalogue. Ranchers often ran more cattle than their pastures could sustain, and almost all eagerly participated in the campaign to exterminate the wolf. Indians, too, could be agents of environmental destruction. Driven not only by their own needs for food, clothing, and shelter, they participated in the fur and bison trades that trapped out beaver in many western streams and dramatically reduced buffalo herds on the plains.[31]

At the same time, however, rural people practiced their own form of conservation. Employing a set of beliefs that the historian Karl Jacoby has termed "moral ecology," they drew clear distinctions between legitimate and illegitimate uses of nature. Providing food or other essentials such as heat for one's self or one's family was a right that justified even trespass on private property. The killing of animals or harvesting of products for cash sale, on the other hand, was viewed with greater suspicion, and if done with recklessness was more likely to result in being turned in to the game warden or even in activating a kind of vigilante conservation. Rural people placed restrictions even on acceptable hunting. Most communities practiced some kind of "law of the woods," which in one rendering emphasized the principle "Never kill anything you do not need." These unwritten laws included sanctions against specific forms of hunting. As one upstate New Yorker recalled of the 1890s, "There was a universal code that deer should not be disturbed while 'yarding,' or in the breeding season, and this applied to game birds as well."[32]

Those who violated the tenets of moral ecology might do so at their own risk. Among the Ojibway Indians of the upper Great Lakes, for example, "rice chiefs" elected by local communities assembled committees to enforce community rules for the critical resource of wild rice. Rice chiefs decided when the crops were ripe enough to be harvested, how many boats would be allowed on a rice lake, which "guest ricers"—those who were not members of local bands—would be allowed to join in, how much of the harvest would be siphoned into a "rice fund" to be drawn upon by destitute or infirm band members, and when the obligations of thanksgiving ceremonies were met. The institution of the rice chief, which survives in some places to this day, had no formal legal sanction in the early twentieth century. But that did not prevent rice chiefs and their committees from enforcing their decisions. Those who harvested past time limits were fined a portion of their proceeds, had their canoes impounded, and were banned from further harvests; or in more extreme cases, or when Ojibway bands could keep non-Indians off their lakes, violators found their boats tipped over or destroyed, and their persons threatened with violence and exile from the reservation. Other, less tightly knit communities practiced their own versions of what might be called folk conservation. William Binkley, a resident of Jackson Hole, Wyoming, found this out the hard way. In the late 1890s, he was arrested for killing an elk outside hunting season in order to give its meat to a sick and hungry neighbor. His neighbors paid the $100 fine. In 1906, however, after Binkley slaughtered hundreds of elk for the sole purpose of harvesting and selling their valuable tusks, a "citizens' committee" in the town ordered Binkley and his partners in crime to leave town or be "left dead . . . for the scavengers to devour."[33]

The kind of folk conservation that disciplined William Binkley's environmental profligacy was viable and widely practiced in local and small-scale disputes where the actors knew one another and where no actor was too large or powerful to ignore community sanctions. They were not adequate to all of the challenges of an industrial economy, where a hydraulic mining company might destroy a hillside in an afternoon, where highly capitalized timber companies could clear-cut hundreds of square miles, where long-range rifles could allow a small number of men to kill hundreds of bison in a day. Nonetheless, conservation leaders might have recognized something of their own concerns and values in this complex thicket of ideas and practices—a chance to enlist others in their crusade, to build broad and deep consensus alongside laws and bureaucracies.

Indian communities, like others, had extralegal regulations of key resources. Here two Ojibway men in northern Minnesota carefully harvest wild rice, a key resource that Ojibway people closely managed for sustainability and equity. *(Courtesy Minnesota Historical Society)*

But generally they did not. Indeed, to the extent that most conservationists acknowledged the plebeian uses of nature that clashed with the new order they ushered in, they typically portrayed their erasure as a positive good, a triumph more than a mere necessity. Forestry advocates such as Emerson Hough and Abbot Kinney looked back on the history of the rational management of woodland resources and saw the extinguishing of communal rights by central authorities as a necessary precondition to enlightened management. "Communal rights in forests, that is, the right of individuals in a community to individually use the forest for personal benefit," Kinney flatly declared, "is fatal to the forests." This was a truism among conservationists, in part because they assumed that plebeian uses of nature were destructive. Emerson Hough, for example, called attention to the "habitually careless and improvident" characteristics of the "unstable and transient . . . class of pioneers."[34]

Moreover, the great respect that many conservationists had for colonial experiments in nature protection helped make them comfortable with authoritarian measures. English forest preserves in India were second only to those in Germany in their influence on American foresters—indeed, the English use of the term "conservancy" for these areas was the inspiration for Pinchot's new definition of "conservation." U.S. acquisition of a formal overseas empire with victory in the Spanish-American War in 1898 meant that there was an empire for U.S. conservation as well. Visiting the Philippines in the wake of the brutal U.S. war against insurgents there, Pinchot finished his early-twentieth-century tour of the islands convinced that they offered "the best opportunity for successful and profitable forest administration of which I have knowledge." He was not perturbed that he had had to travel with a military escort.[35]

Whether abroad or at home, the kind of society that rural usufruct supported, as much as its assumed destructiveness, offended elite conservationists. Indians and backcountry whites and blacks, or so conservationists thought, harvested nature's bounty not in the interests of building a prosperous and modern economy, but rather in perpetuating social ties that were themselves objectionably backward and unenlightened. "Along the fringe of civilization," Abbot Kinney noted in his advocacy of governmental ownership of woodlands, "there is always a tendency to revert to primitive types of life and to primitive types of government and property holdings. Primitive man was everywhere and is everywhere more or less of a socialist. It may be more strictly accurate to say a communist. Most property and all land is held in common in primitive communities." The specters of different sorts of backwardness hung over Charles Askins's portrayal of southern hunting, much of which was reproduced by William Hornaday in the latter's *Our Vanishing Wild Life*. Askins and Hornaday simultaneously indicted black hunters for their "pot-hunting" (killing for food rather than sport) and white southerners for their willingness to tolerate black backwardness: "The white man is telling the black to abide upon the plantation, raising cotton and corn, and further than this nothing will be required of him.

He can cheat a white man or a black, steal in a petty way anything that comes handy, live in marriage or out of it to please himself, kill another negro if he likes, and lastly shoot every wild thing that can be eaten, if only he raises the cotton and the corn." Here, as with Kinney, the presumably wasteful and antisocial practices of the countryside called out for the intervention of enlightened foresters and hunters.[36]

For conservationists, the contrast between primitive and modern use of natural resources was crystal clear. Under conservation, resources would be exchanged in a mutually beneficial capitalist economy, one where technical knowledge and specialized labor would ensure an accumulation of wealth as well as environmental sustainability. As the Minnesota state forester asserted, woodlands were an essential part of a modern economy, in which each segment of society performed a specialized role: "The radiating influence of the standing forests is repeated when they are cut and utilized. The producers of the raw materials which supply the factories, which sell to the wholesalers, distributing to the retailers, who sell their wares to the wage-earners in forest and mill—are, with their employees, and the lumber companies and their employees, all more or less dependent upon the forests." Hunting was depicted similarly: it was pernicious for Indians or black southerners to perpetuate their supposedly distinctive ways of life by snaring and trapping, but sport hunting, on the other hand, could be a valuable part of wholesome consumer markets. "The sportsman, too," claimed a Minnesota agency, "is a medium, together with the lumber companies and the railroads, through which the forests exert an economic influence upon the country. They furnish cover for the game which calls him out. In pursuit of that game he expends quantities of ammunition. He buys guns, tents, canoes and endless other paraphernalia, in the production of which countless citizens gain their living. The ammunition bought from the retailer means renewed activities all along the line back to the charcoal burner."[37]

So cutting down a tree or shooting a bird—or appropriating any other portion of nature's bounty—was pernicious or beneficial according to the context in which it occurred and the networks in which the product circulated. It was one thing for urban sportsmen with their heaps of gear to travel to the country, shoot quail, and enjoy the roasted bird over the evening's fire, but a very different matter for the Blackfeet or plantation laborers to provision themselves, catch the same bird, and enjoy it with their own people or sell it in a nearby town. It was one thing for a timber company to harvest white pine in a national forest, at a volume and location determined by scientific forestry, and to put the timber up for sale, but a very different matter for an Adirondacker to cut the same tree and build himself a house.

This validation of a national market, and the consequent denigration of local communities and their markets and subsistence, revealed a side of conservation that was generally obscured when conservationists did battle with their ideological foes in the formal political arena. When defending the youthful national forest system and other measures against the likes of the National Public Domain League, conservationists looked like critics of American capitalism. And indeed they often were, warning not just of the prospect of resource exhaustion but also of monopoly and labor exploitation, insisting that the rights of the public to security and dignity outweighed the opportunity for private gain and the hollow and pinched constitutional fundamentalism offered by anti-conservationists and other critics of the Progressive state. But when defending the conservation state against the varied demands of rural society, conservationists were staunch advocates of large-scale capitalism—a certain version of it, to be sure, but nonetheless one in which the direct access to nature enjoyed by discrete local communities would be supplanted by a national market. That it often took guns and jails to make this happen did not seem to trouble them.

The social distance between conservationists and many rural Americans contributed to park and forest officials' lack of concern for the social impact of their policies and a lack of respect for the plebeian uses of nature. This disdain was most frequently and starkly displayed when the people in question were Indians. The forest supervisor who banned the Havasupai, for example, fairly dripped with contempt when he justified their expulsion: "The Grand Cañon of the Colorado is becoming so renowned for its wonderful and extensive natural gorge scenery and for its open clean pine woods, that it should be preserved for the everlasting pleasure and instruction of our intelligent citizens as well as those of foreign countries. Henceforth, I deem it just and necessary to keep the wild and unappreciable Indian from off the Reserve and to protect the game." Later in the twentieth century, the invocation of Native Americans' supposedly harmonious relations with nature became a staple of environmentalist rhetoric. Conservationists paid no such homage. John Muir was thus typical in his dismissal of the Yosemite as "mostly ugly, and some of them altogether hideous," and in his celebration that Indian removal from the wilderness meant that "arrows, bullets, scalping-knives, need no longer be feared." Americans could now hear the "solemn call" of the wilderness uninterrupted by savages.[38]

Indian peoples bore the brunt of particular animosity, but did not do so alone. Ethnic Mexicans faced a new degree of economic subordination, cultural chauvinism, and land loss as the turmoil of the Mexican Revolution (circa 1910–20) prompted migration to the United States and heightened Anglo fears. The contemporaneous expansion of the conservation state left them entirely outside the ranks of public lands bureaucrats or agents, subjected instead to the authority of those who saw them with contempt and hostility. Patrolling the mountains of northern New Mexico, Ranger Allen Peters contrasted the scenery with the residents: "This is one of the most beautiful of places I have ever been, how unfortunate that it is populated by the most backward, dirty and brutish people I have ever come across." Conservation bureaucrats and officers, mostly native-born and of northern European descent, harbored similar prejudices against immigrants from southern and eastern Europe. A Minnesota sportsman's diatribe against "pot hunters" characteristically singled out "foreigners" as the major culprits for improper and excessive hunting. "They do not hunt for the sport of it," he insisted, "but merely for a certain class of aliens. . . . It is meat, even if bad meat, and that is all they are after. . . . More game is killed by these people than by Americans who shoot during the closed season." William Hornaday's widely read book *Our Vanishing Wild Life* (1913) was nearly hysterical in its warning about one group of southern European immigrants: "Italians are spreading, spreading, spreading. If you are without them to-day, to-morrow they will be around you. . . . The bird-killing foreigner . . . will surely attack your wild life." The principal national theorists of conservation were more preoccupied with Indians and European migrants than with African Americans. Few of them lived outside of the South, the region of the country where the conservation state had the smallest footprint, and the young Jim Crow system seemed to have fixed their social place in a way that had not been done for immigrants in the East and Midwest. Nevertheless, the discussion of southern blacks by Hornaday, Charles Askins, and other sportsmen displayed a disdain similar to that for the more pressing threats of Italians and Native peoples.[39]

The power of wilderness as an idea—the appeal that a return to untouched nature had for so many Americans—made it easy for conservationists to gloss over or even actively hide the social tensions caused by their policies. Early conservation bureaucrats presented the areas under their control as natural and pristine even when they had abundant reason to know otherwise. In an interview with *Forest and Stream*, for example, the state game commissioner of Minnesota described Superior National Forest as "an absolutely wild and unsettled country," and there were "no settlements or even settlers in the area, and nothing to attract them"—even as the nonexistent settlers harassed and shot at his game wardens. The Forest Service underscored the area's remoteness even as it asserted its accessibility: "Fine camping sites are abundant, and the voyageur can always pitch his tent wherever night overtakes him—at places others have camped before, or perhaps where the ring of the woodsman's ax has never broken the forest silence."[40]

It is tempting to conclude that conservationists' willingness to dispossess the most vulnerable proves that a deep and ineradicable racism and elitism lay at the heart of the movement—in other words, that this elitism was not incidental, but rather fundamental, to the entire project of conservation. Influential scholars of environmental thought and politics working in recent decades have made just such an argument; indeed, they have emphasized the racial blindness and chauvinism of conservation to a much greater extent than they have examined its simultaneous critique of local folkways and unbridled capitalism. Wilderness preservation has been subjected to a particularly thorough critique. William Cronon's "The Trouble with Wilderness" historicizes the concept, arguing that wilderness "is very much the fantasy of people who have never themselves had to work the land to make a living" (a category that does not include the orchardist John Muir, among others) and that contemporary environmental writers and activists should be cognizant of its sharp limitations. Others are more dismissive of the wilderness tradition. Ramachandra Guha unfavorably contrasts American environmentalists' validation of wilderness with the environmental politics of the peasantry of India and other colonized places, which emphasized the coexistence of human and natural communities. Jake Kosek similarly argues that Muir and his apostles "galvanized support for wilderness preservation" by appealing to "racial and class fears surrounding purity and degradation."[41]

These arguments successfully explain the willingness of white conservationists to victimize others. But they obscure some important characteristics of conservation. Many of these claims let wilderness preservation or the fondness for eugenics by a few elite conservationists stand for the whole of the movement, leaving no place for the appeal that conservationist measures had for some African Americans and labor progressives. And they suggest that wilderness preservation, and perhaps conservation more generally, could not be unchained from racism, Indian removal, or whiteness.

But conservation was too complex to be put into one small box. Despite the general contempt for common rights by elite conservationists, for example, at times they did accommodate claims for local rights. In the 1880s, for example, much of the Adirondacks "was controlled by community-based guides' clubs" that tried to shape early conservation policies in ways that left room for the needs and knowledge of local communities. "The forests," proclaimed the Adirondack Guide Association's secretary, "can best be protected by those residing in their borders." Guides helped repopulate the region with beaver and implement new restrictions on the killing of does and black bear. Similarly, local moral ecologies in New England deeply shaped the content and implementation of Progressive-era conservation, particularly by regulating hunting and fishing in the interests of small communities and subsistence users. These arrangements were not uncommon, and did not necessarily serve the interests of the most economically marginalized locals, but they did represent codified versions of piecemeal synergy between state and folk conservation. Across much of the country, informants ratted out environmental profligates to game wardens while remaining mute about subsistence hunters, and juries convicted or failed to convict neighbors charged with environmental crimes according to their own logic. The conservation state was used for local ends that its architects neither anticipated nor welcomed.[42]

The ability of Adirondackers to get a hearing from New York City conservationists such as then governor Theodore Roosevelt no doubt reflected the fact that the guides were native-born whites rather than immigrants, Indians, Mexicans, or African Americans. But conservation, including wilderness preservation, was not implacably racist—or rather, it was neither less nor more racist than native-born white American society as a whole. On this count, the politics and sensibility of Ernest Oberholtzer, one of the founders of the Wilderness Society, for example, flatly contradict the arguments of Kosek and Guha. On the one hand, Oberholtzer's comfortable background as a prosperous midwesterner who attended Harvard, his yearning to replicate earlier feats of exploration, and his discomfort with aspects of modernity all seem to mark him as a conventional white wilderness devotee. "Man was made for broad scenes and tall shadows," he wrote in a tract extolling the virtues of the Ontario-Minnesota border lakes and calling for their protection from industrial development: "Cramp him, and he revolves in an ever narrowing circle, until finally he doubts his own destiny. The song goes out of his heart." This was the yearning that brought him to the lake country west of Lake Superior, where he made his home on land taken from the Ojibway. On the other hand, Oberholtzer was as drawn to the residents of his beloved wilderness, principally the Ojibway, as he was to the landscape. Rather than fantasizing about a northern woods free of human touch, he could not imagine it without a Native presence. To his Harvard classmates, he described his life in the wilderness as "living among the Indians" and promised a "hearty welcome" to those who might care to join him in "sitting in smoky wigwams and recording ancient tales." To the public at large, he extolled the virtues of the landscape as an inhabited as well as a rugged and remote place. "Many traces of the old commerce are still visible," he informed the readers of *American Forests*. "We have much to learn from Indians and no better place to learn it today than on the portages worn smooth by our Indian predecessors."[43]

Oberholtzer became such a connoisseur of Ojibway culture that he

Ernest Oberholtzer's close association with Ojibway people, as captured in a photograph taken during a 1920s camping trip with his longtime guide and friend Taytahpaswaywitong (Billy Magee), demonstrates that a wilderness ethos was no barrier to appreciating the human history of wild places. *(Courtesy Minnesota Historical Society)*

earned the moniker "Atisokan," or "story," from his Native informants. Well after much of the region came to be protected by park and wilderness bureaucracies of both Canada and the United States, he continued hosting and visiting Ojibway friends. He placed a large drum from the Rainy River band in the center of his living room in front of the hearth, which itself featured a stone named after Seine River Ojibway Charlie Friday, the friend and craftsman who once told Atisokan that after his death he would come to live in Oberholtzer's chimney. The beneficiaries of Oberholtzer's will included several Ojibway. Louise Erdrich, a contemporary poet and novelist whose works draw heavily on her Ojibway family history, was a frequent visitor to Oberholtzer's former home on Mallard Island. She described it as "a kind of place that inspires a certain energy that I can only term 'Oberholtzerian'—a combination of erudition, conservation, nativism, and exuberant eccentricity." Oberholtzer's "phenomenally active life benefited his Ojibwe friends in many ways," Erdrich declares, "not the least of which is in the area of conservation.[44]

Atisokan's close ties to Indian people made him as exceptional among conservationists as among the general white populace at large. But his breadth of vision was not unique. Conservationists were hardly free from racism or ignorance, but there was nothing inherent in wilderness appreciation, or conservation politics more generally, that chained its proponents to racism, Indian removal, or whiteness. Later generations of environmentalists demonstrated this truth, even as they had to grapple with some of the bitter legacies bequeathed to them by their Progressive-era forebears.

Natural Challenges

Most elite conservationists of the period, besides being convinced that they could and should replace plebeian uses of nature with formal regulations, were sure that nature itself could be understood and controlled. Gifford Pinchot's stark declaration in *The Fight for Conservation* that "the first duty of the human race is to control the earth it lives upon" expressed a very different sensibility from that found in subsequent environmental movements. At the time, however, Pinchot expressed a faith that cut across many of the divisions among conservationists. Fires reduced magnificent and valuable forests to stumps and ashes—so it was obvious that they should be extinguished, as both Pinchot and his sometime antagonist John Muir agreed. The once great salmon runs could be replenished if only legislatures heeded conservationist calls for fishing limits and funded their proposals for artificially raising salmon to restock decimated rivers. Massive irrigation systems would make productive and beautiful orchards and farms blossom in what previously was desert. Careful management of logging, judicious planting of seedlings, and aggressive fire suppression would ensure healthy forests indefinitely. Hunting regulation and the trapping and shooting of predators would restore game animals to their prelapsarian abundance.[45]

In short, humanity had the knowledge and power to protect the beauty and productivity of nature. Unlike the conflicts between conservation and its foes in Congress and the countryside, this optimistic assumption was rarely contested in the early twentieth century. Yet because nature proved not nearly so malleable or legible, the self-confidence of Progressive conservationists would leave legacies just as enduring and complicated as the political and social conflicts brought on by their accomplishments.

Conservationists' attitudes toward fire epitomized their larger and ultimately misplaced confidence in human power and wisdom. Fire was a principal enemy of the managers of the public domain. The conflagrations of the Great Lakes states, such as the 1871 disaster at Peshtigo, numbered among the most notorious environmental disasters that prompted the rise of conservation in the first instance. And fires continued to destroy vast amounts of property and claim scores of lives each year; the Forest Service proclaimed that the blazes of 1908 alone destroyed enough timber to "provide for a good-sized navy of first-class battleships." Materially minded and Romantic conservationists alike thus found reason to object to fires. Not all fires were rampantly destructive, of course; indeed, close observers of the continent's forests saw abundant evidence of past fires, many set accidentally or deliberately by Indians, even in seemingly healthy forests. But it was difficult for most conservationists and land managers to conceive of fires as natural events to which plant communities had adapted or were even dependent upon, as ecologists realized much later in the twentieth century. Much of this was due to the assumption that nature was timeless and unchanging, which implied that the locally dramatic changes brought by fires (especially when started by people) were always and inherently destructive and preventable. This belief had a genealogy that long predated conservation, and was incorporated into the basic assumptions of the movement. George Perkins Marsh, for example, wrote famously in *Man and Nature* (1864) that "Nature, left undisturbed, so fashions her territory as to give it almost unchanging permanence of form, outline, and proportion." In undisturbed nature, "a condition of equilibrium has been reached which, without the action of man, would remain, with little fluctuation, for countless ages." Although geologists were growing increasingly aware of dramatic past alterations, such as the advance and retreat of glaciers, ecologists in the early twentieth century incorporated this assumption of perfect stability in their model of a climax community, an array of species so well adapted to a particular place that it replicated itself indefinitely.[46]

So perhaps it was inevitable that the new environmental state would devote itself to fire suppression. Yet firefighting was more than a duty for conservationists, and fires meant more than mere disruption and destruction. Conservationists singled out tolerance or indifference to forest fires as one of the most pernicious forms of laxness indulged in by previous generations. Bernhard Fernow labeled fires products of "bad habits and loose morals." Abbot Kinney declared that "the student, philosopher and statesman are all opposed to forest fires." John Muir gave fires a prominent place in his depiction of the environmental profligacy of past generations. The "pious destroyers" of early America, he wrote,

> waged interminable forest wars; chips flew thick and fast; trees in their beauty fell crashing by millions, smashed to confusion, and the smoke of their burning has been rising to heaven more than two hundred years. After the Atlantic coast from Maine to Georgia had been mostly cleared and scorched into melancholy ruins, the overflowing multitude of bread and money seekers poured over the Alleghanies [*sic*] into the fertile middle West. . . . Thence still westward the invading horde of destroyers called settlers made its fiery way over the broad Rocky Mountains, felling and burning more fiercely than ever.[47]

In contrast, the clear-sighted and resolute conservationist knew that fires had to be condemned and combated. Pinchot declared them to be "wholly in the control of man." Writing in *My First Summer in the Sierra,* John Muir inserted a mournful note in his ode to a magnificent grove of sequoias, remarking on "a black charred stump about thirty feet in diameter and eighty or ninety feet high—a venerable impressive old monument of a tree that in its prime may have been the monarch of the grove." Along with the strong impressions of the grace and venerable beauty of the trees, Muir left his readers with the troubling thought that "only fire threatens the existence of these noblest of God's trees." Gifford

Pinchot, though then locked in combat with Muir over the future of the Hetch Hetchy Valley, wholly shared his views on fire: as he warned early in his career, "the question of forest fires, like the question of slavery, may be shelved for a time, at enormous cost in the end, but sooner or later it must be faced."[48]

The faith that even something as powerful and seemingly uncontrollable as forest fires might come under the authority of humanity informed how conservationists understood a number of issues. The geologist and ethnologist W. J. McGee placed the control of nature at the heart of conservation and the work of the trained professionals who enlisted in its ranks. "The course of nature," he proclaimed, "has come to be investigated in order that it may be redirected along lines contributing to human welfare." He saw conservation as a "conscious and purposeful entering into control over nature." Such confidence pervaded conservation. Wolves, mountain lions, grizzly bears, and other predators might have been part of nature, but since they threatened increasingly scarce charismatic game species such as deer and elk—to say nothing of domestic livestock—they should be hunted to the point of extermination. As with so much else in American life, professionals could do better what had once been a folk pursuit; in 1915, Congress established the Predatory Animal and Rodent Control Service. "Large predatory mammals destructive to livestock and game," one of the new bureau's scientists said, "no longer have a place in our advancing civilization." Profligate hunters might have pushed game populations to the brink, but the lethal force brought by government hunters would bring them back. Indeed, wildlife scientists followed the lead of foresters in calculating the total amount of game that a particular region could support, then suppressed predation and set the annual harvest to secure a perpetually sustainable animal resource.[49]

A similar confidence suffused reclamation. The lush fields made possible by irrigation networks in the West were not merely agricultural development; to a host of farmers, engineers, and boosters, they represented nothing less than "conquest," a tribute to the wisdom and power of those who replaced barren deserts with farms that were both productive and beautiful. William Ellsworth Smythe, the chief prophet of irrigation, titled his widely read tract *The Conquest of Arid America*

(1899). Smythe proclaimed "a policy of peaceful conquest over the re-sources of a virgin continent" as the source of American national great-ness, one that irrigation would perpetuate by providing millions more Americans with the opportunity to gain the independence that came only with farm ownership.[50]

Professional foresters approached their work similarly, and not just with regard to fire control. Whereas woods not under professional man-agement were like an unregulated economy beset with inefficiencies and waste, carefully managed forests would produce abundant timber in-definitely. Some of this was a matter of fostering attractive and valuable growth in place of "weed" or "trash" species that provided poor timber, easily fell over in storms, and seemed to attract insects and disease. What purpose could such trees serve in a healthy and productive forest? It was also a matter of the age of trees: since perhaps three-quarters of western forests were made up of older trees and thus lost at least as much wood to decay and tree death as they added in new growth, they needed to be dramatically reworked by heavy cutting that would open the land to the young trees that would become the homes, ships, industry, and suste-nance of future generations. "This logic," observes the forest historian Nancy Langston, "shaped a Forest Service that, in order to protect the forest, believed it necessary to first remove it."[51]

In fire policy as elsewhere, the result of this confidence was dra-matic and aggressive intervention, with little thought that such interven-tions might bring unintended consequences. In the most direct physical sense, this meant extinguishing all fires as soon as possible, arresting the culprits who set anthropogenic blazes, and building an infrastructure of roads and lookout towers to support early detection and rapid response. A reader of park and forest annual reports from the early twentieth century can be forgiven for drawing the impression that public lands conservation bureaucracies were principally firefighting agencies. Fires were central features of these bureaucracies' publications, budgets, and personnel.[52]

This prolonged campaign against wildland fire had its cultural and ideological front. Heroic firefighters became popular icons whose courage and selfless sacrifice were widely invoked in the popular press. Ranger Ed Pulaski became such a hero when he guided his fire crew through a conflagration in the northern Rockies in 1910. Surrounded by fire that blackened the sky and deafened with the "roar of a thousand freight trains," Pulaski led his men into a mineshaft with a small trickle of water in its recesses. Smoke and gas filled the refuge as the fire passed. Pulaski kept his panicked crew inside, at gunpoint, until all lost consciousness. Thirty-nine of the forty-five men survived, including Pulaski, who became, in the fire historian Stephen Pyne's description, "a symbol of the strenuous life bravely battling the reckless waste of natural resources," and for "firefighters . . . a folk hero." The public lands managers who orchestrated the war on fire recognized the value in such stories, for they believed that public culture and awareness constituted one of the critical theaters of battle. National Fire Prevention Day, which marked the deadly Peshtigo and Chicago blazes of 1871, was inaugurated in 1914 to raise consciousness about all kinds of fires. Soon the Forest Service began publishing a series of regularly updated tracts entitled *Forest Fire Prevention Handbook for Children,* distributed moralistic films with such titles as *Trees of Righteousness,* and printed collections of fire poems. The Boy Scouts began preaching the same gospel in the 1910s. The organization's *Handbook for Boys* included prolonged discussions of the virtues of campfires and the skills necessary to make them even in adverse conditions. But the wise boy also made his campfire only well away from flammable vegetation and always ensured it was completely out before breaking camp.[53]

The crusade against fire was deeply bound up in the political disputes over conservation, which helps explain why it became so relentless, intolerant of dissent, and deaf to suggestions that some fires might in fact have a role in maintaining productive and attractive wildlands. Once large portions of the nation were turned over to conservation bureaucracies for safekeeping and wise use, each fire season became a referendum on the wisdom of state conservation. The foes of conservation ensured this. In 1910, even as the conservation state defended itself against agitation in the West and the halls of Congress, a series of catastrophic fires swept across the country. Unlike the grim fire season of 1908, which had burned mostly lands not under the supervision of the Forest Service, the 1910 fires burned an arc across the northern tier of the country, including the new forest reserves of the Pacific Northwest, northern Rockies, and the Upper Midwest. Several thousand individual blazes proved an overwhelming challenge for the youthful Forest Service. In August, heeding pleas from timber companies and conservationists, President Taft called out the army to assist in the suppression campaign. It did little good: the blazes continued, and grew particularly severe in the northern Rockies, where a blaze that came to be known as the "Big Blowup" consumed acreage roughly the size of Connecticut. Several Idaho towns saved themselves from incineration only by burning numerous structures and considerable areas on their outskirts. Trains running out of the town of Avery managed to save perhaps a thousand residents; the last two trains ran desperately over trestles already aflame; soldiers dowsed the inside of the wooden cars as the heat peeled the paint. Eighty-seven lives, mostly firefighters, were lost to the Big Blowup, including an entire fire crew of twenty-eight trapped by flames outside Avery. Farther away, the fires continued to announce themselves: a yellow haze obscured the sun in Boston, and towns hundred of miles from the worst fires of the Rockies were blanketed with ash that fell like snow.[54]

Anti-conservationists were quick to seize the fires as proof of the failure of the conservation state. Montana senator Thomas Carter, one of the leading congressional critics of the Forest Service in the previous few years, used the blazes as an opportunity to condemn the service for driving off the "settlers, prospectors, and miners" who would have made "a splendid fire fighting force within the forests." He argued that economic development, spurred by returning to the policy of converting public lands into private property, was a better solution to the problem of forest fires than was conservation. Interior secretary Richard Ballinger, then in the throes of his struggle with the recently fired Pinchot, speculated to the press that allowing some fires to burn—or even deliberately setting small blazes—might be a more sensible response than a total war on fire. The Forest Service successfully fought off these attacks. Invoking the heroism of men such as Pulaski and the martyrdom of the fallen firefighters, the custodians of the conservation state insisted that the terrible fires were proof of the need for more, not less, conservation, namely, for a fully funded network of trails, telephones, towers, and regular patrols. The charges made by Ballinger, Carter, and others nevertheless had a lasting effect on the service. With battle lines drawn so starkly, conservation bureaucracies lost their earlier tolerance for discussions of the virtues of light burning. Anything less than total fire suppression was now heresy.[55]

Some voices within conservation questioned fire suppression and other measures based on the assumption of complete human under- standing and control of natural processes. These figures embraced the goals of conservation and understood themselves as part of the larger movement, but proposed policies that were premised on a respect for lay knowledge and experimentation. They demonstrated at the time that conservation was not monolithic, but rather something whose exact meaning and content was contested. Although they were roundly de- feated in the policy arena at the time, their advocacy of a humbler ap- proach to land management, and their warnings about the consequences of the quest for mastery of nature, would be validated by results on the ground and embraced by later generations of environmental activists.

The widely read and circulated dissent from the mania for fire sup- pression promulgated by Stewart Edward White of California suggests the contours of this dissident strain of conservation. The author of nu- merous books, both fiction and nonfiction, about western life, camp- ing, and hunting, White would be honored by the Boy Scouts as one of the organization's Honorary Scouts, as one of those "American citizens whose achievements in outdoor activity, exploration and worthwhile adventure are of such an exceptional character as to capture the imagi- nation of boys." In the late 1910s, at the height of his fame, White force- fully inserted himself into popular and scientific discussions of forest fires. Writing in *Sunset,* a popular magazine aimed at a general audience interested in the West, White began his salvo against fire suppression by invoking his support for conservation. He nodded to past resentment of forest rangers over grazing and timber access, but suggested that the days of outright hostility to public lands conservation had passed: "Now, thanks to the devotion and loyalty of a group of these ill-paid men, we know we own our forests, we use them and are proud of them and inter- ested in their preservation and maintenance." Both Romantic and ma- terial conservation, White insisted, were a secure part of the American landscape because of both bureaucratic rationalization and widespread

The novelist, conservationist, and spiritualist Stewart Edward White leveled a withering critique of Forest Service fire suppression as an example of what he regarded as dangerous bureaucratic hubris. *(Library of Congress, Prints and Photographs Division)*

public support: "Cattlemen and sheepmen, formerly hostile, are now happy and satisfied in the regulated rights that have been substituted for the raids and wars of the old days; lumber sales have been worked out on a practical basis until both Government and operator have agreed on methods acceptable to both sides; the wonders of the mountains have been opened by trail, road and sign, by proposed camp-site and reserved horse feed to the great public on whose good will in the final analysis all these things depend."[56]

Having established his support for conservation, White then launched into a frontal assault on fire suppression: "[The] general public, educated for twenty years by the Forest Service, reacts blindly and instinctively against any suggestion of fire. Nevertheless fire—a bad master—is an excellent servant. There are good fires and bad fires. Let us not too blindly condemn one for the misdeeds of the other." Before modern times, he argued, North American forests "were burned over periodically by fires that ran unchecked until the rains put them out."

Since "there is not a mature stand of timber in existence that does not show indications, not of one, but of many forest fires," then it followed that not all forest fires were destructive. Quite the contrary: White drew particular attention to the efficacy of low-intensity fires in combating insect infestations, which he feared would devastate western forests if fire suppression continued unchallenged. These were different matters from the massive blazes associated with industrial logging, which were quite properly a cause for the creation of the Forest Service in the first place. On the other hand, he insisted that the policy of total suppression would end in disaster: "We are painstakingly building a fire-trap that will piecemeal, but in the long run completely, defeat the very aim of fire protection itself. Rigid fire exclusion accumulates kindling, and when you get enough kindling you get a fire that you cannot exclude." The insistence of a high-ranking forester that "with the present perfection of his equipment and personnel he could stop any fire anywhere at any time" was self-deluding hubris.[57]

Despite its sincere and credible invocation of the good of conservation, White's piece was an attack on state conservation as it was practiced, for he threatened the claims to certainty and unquestioned professional expertise relied on by the Forest Service and other conservation bureaucracies. White drew freely on his own knowledge of the woods—the large fire scars on perfectly healthy ponderosa pines, the mounting insect infestations, the fuel buildup in areas of active fire suppression. He invoked his decades of travel in pine woods across the continent as authority enough for his information. Moreover, in White's writings on fire, as in his novels, rural folk were not ignorant and dangerous despoilers, but people with experiences and knowledge of their own, to be taken seriously. He urged respect for the knowledge of "practical woodsmen, intelligent men who are capable of observation and deduction and who have been in the woods all their lives." White referred to the white men whose company he kept, but unlike other conservationists, he was not obsessed with policing the social boundaries of environmental enlightenment. That Indians, for example, started many forest fires before their confinement to reservations, was a matter of fact but not, for him, of moral opprobrium. White was clearly open to nonscientific ways of knowing—he and his wife later wrote books based on knowledge gained through spiritual mediums—but he was by no means critical of scientific truth or of conservation per se.[58]

White assumed that scientists were marked by self-interest as well as thirst for knowledge. And the conservationist crusade against fire led them to distort their work. Government scientists willfully ignored evidence contrary to their positions on fire and insect infestation, White charged, and unfairly discounted the knowledge held by laypeople familiar with western forests: "Once having committed themselves, these scientists were reluctant to back water. They abandoned the scientific for the polemic; they were more interested in procuring facts to bolster their expressed theories than in refitting their theories as fresh facts came to attention." He closed his broadside with an appeal for conservation to be nondogmatic and open to the knowledge and experiences of those who knew nature firsthand. "Our danger," he intoned, again identifying himself as a loyal supporter of conservation, "is that we will become bureaucratic and hidebound and inclined to the closed mind."[59]

White's broadside in *Sunset* appeared in too widely read a publication and from too credible an author for public lands managers to simply dismiss it out of hand. Moreover, his article threatened to make public an ongoing dispute between the Forest Service leadership and local officers, especially in the South, who expressed concerns about total fire exclusion similar to White's. Feeling that their expertise and authority were threatened, orthodox conservationists reacted furiously, insisting that such debates were technical matters that had been decisively settled by experts. Henry Graves, the former dean of Yale's forestry school and Pinchot's replacement as head of the U.S. Forest Service, responded directly with his own piece in *Sunset*. Graves's response reassured the public that the government had examined the question of total fire suppression with great care, and had found conclusive evidence that the perpetuation of even small fires damaged the long-term reproduction of forests across North America. Although he did not explicitly question White's motivations or integrity, the chief forester did carefully and directly link openness to fires with the interests of two types of foes of conservation: Indians and the timber industry. He conceded that White's approach might not harm merchantable standing timber, but insisted that conservationists—unlike private landowners—were concerned with the forests of the future, which would not grow if fires went unchecked. Graves insisted that permitting or even setting regular fires had "its analogy with what the Indians are alleged to have done when they fired the woods every few years." The idea that this practice could protect the forests against massive conflagrations was thus absurd, since "the wisdom and foresight necessary to conceive and apply such a system of deliberate protection seem far from consistent with the relatively low stage of cultural development" of Indians.[60]

Graves and his compatriots at the highest levels of federal conservation were even less charitable in other venues. The Forest Service threatened legal action against *Sunset* until the magazine agreed to run his piece, and brought similar legal pressure and threats of withholding patronage against local governments in the West that seemed sympathetic to White's position. In more specialized venues than *Sunset,* such as the *Timberman,* Graves and his allies were more caustic, branding White's position "Paiute Forestry," which they assumed would be understood as an oxymoron by audiences who shared their contempt for Indians. This dismissal invoked the long tradition of hostility to rural people that had informed conservation from its beginning, a hostility that dismissed the knowledge and experiences of Indians and others. Gifford Pinchot similarly gestured to the specter of backwardness in his comment that "there is no doubt that forest fires encourage a spirit of lawlessness and a disregard for property rights." These statements and actions were part of a larger marginalization of fire dissidents at the highest level of conservation. The Yale forestry professor Henry Chapman, for example, found himself "institutionally isolated, almost quarantined," for his publications suggesting a healthy role for fire in southern forests. He was not imprisoned, as was Eugene Debs for his opposition to joining World War I. Yet the willingness of conservation bureaucrats to suppress and dismiss their critics, even those so well placed as White and Chapman, demonstrated that by the late 1910s they had become as coercive as other Progressives.[61]

Developments in the decades after the battle over light burning in the pages of *Sunset* showed that conservation bureaucrats would have done well to heed Stewart White's caution, both about the specific issue of fires and the more general warning about the seductions of power and orthodoxy. Nature proved far more complex, and their own mastery much more illusory, than the architects of the conservation state believed.

Predator control exemplified the unanticipated consequences of success. Top predators such as wolves, mountain lions, and grizzly bears were hunted to extinction across much of the country, and smaller "varmints" such as prairie dogs declined in the face of the onslaught. But soon the cure seemed worse than the disease. By the 1930s, prairie dogs and other rodents once checked by coyote predation ravaged ranchlands and prevented much new forest growth, prompting the Forest Service to resort to chemical poisoning to replace the lost natural predation. The recovery of elk and deer populations brought similar problems. Government biologists urged the complete elimination of wolves and coyotes in Yellowstone National Park so that the magnificent elk herd would regain its population. As many as thirty thousand elk, up from several thousand in the 1870s, may have lived in the park by 1919. More than five thousand starved to death during the next winter, in a sight that would become depressingly familiar. The overly abundant elk largely eliminated the willows that once grew along Yellowstone's waterways, and with them the beaver. The disappearance of beaver dams and ponds, in turn, dried out much of the park, driving white-tailed deer in the region to extinction by the 1930s.[62]

Irrigation agriculture was similarly beset with the problems of success. The federal backing for irrigation secured by the Reclamation Act of 1902 brought millions of acres under profitable cultivation, made possible by the soaring dams, enormous reservoirs, and extensive networks of irrigation canals carefully designed by engineers. On the surface, the prophecies of conquest seemed to have been fulfilled. But this was not the experience of irrigation farmers, who soon came face-to-face with the unintended consequence of large-scale irrigation. Irrigation ditches, intended to deliver water to crops, also created lush environments for unwanted plants, whose growth in many regions quickly cut ditch capacity in half. Muskrats and beavers found the ditch environments attractive, and their tunneling and dams caused collapses and floods that were the scourge of many an irrigation farmer. Nevertheless, the irrigation systems succeeded in bringing large quantities of water to previously arid fields. But this, too, brought its own problems: rising groundwater and irrigation water that had percolated to river bottoms and other low-lying areas, now called "seeped" land, making them unfit for farm crops. Bottomlands and other places with poor drainage also suffered from salinization, since water leached out salts in the soil and then evaporated, leaving salt crusts behind.[63]

Other policies met with much less success but nonetheless wrought similarly complicated, unexpected, and sometimes destructive results. The preservation of salmon runs by restrictions on fishing and augmentation by artificial hatcheries were precocious conservation efforts, predating the embrace of federal power and the political opportunity of the Progressive moment in the 1900s and 1910s. Hatchery programs were continually appealing because their promise of abundant fish seemed a painless way to avoid choosing between the claims of net fishers, operators of fish traps, Indians, and sportsmen. But they did not succeed in augmenting fish populations, in part because biologists did not yet understand that Pacific salmon returned to their natal streams in discrete runs for spawning, and that the indiscriminate dumping of fry and hatchlings into mountain streams was therefore unlikely to have any lasting effect.[64]

Predominantly urban sportsmen claimed the mantle of conservation in order to make themselves increasingly powerful in salmon regulation in the early twentieth century. In western states, they used the Progressive tool of the ballot initiative to severely restrict the use of nets and traps in favor of recreational fishermen's hook and line. As with conservationist restrictions on timber harvesting and hunting, these measures helped foster a recreational market for urbanites with cash to spend, to the detriment of humbler fishermen who caught their own food or sold the fruits of their labor. Even by the declared standard of protecting fishing stocks, measures against nets and traps failed. They pushed commercial fishing out of rivers and streams and into the ocean, where managers were powerless to regulate specific salmon runs and where trolling killed huge numbers of fish, which went unharvested. Salmon runs declined, and some types of salmon evolved to be smaller and shorter-lived. After more than a century of active conservation directed at preserving and restoring salmon, it is not clear that conservation has helped salmon—or fishermen—at all.[65]

Fire suppression, of such critical importance to conservation's self-conception, was initially successful. Later, however, the practice encountered problems similar to those seen in the 1910s, and brought similarly complicated results. In later decades, blazes consumed less acreage and destroyed less property than before. But particularly when combined with the heavy cutting of senescent forests for new growth, fire suppression transformed enormous tracts of western forests into dense stands of small trees. This heavy undergrowth provided neither the timber so important to the materialist side of conservation nor the serene, parklike understories and soaring giants that inspired so many. (And just as White had warned, these forests were more vulnerable to insect infestation because of poor general tree health and greater uniformity of species.) In many places, the removal of fires fostered the growth of fir, to the detriment of the pines that, ironically, were so favored by the foresters. And as fire suppression continued for decades, it created the very conditions of its own undoing: the accumulation of forest litter made the floor more moist, encouraging shallower growth of roots, which then could be more easily killed by the surface fires that eventually occurred. Over the decades, fuel loads built to enormous levels, resulting in fires that were both more catastrophic—some destroyed the soil's organic matter as well as vegetation—and impossible to stop, even with military aircraft and chemical fire retardants. By the 1960s, acceptance of wildland fires had regained its intellectual credibility in scientific, policy, and bureaucratic circles. Conservation declared war on fire. Fire won.[66]

A Legacy of Progressivism

The first conservationists fought long and hard for intellectual credibility, public support, and laws and policies to benefit humanity by protecting and cultivating nature. In a sense, the opposition they provoked in the 1910s was a testimony to their success in achieving all of these things. The opponents of conservation jeered at the idea of resource scarcity and decried the turn to state power as unconstitutional and antirepublican. The new conservation agencies, however, survived the decade's political vicissitudes, and conservation secured an active and effective electoral constituency, even in the West. The contempt and violence directed at rangers by Indians and backcountry whites and Hispanics reflected the very real power that the conservation state came to wield. So did the confidence of most conservationists that they could control fires and predators, and restore, or even create out of whole cloth, profitable and attractive forests and farms.

The challenges to conservation posed by its foes and by the complexity of nature itself never went away, and in the case of such policies as fire suppression would return with a vengeance. But the fact that conservation defeated these challenges in the 1910s, even as other aspects of Progressivism met with much less success, marks it as one of the signal and lasting achievements of the Progressive era. What bound together diverse and sometimes contradictory aims under the banner of Progressivism was the effort to engage the public and the attentions of an empowered government to address the problems of urban-industrial life. In this sense, the first two decades of the twentieth century are often called the "Progressive era" precisely because Progressivism was—for better or for worse—such a powerful force. Progressives enfranchised women; instituted the income tax; brought popular sentiment more directly into formal politics through such measures as the initiative, referendum, and direct election of U.S. senators; banned the consumption of alcohol; discredited and limited some monopolies; enticed and sometimes coerced immigrants into seeing themselves as members of a national society; and provided some protection for vulnerable laborers, widows, and orphans.

Historians and pundits alike often portray the United States as a nation with an entrenched political tradition more hostile to state action and more deferential to laissez-faire than other advanced industrial states. This is consistent with the failure of the United States to establish robust unemployment, pension, workers' compensation, and health insurance programs in this period, in contrast to much of the industrial world. This depiction also reflects the reality that unions failed to achieve a secure position, particularly in key industries such as railroads, coal mining, and steel manufacturing, as they did in much of western Europe, Australasia, and Canada. But the idea of the United States as a nation with a weak state and a strong market—as the German sociologist Werner Sombart put it in 1904, "Why is there no socialism in the United States?"—focuses on what the American state did not do rather than what it actually did. The creation, consolidation, and survival of what Adam Rome has dubbed the "environmental management state" was one of the signal achievements of the era, and one premised precisely on the rejection of laissez-faire as inadequate to the demands of an industrial age.[67]

But wars change the victor as much as they vanquish the defeated. Conservation had become more bureaucratic and less democratic by 1920. The transformation of the countryside brought forth its more authoritarian streak, and the battles it fought with those who rejected the idea of environmental vulnerability and the Progressive state left it less tolerant of internal dissent and diversity. As in so much else, here conservation tracked the larger course of Progressivism. Excited by the prospects that the entry into World War I offered for the forging of a common purpose and social solidarity, many Progressives, including such key intellectual figures as the philosopher John Dewey, came to place more hope in the power of the state than they had before. Yet the wartime state proved more coercive than liberating, subjecting ethnic pluralism and the labor left to intense and prolonged suppression. The war to save democracy abroad left it in shambles at home. By the 1920s, national conservation was closer to its portrayal by most later historians: a technocratic effort concerned mostly about the countryside, using state power to impose its will on a heterogeneous and not always willing society. Later generations of Americans motivated by similar concerns about the environmental destructiveness and alienation of modern life repeatedly turned back to conservation for inspiration and instruction, but they also tried to learn from its mistakes and shortcomings.[68]

Epilogue

In August 1912, the editors of *Scientific American* alerted their readers to a "prophecy of what is claimed by many to be the increasing temperature of the earth and an explanation of the recent prevalence of hot summers." The popular magazine called attention to a discussion by Charles Van Hise, president of the University of Wisconsin, of the effects of burning coal. The Progressive luminary Van Hise observed that "the carbon dioxide of the atmosphere serves as does the glass of a hothouse to save the heat of the sun." Drawing on the more technical work of the Swedish physicist Svante Arrhenius from the 1890s, Van Hise calculated the impact that the increasingly rapid rate of the burning of coal might have on atmospheric levels of carbon dioxide. Although his conclusions were couched in the sober and restrained tones of the discipline of geology, they pointed to the dramatic and rapid changes that this burning could bring to the planet. "It appears probable that within a comparatively short time in the future, as compared with a single geological period, or even an epoch, the amount of carbon in one of its great reservoirs, the atmosphere, will be increased to an important extent." Van Hise showed that the continued burning of coal—at the time, overwhelmingly the most extensively used fossil fuel—would eventually triple the amount of CO_2 in the atmosphere and thereby "produce a climate as mild as that of the Eocene period," or some 14–15 degrees Fahrenheit warmer than before the Industrial Revolution. Briefly pointing to these temperature changes, the spur to vegetative growth of a more carbon-rich atmosphere, and possible impacts on chemical weathering, Van Hise concluded that "it therefore appears probable that the artificial oxidation of coal will result in some of the most profound and far-reaching geological consequences which are due to the agency of man." The *Scientific American* article endorsed this conclusion, noting only that the accelerated rate of coal consumption since it was originally published meant that these "profound and far-reaching" changes lay sooner ahead in humanity's path than was previously realized.[1]

Global warming, now generally referred to as climate change, did not become an issue in the United States or elsewhere in the early twentieth century. A few scientists and policy experts like Arrhenius and Van Hise offered the first description of the basic dynamic of what came to be recognized as one of the most pressing global environmental problems a century later. Their calculations may have prompted some readers of such publications as *Scientific American* to fear for the future of their planet, but unlike forest fires or calls for national parks, this was not an issue that prompted outcry or mobilization. Perhaps this was partly a result of the time frame that Van Hise offered: by his calculations, it would take exactly 1,624 years at current rates of coal use for levels of atmospheric carbon dioxide to triple. *Scientific American*'s estimation that this would take more like 812 years still left global warming far in the future.[2]

If they were wrong about the timing, these observers were tragically right about the changes in the atmosphere. Contemporary climate scientists now estimate that atmospheric carbon dioxide is about 1.4 times as abundant as before industrialization, and that the earth will be 2.7–8.6 degrees Fahrenheit warmer by 2100, with a continual rise unless and until humanity stops releasing carbon dioxide or finds some way to sequester the vast quantity produced by our livestock, automobiles, airplanes, and power plants. The known consequences of such elevated average temperatures include drought in some places, destructively higher rainfall in others, increasingly powerful hurricanes and typhoons, elevated sea levels that will threaten large portions of the human population, and mass species extinction. If the worse of these scenarios come true, the Industrial Revolution will have proved to be one of humanity's greatest follies, a kind of bitter and violent prank that it played on itself.[3]

What does it say about conservation that some of its adherents predicted global climate change, the most serious environmental threat that humanity faces a century later? This foresight does not suggest that conservationists had all the answers, or that they built an Eden of environmental reform from which we were later evicted. Subsequent generations have seen much that Progressive-era conservationists missed. Charles Van Hise may have grasped the fundamental geochemical dynamics of carbon dioxide and climate change, for example, but he remained unaware of the enormous implications of his dry mathematical calculations. The only real consequence that he foresaw was a future abatement in demand of coal for heating purposes, since Americans of future centuries would enjoy warmer winters. It was left to later generations to ascertain the scope of this problem and to again incite the public and political leaders to respond to it.[4]

Environmental reform hardly ceased with the close of the 1910s. While the general expansion of the environmental state at the federal level paused with the eclipse of Progressivism as a whole during World War I, and became more coercive and reliant on state power, there was no abrupt or neat end to conservation. Americans still sought to address the concerns about artificiality and resource scarcity that had animated the movement. This attitude was evident in social developments and formal politics alike. The environmental cast of real estate development continued in full force, at least for those who could afford it. The aesthetics and plantings that landscape architects like Wilhelm Miller had seen as part of a wider movement enjoyed increased circulation as commodities shorn of Progressive commitments. The face of numerous communities reflected this: when lots in Palos Verdes Estates went on sale in 1923, for example, the wealthiest residents of the Los Angeles region could move to a community where groves of carefully selected eucalyptus and pepper trees dotted the landscape, more than a quarter of the acreage was contained in parks, and roads laid out by the Olmsted brothers emphasized the peninsula's natural contours and spectacular ocean vistas. The deed restrictions that mandated muted colors and re-

gionally appropriate architectural fixtures consistent with the past decade's naturalistic push in park design and landscape architecture also
promised that they would not have to endure the presence of neighbors
"not of the white or Caucasian race." Picturesque suburbs helped nur-
ture a public critique of industrial capitalism, but also undermined that
critique by offering a private escape for the fortunate few.[5]

In other realms, private property fostered an inclusive culture of
nature that continued the political programs of Progressive-era conservation. The proliferating automobile ownership of the 1920s helped put vis-
its to national parks and other sites of a wilder nature within the reach of
an ever growing portion of the national population. A *New York Times*
survey in the early 1920s revealed that about half of the nation's automobiles were used for camping. A few years later, another study concluded
that 10–15 percent of Americans went auto camping. The public lands bureaucracies established by Progressive-era conservationists, particularly
the National Park Service, capitalized on this growing demand, which
rose to greater heights in the next generation, buoyed by the interstate
highway system and postwar prosperity. On the state level, similar agencies enjoyed robust support. New York's governor Al Smith, for example, whose electoral coalition of European ethnics, reformers, and labor
advocates anticipated the later coalition of the New Deal, aggressively
pursued both public electrical power and a rationalized statewide park
system, a bond issue that enjoyed heavy support from New York City
voters. He blasted opponents of such measures as a small elite out of
touch with the needs and desires of urbanites for wild nature.[6]

Ambitious proposals from the 1920s that were not fulfilled, at least
in the breadth of their conception, similarly reflected the persistence of
the urban-populist strain of conservation epitomized by Horace McFarland, Mira Lloyd Dock, and Dana Bartlett. The Los Angeles Chamber of
Commerce commissioned landscape architects, including the Olmsted
brothers, to prepare a study of parks and natural spaces across Los Angeles County. The result was a breathtakingly ambitious plan to create
new public spaces, especially parks, by regulating real estate development and heavily funding city government. The chamber recoiled from
this vision, which was grossly at odds with the embrace of an unfettered
market—the key to its successful crusade against organized labor in any

form. Perhaps chamber members believed that the contact with natural
beauty ensured by workers' access to places such as Palos Verdes Estates obviated the need for such a plan. This decision and the coming of
the Great Depression buried the plan, though its calls for a green space
along the Los Angeles River was taken up by later generations. Benton
MacKaye's proposal for an Appalachian Trail enjoyed greater success:
by the mid-1930s, one could walk from Georgia to Maine on the con-
tiguous trail. MacKaye's hopes that the trail would be the linchpin for
comprehensive natural resource development and regional planning,
however, went as unfulfilled as the Olmsted pan for Los Angeles parks.
As in the city of angels, the laissez-faire politics of the 1920s made it a
challenging time for a vigorous conservation that sought not only wilderness recreation but also a materially sustainable economy.[7]

In the next decade, the crisis of the Depression and the politics of
the New Deal brought a kind of rebirth to conservation. Economic collapse and the environmental disasters of the Dust Bowl and Mississippi
flooding underscored the connections between economic, social, and
ecological problems. Consistent with its expansion of federal power in
legalizing labor organizing, creating a safety net through such programs
as Social Security, and directly employing millions, the administration
of President Franklin D. Roosevelt embraced the active management
of natural resources. The expansion of national forests, the planting of
shelterbelts of trees, programs to encourage soil conservation, the regulation of grazing on federal lands, model "greenbelt" cities, and a host
of agricultural programs designed to shore up a devastated farm sector
constituted the foundation of New Deal conservation. Americans would
live in a society more self-conscious and efficient than before in its use
of natural resources. Soil and range scientists provided advice (and dispensed subsidies and other economic incentives) to farmers, natural scientists managed more lands for timber and forage production, and city
planners developed three model urban "greenbelt" settlements, which
they hoped would showcase the combination of urban life, easy access
to nature, and social and economic cooperation. Hundreds of dams
built by the Army Corps of Engineers and the Bureau of Reclamation
controlled flooding and produced both water for irrigation and electricity for homes and industry. More than three million young Americans

were employed in building trails and roads, new park buildings, and fighting fires as part of the Civilian Conservation Corps. The comprehensive regional economic development aimed for by the Tennessee Valley Authority sought to use the centralized management of natural resources to foster economic development in one of the regions most devastated by economic collapse and environmental damage.[8]

On one hand, the New Deal conservation state was the apotheosis of Progressive-era conservation. Its policies were premised on a similar hostility to unregulated markets, a confidence in scientific resource management, and a belief that human and natural welfare were deeply tied. These policies encompassed urban design, agriculture, and the nation's most remote and scenic areas. But the New Deal measures also departed from earlier conservation. They were nurtured in the shadow of the Depression, aiming at restoring economic growth rather than limiting and channeling it. Agriculture thus occupied a more prominent place as a site of state intervention. And conservation in the era of Franklin D. Roosevelt was on the whole more statist than were earlier environmental politics. The strand of Progressivism that validated cultural revitalization and faith in grassroots activism by civic organizations, critically important to earlier conservationists such as Liberty Hyde Bailey and political theorists such as Mary Parker Follett, was an even more frayed thread in the New Deal than it was in late-1910s conservation.

Some of the writers most important in the development of environmentalism after World War II turned to marginalized aspects of Progressive conservation to help develop positions that were critical both of American environmental profligacy and of the conservation state built by Progressives and New Dealers. Aldo Leopold was a key bridge figure between conservation and what would come (after his untimely death in 1948) to be called "environmentalism." His early career epitomized success at the Pinchotian end of the conservation spectrum: his training as an early graduate of Yale's forestry school led him to work for the Forest Service in Arizona and New Mexico, where his hunting and outdoor exploits earned him recognition by the Boone and Crockett Club. While working in the Southwest, he proposed the creation of formally designated wilderness areas, reflecting the deep hold of the Romantic,

Muirian strain of conservation. Yet he retained his interest in nature as an economically productive force, moving in 1924 to Madison, Wisconsin, to work at the U.S. Forest Products laboratory. Nine years later, he became professor of game management at the University of Wisconsin, assuming the first such professorship in the country. In these positions, he participated at the highest levels in the implementation of Pinchot's dictates of the most efficient use of natural resources: the government would exterminate wolves, mountain lions, grizzly bears, and other predators in order to produce more valuable deer and other game animals, just as it suppressed fires and cut old and undesirable trees in order to produce more timber.

Having mastered this approach early in his career, Leopold then rejected it—or rather, transcended it. Writing in the 1940s, he attributed some of his transformation to an earlier encounter with wolves. He and his companions saw a pack playing down the mountain, and instinctively opened fire on them, since "in those days we had never heard of passing up a chance to kill a wolf." Whatever sense of triumph he felt evaporated when he reached the site and saw "a fierce green fire dying in the eyes" of one of the wolves. "I realized then, and have known ever since," Leopold wrote, "that there was something new to me in those eyes—something known only to her and to the mountain. I was young then, and full of trigger-itch; I thought that because fewer wolves meant more deer, that no wolves would mean hunters' paradise. But after seeing the green fire die, I sensed that neither the wolf nor the mountain agreed with such a view." Later experiences augmented this spiritual awakening, giving him practical reasons to regret the reflexive destruction of predators and the logic behind it: "Since then," Leopold continued, "I have lived to see state after state extirpate its wolves. I have watched the face of many a newly wolfless mountain, and seen the south-facing slopes wrinkle with a maze of new deer trails. I have seen every edible bush and seedling browsed, first to anaemic desuetude, and then to death."[9]

This shift to ecological holism from mechanistic resource manipulation was Leopold's first critical revision of bureaucratic conservationist orthodoxy. It would later be seen as a sensibility that distinguished environmentalism from conservation, but it was also an argument against one strain of conservation based on the premise of another. Leopold's point would have been familiar to Stewart Edward White or to John Muir, whose observation, "When we try to pick out anything by itself, we find it hitched to everything else in the Universe," became a favorite quotation of environmental activists and ecologists decades after Leopold's death. The second important revision that Leopold made similarly harked back to Progressive-era conservation. He forcefully reasserted the importance of culture and ethics in environmental matters. The conservation state painstakingly assembled by Progressives and New Dealers was not so much misguided as inadequate. "Despite nearly a century of propaganda," he wrote, "conservation still proceeds at a snail's pace." As he understood it, the message of orthodox conservation was "obey the law, vote right, join some organizations, and practice what conservation is profitable on your own land; the government will do the rest." Leopold instead maintained that true conservation was beyond the reach of state power, since conventional conservation "tends to relegate to government many functions eventually too large, too complex, or too widely dispersed to be performed by the government." Instead, he argued, the modern world needed a culture and ethics that fostered judiciousness, humility, and values higher than mere economic efficiency. Just as the nineteenth-century Audubon Society both sponsored legislation and stigmatized the wearing of bird hats, just as W. J. McGee proclaimed a "cult of conservation," so could what Leopold called a "land ethic" take conservation to places where the state could not.[10]

The science writer Rachel Carson was, if anything, even more influential than Leopold. Her seminal book *Silent Spring* (1962)—once called the "Uncle Tom's Cabin of environmentalism"—was more oriented toward criticizing environmentally destructive chemicals than the conservation state, but like Leopold she refitted aspects of Progressive conservation to meet newer environmental problems. The powerful opening passages of *Silent Spring* reflected her indebtedness to Dallas Lore Sharp and other poets of the subtle beauties and natural pleasures of suburban life. "There was once a town in the heart of America," she wrote, "where all life seemed to live in harmony with its surroundings. The town lay in the midst of a checkerboard of prosperous farms, with fields of grain and hillsides of orchards where, in spring, white cloud of bloom drifted above the green fields." It was into this domesticated landscape, rather than into the remote mountains, forests, and farm fields that preoccupied Leopold, that "a strange blight crept" and the deaths of animals, children, and adults signaled the casting of "some evil spell." Because of it, in much of the country, "spring now comes unheralded by the return of the birds." That spell was cast by DDT and a host of other chemicals, as Carson painstakingly detailed. Her book contained a shocking amount of technical discussion of chemistry for a best seller, which was made possible by how she linked the results of chemical interactions in the food chain with the bodies and neighborhoods of her readers. Carson broke new ground in her focus on the harms of modern chemicals and with her withering critique of the companies and the lax or nonexistent regulations that enabled them, but she did so by tapping into the older validation of the suburban and domestic landscapes as places of natural beauty.[11]

Carson also criticized reductionist scientific thinking and the hubris that often accompanied it. Like Leopold, she was herself a scientist—trained as a marine biologist, she spent her early career in the employ of the U.S. Bureau of Fisheries. "This is an era of specialists," she wrote early in the book, "each of whom sees his own problem and is unaware of or intolerant of the larger frame into which it fits." The solution was not the abandonment of expert knowledge, but rather its integration into a holistic understanding of the ways that plants, animals, and humans were connected in ecosystems. This holism, in turn, fostered an attitude of humility and respect rather than of hubris and domination.[12]

The environmental movement that emerged in the 1960s is generally understood as a break with Progressive conservation in its mass character, skepticism of expertise, and preoccupation with the effects of pollution on humans and nature. Yet contrary to this conventional wisdom, environmentalism, as the influence of Leopold and Carson suggests, was both an extension and a repudiation of Progressive-era conservation. The protection of wild nature spearheaded by Muir experienced a rebirth: the Sierra Club transformed itself into a national organization in the struggle to protect iconic places such as the Grand Canyon from damming, and wilderness advocates succeeded in passing the Wilderness Act of 1964, creating a formal system for defining and protecting wilderness areas, which by 2009 had reached just shy of 110

million acres. Appreciation for the more quotidian beauty of the suburbs also continued in environmentalism, leading to protests against development on open space, the pollution of water supplies, and the spray-
ing of insecticides. The strong legal protections for threatened species
created by the Endangered Species Act of 1973 offered a comprehensive
version of the bird-protection campaigns that the Audubon Society and
others waged in the late nineteenth century. Environmentalists saw cultural changes—the return to natural and organic foods, the validation
of authenticity over superficiality, ecological education—as important
means to their ends. The sensibility peddled in the *Whole Earth Catalogue* was not so different from the promises of the bungalow or the bird-
less hat. And their movement was part of a larger opening in American
culture and politics: like its Progressive forebear, it floated on the tides
of feminism and deep hostility to corporate power.[13]

Environmentalism also differed from conservation in important
ways. It inherited much of Leopold's and Carson's hostility to narrow,
technocratic thinking, but little of Pinchotian conservation's validation
of scientific expertise. In large part this was because by the 1960s the
increasing mastery over nature delivered by scientific progress looked
more ominous than emancipatory. Unlocking the secret of the atom
was an astounding achievement for state-sponsored science, but one
that gave humanity the dubious gift of the power of self-destruction.
The synthesis of artificial substances such as DDT led to a host of environmental and health issues. Amid mounting concerns over radio-
active fallout, nuclear annihilation, and the spread of toxins through
ecosystems and human bodies, Gifford Pinchot's declaration that "the
first duty of the human race is to control the earth it lives upon" seemed
more like madness than wisdom.[14]

In addition to being more pessimistic about scientific expertise,
environmentalism was generally broader than conservation in its understanding of the problems that it confronted. Warnings about toxic
pollution and health threats dated back to the Progressive era, but
played virtually no role in conservation. Postwar environmentalists
added the protection of humans from a range of hazards such as pollution and toxic chemicals to questions of the protection of wild spaces
and animals. As with the rise of the term "conservation" in 1907, the 1964

proliferation of the term "environment" to describe this movement was revealing. Environmental politics had departed enough from Progressive conservation to warrant its own name.[15]

Yet in an important sense, environmentalism was narrower than conservation: conservation had included a deep interest in economic development, particularly the sensible expansion of agriculture in places once too dry to grow crops, the sustainable production of timber, and the integration of the wider natural world into the lives of cities. Environmentalism was much more about constraints on development, and environmentalists often found themselves at odd with the parts of the environmental state, particularly the Forest Service and the Bureau of Reclamation, designed to foster the sustainable use of natural resources. And this wave of environmental reform had much less invested in cities than did the Progressives.

The environmental organizations renewed or born in the 1960s did a poor job of addressing the concerns or incorporating the activism of nonwhites, even as the civil rights revolution brought African Americans, Latinos, Native Americans, and others increased political power. Almost all the membership and leadership of mainline environmental groups such as the Sierra Club remained white. A growing number of critics charged that this contributed to their general neglect of toxic threats that disproportionately targeted people of color, in favor of a traditional focus on the protection of charismatic species and wild places. Chapters of these groups in major cities ignored or rebuffed smaller grassroots efforts, such as calls from South Central Los Angeles and the city's Chinatown for the creation of neighborhood parks. Some of these activists coined the term "environmental racism" to signify racially disproportionate exposures to environmental hazards and the exclusion of nonwhites from environmental decision making. Large protests in North Carolina against toxic waste landfills in an overwhelmingly African American area galvanized African American civil rights organizations, just as parallel movements in Los Angeles did for Latino groups, helping elevate Benjamin Chavis, one of the authors of a key study of race and the siting of toxic waste dumps, to the presidency of the NAACP in the early 1990s.[16]

What was dubbed the "environmental justice" movement made

some headway in changing the practices of the environmental state and the concerns of national environmental organizations. Indians were on the leading edge, even before the term "environmental justice" came into wide circulation. The Taos regained exclusive control of their sacred Blue Lake in 1970. Later that decade, the Blackfeet nation secured the waiver of camping and entrance fees for Glacier National Park. Badlands National Park was doubled in size, but the Sioux "retained ownership of all reservation land within the new park boundaries." The Havasupai benefited from a similar arrangement with Grand Canyon National Park, regaining "traditional usage" rights and an outright expansion in the size of their reservation as the park and its portion under wilderness protections grew. In 1994, President Bill Clinton issued an executive order that committed the federal government to "make achieving environmental justice a part of its mission by identifying and addressing . . . disproportionately high and adverse human health of environmental effects of its programs, policies, and activities on minority populations and low-income populations." More than thirty states adopted similar measures. In the 1990s, African Americans and Asian Americans ascended to high positions on the Sierra Club's board. In 2013, the organization bestowed its John Muir Award, its highest honor for "achievement in national or international conservation causes," on the sociologist Robert Bullard, whose work on the siting of toxic waste dumps made him a pioneer of the environmental justice movement.[17]

Bullard, Chavis, and their cohorts understood environmental justice as a challenge to the very white history of American environmentalism. Surely it was: the fact that they could press their claims vigorously reflected the cultural and political achievements of the civil rights revolution. It became an embarrassment and a practical liability for such organizations as the Sierra Club to remain almost entirely white. Environmental justice advocates insisted that those without race and class privilege had their own, distinctive environmental concerns, and that their mobilization and inclusion in larger political movements were necessary for addressing those concerns. On these counts, environmental justice was a new turn for a much older tradition. A century earlier, A. Wilberforce Williams and George Washington Carver forged their own visions of Romantic and utilitarian conservation to meet the needs of urban and rural African Americans. Labor leaders such as Job Harriman and Industrial Workers of the World chapters developed conservation programs to serve the needs of wage laborers. Mira Lloyd Dock and Dana Bartlett, who fought ferociously for access to parks and natural beauty for the most marginalized, and Horace McFarland, who similarly argued with Gifford Pinchot that the "aesthetic side" of conservation in cities ought to be a top priority, surely would have recognized environmental justice as congruent with their own blend of environmental and social justice. Indeed, the efforts in recent decades to restore the Los Angeles River to something resembling a natural channel, with public space and recreation for the residents of some of the city's densest and poorest neighborhoods, were resurrections of plans for the river articulated by Bartlett and others in his circle early in the twentieth century. History may not repeat itself, but it often rhymes.[18]

The achievements of post-1960s environmentalism are legion: dramatic improvements in the air quality of cities, strong and diverse movements for city parks, rapid abatement in lead poisoning, much cleaner water in countless streams and lakes, revitalized wilderness protection, strong legal protection for endangered species, provisions for the amelioration of toxic waste, an abatement of acid rain across most of the country, and the creation of dynamic local and organic farm sectors. Yet older environmental problems continue, joined by newer ones. Hydraulic fracturing causes massive pollution and the poisoning of waterways. Many urbanites lack access to anything resembling natural spaces. The poor, especially poor African Americans, are still disproportionately exposed to air pollution and environmental toxins. Lake Erie once again blooms with algae, fed by runoff from the same sort of wasteful and energy-intensive agriculture that remains dependent on dangerous, lightly regulated chemicals. And climate change threatens a global undoing of many of the local and national achievements of environmentalism.

Addressing these environmental problems will require the resurrection and adoption of central aspects of the conservation movement. The idea that humans can dramatically and adversely change nature because we are so numerous and armed with such powerful technologies has never been more relevant than in the era of climate change. Nor has Progressives' skepticism toward the justice of market outcomes. The unrestrained consumption of fossil fuels may well jeopardize civilization, yet the market continues to reward it handsomely. Moreover, the ability of energy companies to block carbon regulation through enormous campaign donations and by funding bogus science supports the Progressive assumption that concentrated economic power is a threat to political democracy. Such measures as carbon taxes and international agreements to limit greenhouse gas emissions are premised on the idea that state power can tame the excesses of the market, a belief widely shared by Progressives and conservationists as diverse as Gifford Pinchot, Dana Bartlett, and Mira Lloyd Dock.[19]

These environmental problems are about people as much as nature. Any effective remediation will be a triumph of social justice as much as a reflection of respect for nature. Limiting carbon dioxide emissions by burning less fossil fuel, for example, has proved extraordinarily difficult, not only because of the global scale of the issue and the deliberate resistance of much of the oil industry, but also because of the myriad ways in which limiting carbon emissions would forces changes to daily life—how we get to work, shop, heat and cool our homes and workplaces, construct buildings, and grow and raise the plants and animals we eat. Climate change is often described as an environmental issue, but it is just as much an issue of transportation planning, urban design, architecture, agriculture, foodways, campaign finance, and capitalism. As Henry George and Liberty Hyde Bailey argued more than a century ago, there is no line between the social and the environmental.

Protecting endangered species, ameliorating toxic pollution, preserving remaining wild nature, creating places of refuge from the built world of the city, and minimizing and abating climate change will happen, if they do at all, because people pass laws that regulate the market, but also because they awaken and inform their consciences. A better society and better laws depend on better people, as Progressive activists and theorists so acutely observed. Conservation, particularly when shorn of its hubris and animated by a respect for democracy, remains pressingly relevant a century after its heyday.

Timeline: Selected Events in the History of U.S. Conservation

1830s–90s	Periodic cholera epidemics wrack large cities
1847	George Perkins Marsh warns of threats of deforestation, erosion
1860s	Widespread complaints about smell, diseases spread by the Chicago River
1864	George Perkins Marsh publishes *Man and Nature*
1868	John Muir sees Yosemite Valley while hiking the West, an experience that helps make wild nature his lifelong calling
1870s	Euro-Americans using large-gauge rifles rapidly diminish the number of bison
1871	Catastrophic fires kill more than 1,500 in Peshtigo, Wisconsin, and destroy the heart of Chicago
1876	Appalachian Mountain Club founded in Boston to protect and foster the enjoyment of New England mountains and forests
1879	Henry George's *Progress and Poverty* points to connections between urbanization, social inequality, and environmental destruction
1882	Ignatius Donnelly's *Atlantis* invokes a lost world of environmental and social harmony
	The forester Franklin Hough warns of the environmental profligacy of frontier settlers
	Massachusetts's Forest Law allows municipalities to buy and condemn land to protect forests and water supplies
1885	State of New York creates the Adirondacks Forest Preserve, citing the importance of urban water supplies
1886	Harvard zoologist Joel Allen and the American Ornithological Union

warn of the possible extinction of the passenger pigeon, and other bird species

The naturalist William Temple Hornaday warns of the imminent extinction of American bison, fewer than 300 of which survive

1888–97   *Garden and Forest* magazine presents a vision of conservation marked by urban concerns

1890   Congress establishes Yosemite and Sequoia National Parks, which join Yellowstone as the first three such parks

1891   Congress authorizes the creation of forest reserves, which reach 46 million acres by 1900

Trustees of Reservations is founded in Boston to preserve places of natural and historical importance in Massachusetts

1892   The historian Frederick Jackson Turner points to the "closing" of the frontier as the advent of a new age in U.S. history

Sierra Club is founded in San Francisco

1893   Creation of Boston's Metropolitan Park Commission, which becomes a national model of urban park administration

1895   Founding of the Trustees of Scenic and Historical Places and Objects in New York

1899   William Ellsworth Smythe presents utopian vision of irrigation in the West in *The Conquest of Arid America*

1900   Engineers reverse the flow of the Chicago River to carry wastes away from Lake Michigan, the city's water supply

Congress passes the Lacey Act, the first national wildlife legislation, which effectively federalizes state bans on bird and animal killing

Yale School of Forestry is founded

1902   Bernhard Fernow's *Economics of Forestry* documents the rapid rise of market-driven forest exploitation

Reclamation Service is founded, soon brings irrigation water to two million acres

1905   Establishment of the U.S. Forest Service, with Gifford Pinchot as its first head

Founding of the National Association of Audubon Societies

1906   Blue Lake, sacred to Taos Pueblo, is incorporated into the National Forest System

San Francisco earthquake and subsequent fires underscore urban vulnerability, prompt renewed push for a municipal reservoir

1907   Gifford Pinchot makes the word "conservation" a commonplace for the shepherding and preservation of the natural world

Dana Bartlett makes a case for urban conservation in *The Better City*

American Nature Study Society founded

1908   Gifford Pinchot and Theodore Roosevelt convene a national meeting
       of governors on conservation

       Society for Preservation of National Parks established in response to
       effort to dam the Hetch Hetchy Valley in Yosemite National Park

1909   First National Conservation Congress held in Seattle

       Federal conservation domain (national forests, monuments, game
       preserves, and bird reservations) reaches 230 million acres, nearly a
       tenth of national territory

       Gifford Pinchot forms the National Conservation Association, to move
       beyond the narrower focus of the American Forestry Association

       Horace McFarland and Gifford Pinchot explore joining forces to
       found a national conservation association that would address both
       metropolitan and rural landscapes

1910   Boy Scouts of America founded

       Leaders of the American Forestry Association begins to limit women's
       roles

       Extensive forest fires in the West and Midwest challenge the Forest
       Service's credibility

       Ranger Ed Pulaski achieves lasting fame by saving his fire crew

1912   Presidential election includes three candidates—Democrat Woodrow
       Wilson, Progressive Theodore Roosevelt, and Socialist Eugene V.
       Debs—running on strong conservation platforms

1913   Congress authorizes the creation of a reservoir in the Hetch Hetchy
       Valley

1914   Death of Martha, the last known passenger pigeon, in a Cincinnati
       zoo

       Split between Horace McFarland and Gifford Pinchot destroys
       chances for a strong national conservation organization, along the
       lines of the Woman's Christian Temperance Union

       National Fire Prevention Day inaugurated

1915   Liberty Hyde Bailey warns of dangers of alienation from nature in *The
       Holy Earth*

       The landscape architect Wilhelm Miller fuses the politics and culture
       of conservation in landscaping advice to homeowners

1916   Socialist Daniel Hoan elected mayor of Milwaukee, prioritizes urban
       conservation

       Establishment of the National Park Service

1917   Frank Waugh urges homeowners to "capture the spirit of the native
       landscape" in *The Natural Style in Landscape Gardening*

Progressive economist Richard Ely frames conservation as an important part of economic growth in *The Foundations of National Prosperity*

Founding of the Save-the-Redwoods League

United States enters World War I

1920   Stewart Edward White attacks Forest Service policy of fire suppression

Notes

Introduction

1. Cohen, *The Pathless Way;* Fox, *John Muir and His Legacy;* Nash, *Wilderness and the American Mind;* Searle, *Saving Quetico-Superior.*

2. R. White, "Environmental History"; Cronon, "The Trouble with Wilderness"; Langston, *Forest Dreams, Forest Nightmares;* Warren, *Hunter's Game;* Spence, *Dispossessing the Wilderness;* Jacoby, *Crimes Against Nature;* Taylor, *Making Salmon.*

3. For example, Donald Worster's *A Passion for Nature,* a biography of John Muir, ignores the dispossession of Indians and others, which is thoroughly documented by Warren, Spence, and Jacoby.

4. Dawley, *Changing the World;* Flanagan, *America Reformed;* Lears, *Rebirth of a Nation;* McGerr, *A Fierce Discontent;* Rodgers, *Atlantic Crossings.*

5. *The Daily Show with John Stewart,* "Rage Within the Machine—Progressivism."

6. Hays, *Conservation and the Gospel of Efficiency.*

ONE Frontier, Market, and Environmental Crisis

1. Yablon, *Untimely Ruins,* especially 148; for the wild popularity of accounts of Atlantis, see Sachs, *Arcadian America,* 302, 321.

2. Marsh, *Address Delivered Before the Agricultural Society,* 18, 2.

3. Ibid., 18–19.

4. Pinchot, *Breaking New Ground,* xvi; Mumford, *Brown Decades,* 78; Lowenthal, *George Perkins Marsh;* Jacoby, *Crimes Against Nature,* 15.

5. U.S. Forest Service, *Report on Forestry,* 3:231–32; Pyne, *Fire in America,* 204.

6. Quoted in U.S. Forest Service, *Report on Forestry,* 3:233–34.

7. Ibid., 3:234.

8. Smith, *Urban Disorder and Belief,* 22; R. Miller, *American Apocalypse,* 4.

9. U.S. Forest Service, *Report on Forestry*, 3:242; Pyne, *Fire in America*, 200, 216, 60.

10. Quoted in Barrow, *Nature's Ghosts*, 54.

11. Merson, *Passenger Pigeon*, 2.

12. Audubon, *Ornithological Biography*, 320–22, 324; *Indianapolis News* quoted in the *Friends' Intelligencer*, "The Extinct Wild Pigeon," 925.

13. Allen, "Wholesale Destruction of Bird-Life," 191.

14. *Forest and Stream*, "To Save the Passenger Pigeon," 2.

15. Allen, "Wholesale Destruction of Bird-Life," 191.

16. A. Wright, "Martha the Last Passenger Pigeon Dead," 337.

17. Quoted in Isenberg, *Destruction of the Bison*, 23.

18. Flores, "Bison Ecology and Bison Diplomacy."

19. Isenberg, *Destruction of the Bison*, 137.

20. Barrow, *Nature's Ghosts*, 108 (quotation), 115, 118.

21. Quoted in ibid., 120–21.

22. Isenberg, *Destruction of the Bison*, 169; Wrobel, *End of American Exceptionalism*, 22–23; F. Turner, *Rereading Frederick Jackson Turner*, 59.

23. Quoted in Barrow, *Nature's Ghosts*, 121.

24. Weber, *Growth of Cities*, 21–23, 152.

25. Jefferson, *Notes on the State of Virginia*, 274; Strong, *Twentieth-Century City*, 53, 82; Strong, *Our Country*, 43, 129, 141–42.

26. Foreman, *Recreation Needs of Chicago*, 9; Hunter, *Tenement Conditions in Chicago*, 49–50.

27. Steinberg, *Down to Earth*, 162–63; Taylor, *Environment and People in Cities*, 82–83; Weber, *Growth of Cities*, 355; McNeill, *Something New Under the Sun*, 282; Preston and Haines, *Fatal Years*, 55. This calculation of life expectancy is based on data from New England, New York, Pennsylvania, Michigan, Indiana, and the District of Columbia.

28. H. Platt, *Shock Cities*, 142–44; quotation (with ellipses) on 144.

29. Hunter, *Tenement Conditions in Chicago*, 181–82.

30. Rodgers, *Atlantic Crossings*, 112; Strong, introduction, 6.

31. Rodgers, *Atlantic Crossings*, 112–14.

32. George, *Progress and Poverty*, 254; Bryson, *Economics of Henry George*, 192; Sachs, *Arcadian America*, 225–27, 279–81.

33. George, *Progress and Poverty*, 9, 7, 33; Lipin, "Nature, the City, and the Family Circle."

34. George, *Social Problems*, 309.

35. Ibid., 310.

36. Marsh, *Man and Nature*, 44; Kinney, *Forest and Water*, 80, 82.

37. Yablon, *Untimely Ruins*, 148.

38. Ibid., 163–65; London, *The Iron Heel*, 334–42.

39. George, *Social Problems*, 7–8.

40. "National People's Party Platform," 83; Sachs, *Arcadian America*, 300–301; Donnelly, *Caesar's Column*.

41. Donnelly, *Atlantis*, 17, 157; Sachs, *Arcadian America*, 302, 305–6.

42. Donnelly, *Atlantis*, 198; Sachs, *Arcadian America*, 321; R. Williams, *Triumph of the Human Empire*, 77; Verne, *Paris in the Twentieth Century*.

43. Buchanan, "Coming Cataclysm of American and Europe," 304–5.

44. Ibid., 300, 304, 312.

45. Pernin, "The Finger of God Is There," 159.

46. U.S. Forest Service, *Report on Forestry*, 3:207.

47. Allen, "Wholesale Destruction of Bird-Life," 191; Judd, *Common Lands, Common People*, 93–95.

48. R. Williams, *Triumph of the Human Empire*, ix; see also Osterhammel, *Transformation of the World*, 375–91.

49. U.S. Forest Service, *Report on Forestry*, 3:130 (Hough was the principal author of the report).

50. Allen, "Wholesale Destruction of Bird-Life," 192.

51. George, *Social Problems*, 8.

52. George, *Progress and Poverty*, 313, 389.

53. Ibid., 359–61; Sachs, *Arcadian America*, 276.

54. Fernow, *Economics of Forestry*, 1–2.

55. Ibid., 372–73.

56. Hornaday, *Wild Life Conservation*, 6, 1, 7; Barrow, *Nature's Ghosts*, 7.

57. Hornaday, *Wild Life Conservation*, 8–9 (emphasis in original); Hornaday, *Our Vanishing Wild Life*, 14.

TWO Landscapes of Reform

1. "Plan the Preservation of Appalachian Forests," *Atlanta Constitution*, January 16, 1908; Drummond, *Enos Mills*, 190, 195.

2. Drummond, *Enos Mills*, 197.

3. Rimby, "'Better Housekeeping Out of Doors,'" 13–14; Rimby, *Mira Lloyd Dock*, 17, 21; Wild, *Street Meeting*, 73–74; James, *Birthday Book*, n.p.

4. Bartlett, *The Better City*; Bartlett, *The Better Country*; Bartlett, *The Bush Aflame*; Hou, *The City Natural*, 2, 29, 41, 71, 78, 135, 159.

5. Bartlett, *Better City*, 17.

6. Bartlett, *Better City*, 37; Dock quoted in Rimby, *Mira Lloyd Dock*, 37; McFarland, "Value of Natural Scenery," 66.

7. Rawson, *Eden on the Charles*, 262, 264; Hou, *City Natural*, 82; Bartlett, *Better City*, 17, 32, 34; Gumphrecht, *Los Angeles River*, 116–17.

8. Young, *Building San Francisco's Parks*, xi; Rawson, *Eden on the Charles*, 264, 270; Grese, "Jens Jensen," 131; Cranz, *Politics of Park Design*, 85–93; Griffith, *Parks, Boulevards, and Playgrounds*, 15.

9. Rawson, *Eden on the Charles*, 270; Griffith, *Parks, Boulevards, and Playgrounds*, 7.

10. Quoted in Rimby, *Mira Lloyd Dock*, 2; Bartlett, *Better City*, 17, 35; Stroud, *Nature Next Door*, 50, 54, 73.

11. Klingle, *Emerald City*, 162–63; Melosi, *Sanitary City*, 117.

12. Rawson, *Eden on the Charles,* 249; Stradling, *Nature of New York,* 102; Kinney, *Forest and Water,* 22, 93; Stroud, *Nature Next Door,* 46; Lukens, *Forestry in Relation to City Building,* 5.

13. Kinney, *Forest and Water,* 93;

14. Worster, *Passion for Nature,* 332.

15. Ibid., 111–14, 383–84; Sachs, *Humboldt Current,* 313–14, 317; Muir, *My First Summer in the Sierras,* 280.

16. Worster, *Passion for Nature,* 321, 327, 349; Robbins, *Our Landed Heritage,* 305; Gates, *Public Land Law Development,* 580.

17. Worster, *Passion for Nature,* 329; Hou, *City Natural,* 79; Rawson, *Eden on the Charles,* 249; Stradling, *Nature of New York,* 102.

18. Muir, *Our National Parks,* iv, 335–36, 2, 340; Worster, *Passion for Nature,* 372.

19. Sachs, *Humboldt Current,* 314–16; Muir, *Our National Parks,* 335, 1.

20. Muir, *Our National Parks,* 337.

21. Worster, *Passion for Nature,* 351–52; C. Miller, *Gifford Pinchot and the Making of Modern Environmentalism,* 23, 55, 68, 71.

22. C. Miller, *Gifford Pinchot,* 92–94.

23. Ibid., 196, 156; Worster, *Passion for Nature,* 353–54; Robbins, *Our Landed Heritage,* 349; Gates, *Public Land Law Development,* 580; Schulman, "Governing Nature, Nurturing Government."

24. Pinchot, *Fight for Conservation,* 6, 10, 4.

25. Tyrell, *Crisis of the Wasteful Nation,* 14, 18, 21, 34, 48.

26. Hays, *Conservation and Efficiency,* 2, 69; Tyrrell, *Crisis of the Wasteful Nation,* 14, 30, 34; Pinchot, *Fight for Conservation,* 1, 4.

27. Pinchot, *Fight for Conservation,* 26, 43–45.

28. Rawson, *Eden on the Charles,* 235, 252–57.

29. Ibid., 257; Stradling, *Nature of New York,* 104.

30. Saunders, *Under the Sky in California,* 50, preface, 68, 101. For a discussion of the wider phenomena of place making and (largely invented) Native histories, see Farmer, *On Zion's Mount,* 322.

31. Saunders, *Southern Sierras of California,* 74, 102, 341, 357, 90.

32. Bailey, *Holy Earth,* 1, 118.

33. U.S. Country Life Commission, *Report of the Commission,* 31, 34; Danbom, *Resisted Revolution,* 43–44.

34. Danbom, *Resisted Revolution,* 43–46; for a rejoinder, see Peters and Morgan, "Country Life Commission," 292, 298; Bailey, *Holy Earth,* 2.

35. Bailey, *Holy Earth,* 2–3; Cronon, *Nature's Metropolis,* 256–57; Benjamin Johnson, "Environment."

36. U.S. Department of Commerce, *Historical Statistics of the United States, 1789–1945,* 25; Peters and Morgan, "Country Life Commission," 292, 303; Bailey, *Holy Earth,* 23, 27. For the contrast between nostalgia as an antireform sensibility and historical memory, see Lasch, *True and Only Heaven,* 82–83.

37. Bailey quoted in Kates, "Liberty Hyde Bailey," 214; Sellers, *Crabgrass Crucible*, 17–22.

38. Minteer, "Regional Planning as Pragmatic Conservationism," 95–100; Steele, *Ecological Architecture*, 51–55; Rodgers, *Atlantic Crossings*, 33.

39. Howard, *Garden Cities of To-morrow*, 17–18, 113.

40. *California Outlook*, "Forward to the Land," 5.

41. Pinchot, *Fight for Conservation*, 31.

42. Smythe, *Conquest of Arid America*, 330, 46.

43. Saunders, *Under the Sky in California*, 212–13, 6.

44. Saunders, *Southern Sierras of California*, 206; Saunders, *With the Flowers and Trees in California*, 246. For a similar argument about the blend of human artifice and natural beauty, see Olmsted Brothers, *Development of Public Grounds for Baltimore*, 33; for an exploration of this tradition of blending wild and cultural landscapes, see Simo, *Forest and Garden*. The environmental sensibility of the Olmsted brothers and Saunders indicates that not all nature writers or conservationists lived in thrall to the idea that nature was a stable, timeless entity that existed outside human history, as William Cronon argues; see Cronon's introduction to *Uncommon Ground* and his essay "The Trouble with Wilderness" in the same volume, especially 25–56, 80.

45. Orth, "Directing Nature's Creative Forces," 202, 204; Gardner, "Constructing a Technological Forest," 284; Lukens, *Forestry in Relation to City Building*, 22.

46. Pisani, *To Reclaim a Divided West*, 322; Fiege, *Irrigated Eden*, 45, 23; John Muir to Lukens, June 21, 1900, and Lukens to Miner, October 14, 1910, box 2, Theodore Parker Lukens Papers (hereafter Lukens Papers); Gardner, "Constructing a Technological Forest," 288, 292.

47. Bartlett, *Better Country*, 166–67.

48. Stern, *Eugenic Nation*, 121, 124.

49. Spiro, *Defending the Master Race*, xiii, 391–92; Grant, *Passing of the Great Race*, 50–51; Farmer, *Trees in Paradise*, 68–72.

50. Kinney, *Conquest of Death*, vii; National Conservation Congress, *Proceedings of the Congress*, 274–75 (Scott quotation); Brechin, "Conserving the Race," 237–38. Stern, *Eugenic Nation*, esp. 148; Kosek, *Understories*, 152–54.

51. H. H. Laughlin to Gifford Pinchot, February 6, 1912; Pinchot to Laughlin, February 9, 1912, Gifford Pinchot Papers (hereafter GP Papers), box 153.

52. Dorr, "Fighting Fire with Fire"; Bartlett, *Better City*, 112–13; Bartlett, *Better Country*, 364–65.

53. For an argument to the contrary—that eugenics is an "apparition" that "sits restlessly at the heart of American environmentalism"—see Stern, *Eugenic Nation*, 148.

54. Sachs, *Arcadian America*, 23, 333; Hickman, "John Muir's Orchard Home," 335–36, 360.

55. Rosenzweig and Blackmar, *The Park and the People*, 131; Rybczynski, *Clearing in the Distance*, 257–58; Simo, *Forest and Garden*, xi.

56. Sachs, *Arcadian America*, 192–93; *Wikipedia*, s.v., "Frederick Law Olmsted,"

accessed May 29, 2015; Rybczynski, *Clearing in the Distance,* 406–8; Simo, *Forest and Garden,* 137–38, 148, 155.

57. Muir, *Our National Parks,* 362; Pinchot, *Fight for Conservation,* 114–15.

58. Rawson, *Eden on the Charles,* 252; Bartlett, *Better City,* 44–45, 166.

59. Muir, *Our National Parks,* 365; Pinchot, *Fight for Conservation,* 84, 46–47.

60. Smythe, *Conquest of Arid America,* 43, 61; Bartlett, *Better City,* 190.

61. Price, "Thirteen Ways of Seeing Nature in L.A."

62. Cronon, "Trouble with Wilderness"; Price, "Thirteen Ways of Seeing Nature in L.A."; Shellenberger and Nordhaus, "Death of Environmentalism"; Kosek, *Understories,* 155; DeLuca and Demo, "Imagining Nature and Erasing Class and Race"; and Lovett, *Conceiving the Future,* 111–14, 124.

63. Rawson, *Eden on the Charles,* 257; Tyrrell, *True Gardens of the Gods,* 39, 138; Tyrrell, *Crisis of the Wasteful Nation,* 108–9.

THREE Back to Nature

1. McGee, "Conservation of Natural Resources," 376; Armitage, *Nature Study Movement,* 10.

2. Canby quoted in Shi, *Simple Life,* 214; Canby, "Back to Nature," 756; Willcox, "Outdoor Books," 116, 119.

3. U.S. Forest Service, *Vacation Land of Lakes and Woods,* 3.

4. Schmitt, *Back to Nature,* 155; Carr, *Wilderness by Design,* 63.

5. Klingle, *Emerald City,* 168; Shi, *Simple Life,* 205, 207.

6. *Sierra Club Bulletin,* "Memorial," 63.

7. Beard quoted in Jordan, "'Conservation of Boyhood,'" 616.

8. Ibid., 616, 618–23.

9. Quoted in Lipin, *Workers and the Wild,* 91–92, 97, 44. For more evidence of the appreciation of accessible parks by working-class urbanites (and also the attendant class tensions), see Klingle, *Emerald City,* 125, 129, 136.

10. *Western Comrade,* "Nature's Banquet Table," April 1913, 25.

11. Saunders, *Under the Sky in California,* 50; Muir, "San Gabriel Mountains," 149; John Muir to Theodore Parker Lukens, November 12, 1897, Lukens Papers, box 2. For the paradox of consumption and protection, see Klingle, *Emerald City,* 178–79.

12. Armitage, "'Child Is Born a Naturalist,'" 8, 4; Armitage, *Nature Study Movement,* 62, 7; A. Comstock, *Handbook of Nature-Study,* 1; Scott, *Nature Study and the Child,* 123.

13. Scott, *Nature Study and the Child,* 126; Armitage, *Nature Study Movement,* 38.

14. Armitage, *Nature Study Movement,* 26.

15. Cooke, *Girl Who Lived in the Woods,* 70.

16. Garland, *Cavanagh,* 175–76; Garland, *Son of the Middle Border,* 172.

17. Garland, *Cavanagh,* 267.

18. Ibid., 152.

19. Stratton-Porter, *Freckles,* 23; Green, "'She Touched Fifty Million Lives,'" 221, 228, 232.

20. Stratton-Porter, *Freckles,* 151.

21. Stratton-Porter, "My Life and My Books," 13.

22. Goss, "Ever-Popular Bungalow," 6; King, *Bungalow,* 130; F. Wright, "Home in a Prairie Town," 17; De Long, *Frank Lloyd Wright,* 178–80.

23. King, *Bungalow,* 134–35, Stickley quoted on 134; Boris, *Art and Labor,* xi; see also Burges Johnson, "Bungal-Ode," and Ore, *The Seattle Bungalow,* 28–29.

24. Ore, *Seattle Bungalow,* 36–39.

25. De Wit, "Apartment Houses and Bungalows"; Stickley quoted in King, *Bungalow,* 145.

26. Bartlett, *Better City,* 18.

27. Steele, *Ecological Architecture,* 78; Schindler quoted in Gebhardt, *Schindler,* 48, 192.

28. Carr, *Wilderness by Design,* 62, 122; Harrison, *Architecture in the Parks,* introduction; Hubbard and Kimball, *Study of Landscape Design,* 189–90.

29. Saunders, *Under the Sky in California,* 238–39, 244.

30. Gisel, *Kindred and Related Spirits,* 268–69; Saunders, *Story of Carmelita.*

31. Paddock, *Keeper of the Wild,* 29, 30, 144, 244; Driapsa, "Cultural Landscape of Mallard Island," 7–8.

32. *California Outlook* 13, no. 12 (September 14, 1912), 2.

33. *California Outlook* 13, no. 11 (September 7, 1912), 12.

34. See *California Outlook* 13, no. 4 (July 20, 1912), 23, for the ad's first appearance.

35. Ibid.

36. Shi, *Simple Life,* 182–83; Stilgoe, *Borderland,* 192, 196, 219; Saylor, *Bungalows,* 54, 62; Gill quoted in Hines, *Irving Gill,* 11; Banham, *Los Angeles,* 43–47.

37. Tyrrell, *True Gardens of the Gods,* 13, 66–67; Kinney, *Forest and Water;* Kinney, *Eucalyptus* 24, 131, 50; Farmer, *Trees in Paradise,* 134–35.

38. Saunders, *Under the Sky in California,* 212–13, 6.

39. W. Miller, *Prairie Spirit in Landscape Gardening,* frontispiece, 1, 5, 20–22.

40. Ibid., 6.

41. Waugh, *Natural Style in Landscape Gardening,* 32, 129–30; Carr, *Wilderness by Design,* 99.

42. Sharp, *Lay of the Land,* 114–15.

43. Ibid., 209.

44. McGee, "Conservation of Natural Resources," 378; A. Comstock, "Conservation and Nature-Study," 299; see also Hornaday, *Our Vanishing Wild Life,* vii.

45. Weyl, *New Democracy,* 319. For similar discussions by key Progressive intellectuals, see Gladden, *New Idolatry,* 209–10.

FOUR Fighting for Conservation

1. Pinchot, *Fight for Conservation,* 41, 132.

2. Gifford Pinchot to Gilbert Rogers, December 23, 1907, GP Papers, box 109; Horace McFarland to Gifford Pinchot, October 18, 1909, McFarland Papers, box 119; Horace McFarland to Lawrence Abbott, March 3, 1911, McFarland Papers, box 16; James Moser to Pinchot, January 25, 1910, GP Papers, box 135, folder 4.

3. The National Park Service calculates that 230 million acres of public land was put under the administration of conservation bureaucracies during the Theodore Roosevelt administration. The United States has a national territory of 3.79 million square miles, and since there are 640 acres per square mile, just under 10 percent of the nation's territory was thus administered; see https://www.nps.gov/thro/learn/historyculture/theodore-roosevelt-and-conservation.htm (accessed May 13, 2016); see also Brinkley, *Wilderness Warrior*, esp. 777–79; Gates, *Public Land Law Development*, 580; U.S. Department of the Interior, *Reports of the Department of Interior*, 107; U.S. Reclamation Service, *Nineteenth Annual Report of the Reclamation Service.*

4. Fernow, *Economics of Forestry*; Ely et al., *Foundations of National Prosperity*, 3, 11–12; Rodgers, *Atlantic Crossings*, 77, 102.

5. Pinchot, *Fight for Conservation*; Van Hise, *Conservation of Natural Resources*, v; Worster, *Passion for Nature*, 160; Hornaday, *Our Vanishing Wild Life*, 1.

6. Ely, *Foundations of National Prosperity*, 14–15; Fernow, *Economics of Forestry*, 1.

7. Filene, "Obituary for 'The Progressive Movement,'" 24; DeWitt, *Progressive Movement*, 186, 163; Bates, "Fulfilling American Democracy."

8. *New York Times*, "Music Heard Yesterday" and "Future of the State's Forests."

9. *New York Times*, "Western Civilization."

10. Du Bois, *Conservation of Races*, 10.

11. *New York Times*, "Future of the State's Forests"; *Chicago Daily Tribune*, "Will Discuss Outdoor Art."

12. Pinchot, *Breaking New Ground*, 322, 326.

13. Hays, *Conservation and Efficiency*, 179. The frequency of the term's use was calculated with a ProQuest search of the *New York Times* and *Chicago Tribune* for the use of the word "conservation" from 1890 to 1920; ProQuest database accessed April 8, 2012.

14. Babson, "Famous Panics of America."

15. Nathan to Pinchot, December 8, 1910, GP Papers, box 135, folder 7; Weyl, *New Democracy*, 320.

16. Pinchot, *Fight For Conservation*, 49–50.

17. Rix, "Gender and Reconstitution," 212; Minnesota State Board of Control, *Proceedings*, 30; American Child Hygiene Association, *Transactions*; Lansing, "'Salvaging the Man Power of America,'" 35.

18. English to Pinchot, February 28, 1911, GP Papers, box 144, folder 10; Lansing, "'Salvaging the Man Power of America,'" 36; Vessey quoted in National Conservation Congress, *Proceedings of the Third Congress*, 111; H. Mock, "Human Conservation and Reclamation," 8.

19. Rome, "Nature Wars, Culture Wars," 432–33; Scudder, *Listener in Babel*, 71.

20. Bartlett, *Bush Aflame*, 101.

21. Gompers quoted in *Proceedings of a Conference of Governors*, 399, 401–2; Lansing, "'Salvaging the Man Power of America,'" 35.

22. Collier, "Leisure Time," 94, 104.

23. Gompers, "Conservation of Natural Resources," 535.

24. McFarland to William Badé, October 4, 1909, McFarland Papers, box 16; Pinchot, *Breaking New Ground,* 33; Tyrell, *Crisis of the Wasteful Nation,* 156.

25. McFarland to Pinchot, November 26, 1909, GP Papers, box 468; Pinchot to McFarland, November 24, 1909, ibid.; Hays, *Conservation and Efficiency,* 138.

26. Merriam, *American Political Ideals,* 306; Follett, *New State,* 1; more generally, see Mattson, *Creating a Democratic Public.*

27. Skocpol, Ganz, and Munson, "Nation of Organizers," 541; Tocqueville quoted in Gramm and Putnam, "Voluntary Associations in America," 512; Balogh, *Government Out of Sight,* 353.

28. Tichenor and Harris, "Organized Interests and Political Development," 307–8; Merriam, *American Political Ideals,* 308.

29. McFarland to Pinchot, January 19, 1910, GP Papers, box 465.

30. Adams-Williams, "Conservation," 350; Unger, *Beyond Nature's Housekeepers,* 83.

31. Rome, "'Political Hermaphrodites,'" 443; Merchant, "Women of the Conservation Movement, 1900–1916," 64, 59; Rimby, "'Better Housekeeping Out of Doors,'" 13, 14, 19; Conrad, *Places of Quiet Beauty,* 26–30.

32. Merchant, "Women of the Conservation Movement," 63; Rome, "'Political Hermaphrodites,'" 441; Adams-Williams, "Conservation," 351; Pinchot, *Fight for Conservation,* 104–5.

33. Merchant, "Grinnell's Audubon Society," 18; Price, *Flight Maps,* 64.

34. Adams-Williams, "Conservation," 351.

35. Price, *Flight Maps,* 98–99; Adams-Williams, "Conservation," 351.

36. Quoted in Bederman, *Manliness and Civilization,* 186; quoted in Nash, *Wilderness and the American Mind,* 150.

37. Jordan, "'Conservation of Boyhood,'" 619; Smalley, "'Our Lady Sportsmen,'" 356–57; "Rome, "'Political Hermaphrodites,'" 441.

38. Hays, *Conservation and Efficiency,* 123–24; McGee, "Water as a Resource," quoted in ibid., 124.

39. Des Jardins, *Madame Curie Complex;* Gottlieb, *Forcing the Spring,* 47–51, 216–17.

40. Grant, *Passing of the Great Race,* xx, 263.

41. Tyrell, *True Garden of the Gods,* 39; Lovett, *Conceiving the Future;* Southern, *Progressive Era and Race,* 47; Beveridge quoted in Leuchtenburg, "Progressivism and Imperialism," 484.

42. Ely, *Foundations of National Prosperity,* 58.

43. Wright quoted in Armitage, *Nature-Study Movement,* 128; Jacoby, *Crimes Against Nature,* 175.

44. Johnston, "Re-Democratizing the Progressive Era," 84; Benjamin Johnson, *Revolution in Texas,* 42–48; Maddox, *Citizen Indian,* 9–12.

45. Blum, "Women, Environmental Rationale, and Activism," 79, 90; Williams quoted in Fisher, "African Americans, Outdoor Recreation," 69.

46. Fisher, ""African Americans, Outdoor Recreation," 70; A. Williams, "Keep Healthy," 7.

47. Washington to Pinchot, June 2, 1908, GP Papers, box 118; Armitage, *Nature-Study Movement*, 131–33.

48. Hersey, *My Work Is Conservation*, 107, 219; Hersey, "Hints and Suggestions to Farmers," 240, 246, 248, 251.

49. Commercial Club of Minneapolis and St. Paul, *Memorial and Appeal*, n.p.; Clar, *California Government and Forestry*, 104, 172, 268–69, 544–45, 397; Sargeant, *Theodore Parker Lukens*, 58; Lockmann, "Forests and Watershed," 84; *Pacific Outlook*, "Pinchot Warns Us Against Predatory Interests," 6.

50. Copy of address enclosed in J. B. White to Gifford Pinchot, September 13, 1910, GP Papers, box 467.

51. Runte, *National Parks*, 44–45, 83, 100; Hill, *Highways of Progress*, 6, 9, 287; Worster, "Muir and the Passion for Nature," 16.

52. Stickney, *New Comers*, n.p. For Stickney's deep conservatism on major economic and political questions of the day, see Stickney, *Economic Problems*.

53. Quoted in *From Pueblo to City*, 68.

54. Letterhead of Forest and Water Society of Los Angeles County [1900], Lukens Papers, box 1, folder 10; *Pacific Outlook*, "Judge Silent's Report on Parks," 7; *A History of California and an Extended History of Los Angeles and Environs*, 2:456–57.

55. Runte, *National Parks*, 100; McFarland, "Value of Natural Scenery," 66, 68.

56. Wirth, *Minneapolis Park System*, 20; Klingle, *Emerald City*, 129; Lipin, *Workers and the Wild*, 3, 46, 52, 61, 66.

57. *The Lumber Industry and Its Workers*, 48–49, 86.

58. McGuinness, "Revolution Begins Here," 84, 90; Whitehall quoted in J. McCarthy, "Dreaming of a Decentralized Metropolis," 46; L. Platt, "Planning Ideology and Geographic Thought," 782–83.

59. Stevens, "Mother Earth," 24.

60. *Western Comrade*, "Nature's Banquet Table," 25; Harriman, "Making Dreams Come True," 54–56.

FIVE Fighting over Conservation

1. McFarland to Lawrence Abbott, January 12, 1914, McFarland Papers, box 16; McFarland to Charles Sargent, October 27, 1913, McFarland Papers, box 17; Pinchot to Olmsted, December 26, 1912, GP Papers, box 473.

2. McFarland, "Are National Parks Worth While?," 237.

3. Ibid.; McFarland to Pinchot, February 13, 1911, GP Papers, box 142, folder 3.

4. Charles Eliot to Pinchot, October 5, 1910, GP Papers, box 457.

5. C. Miller, *Gifford Pinchot*, 108–10; Gifford Pinchot to Horace McFarland, March 4, 1911, GP Papers, box 142, folder 3.

6. Muir, "Hetch Hetchy Valley," 214, quoted in Righter, *Battle over Hetch Hetchy*, 18 (Whitney quotation), 49.

7. Righter, *Battle over Hetch Hetchy*, 39, 41.

8. Ibid., 72, 74, 75, 85; Muir, "Hetch Hetchy Valley," 211.

9. U.S. House of Representatives, Committee on the Public Lands, *Hetch Hetchy Dam Site*, 25–29; C. Miller, *Gifford Pinchot*, 141.

10. Hyde, "William Kent," 36–39, 47, 52; Runte, *National Parks*, 148.

11. Olmsted quoted in Morrison, *J. Horace McFarland*, 170.

12. Hyde, "William Kent," 52; Winks, "National Park Service Act," 18.

13. Muir, "Hetch Hetchy Valley," 211; Righter, *Battle over Hetch Hetchy*, 92; Manson quoted in Clements, "Engineers and Conservationists," 284, 294–95.

14. Righter, *Battle over Hetch Hetchy*, 67, 84.

15. Richard Watrous to McFarland, March 21, 1913, McFarland Papers, box 16.

16. Muir, *Our National Parks*, 1–2; Worster, *Passion for Nature*, 276–304; Hickman, "John Muir's Orchard Home," 340–42.

17. Sharp, *Face of the Fields*, 24–25; Lytle, *Gentle Subversive*, 31.

18. Sharp, *Face of the Fields*, 239, 236.

19. Sharp, *Lay of the Land*, 114, 39, 46; Sharp, *Face of the Fields*, 230.

20. Bartlett, *Better Country*, 191, 135, 40; Bartlett, *Better City*, 26; Sharp, *Face of the Fields*, 234.

21. Rome, "'Political Hermaphrodites,'" 450–51; *American Forestry*, "Women's Clubs and the Forests," 363.

22. Rome, "'Political Hermaphrodites,'" 451; Merchant, "Women of the Conservation Movement," 77; Hays, *Conservation and Efficiency*, 178–79.

23. Merchant, "Women of the Conservation Movement," 76; Rome, "'Political Hermaphrodites,'" 451–52.

24. Rome, "'Political Hermaphrodites,'" 451; Drummond, *Enos Mills*, 183, 186; Draper to Pinchot, October 23, 1909, GP Papers, box 468.

25. Pinchot, *Breaking New Ground*, 27; Merchant, "Women of the Progressive Movement," 78; Rome, "'Political Hermaphrodites,'" 441, 450.

26. C. Miller, *Gifford Pinchot*, 255, 259, 265, 288–89.

27. Ibid., 228; Horace McFarland to William Colby, March 22, 1913, McFarland Papers, box 16; Hays, *Conservation and Efficiency*, 180–82; McGeart, *Gifford Pinchot*, 200.

28. Ishii, "'Not a Wigwam Nor Blanket Nor Warhoop.'"

29. Binkley, "'No Better Heritage than Living Trees,'" 182, 191, 193, 196–97.

30. Righter, *Battle over Hetch Hetchy*, 82–83.

31. Morrison, *J. Horace McFarland*, 174; U.S. House of Representatives, Committee on the Public Lands, *Hearings on HR 434 and HR 8668*, 11.

32. *U.S. Statutes at Large*, "An Act to Establish a National Park Service, and for Other Purposes"; Righter, *Battle over Hetch Hetchy*, 194–95; Merchant, "Women of the Conservation Movement," 79.

33. McFarland quoted in Morrison, *J. Horace McFarland*, 181–82.

34. Foreman, "Recreation Needs of Chicago," 5, 6, 9.

35. Ibid., 8, 10.

36. Keith, *Pipes o' Pan in a City Park*, 11–12.

37. Ibid., 77–78.

38. Ibid., 78, 92; on Keith and the class dynamics surrounding Minneapolis parks, see Murray, "Making a Model Metropolis," esp. 302–4.

39. Erie, "How the Urban West Was Won," 520, 547–48; Dear, "In the City, Time Becomes Visible," 94; Culver, *Frontier of Leisure.*

40. Minutes, Los Angeles Board of Park Commissioners, July 5, 1910, March 21, 1911, November 13, 1911, December 11, 1911, April 22, 1912, L.A. City Archive; *Pacific Outlook,* "Parks by Assessment," 3.

41. Wild, *Street Meeting,* 155–57; Greenstein, Lennon, and Rolfe, *Bread and Hyacinths,* 37.

42. Cooke, *Girl Who Lived in the Woods,* 214.

43. Ibid., 288–89, 125.

44. Smalley, "'Our Lady Sportsmen,'" 361 (Hallock quotation), 364.

45. Price, *Flight Maps,* 79–80; Boy Scouts' *Handbook* (1914 ed.) quoted in Jordan, "'Conservation of Boyhood,'" 629; Boy Scouts of America, *Official Handbook for Boys* (1919 ed.), 227–28.

SIX Fighting Against Conservation

1. Ise, *United States Forest Policy,* 161–62, 196; Richardson, *Politics of Conservation,* 89–90, 99–101.

2. *Proceedings of the Public Land Convention,* 48; Eddy, *Conservation Alarms,* 1. Thanks to Allison Bryant for calling Eddy to my attention.

3. Robbins, *Our Landed Heritage,* 314, 322; *Proceedings of the Public Land Convention,* 6.

4. Walsh quoted in *Proceedings of the Public Land Convention,* 71.

5. Eddy, *Conservation Alarms,* 9.

6. Ise, *United States Forest Policy,* 159; *Congressional Record,* 62nd Cong., 2nd sess., vol. 48, March 7, 1912, 2988, 2975, 2993.

7. Knapp, "Other Side of Conservation"; Knapp's article was reproduced in Fanning, *Selected Articles on Conservation,* 22–38.

8. Knapp, "Other Side of Conservation," in Fanning, *Selected Articles on Conservation,* 38.

9. *Proceedings of the Pubic Land Convention,* 47, 23.

10. Richardson, *Politics of Conservation,* 120, 124; Ise, *United States Forest Policy,* 201; Rakestraw, "The West, States' Rights, and Conservation," 90, 97, 99.

11. Richardson, *Politics of Conservation,* 101, 124–29.

12. Nickerson, *Mothers of Conservatism,* 3–4, 170; Turner, "'Specter of Environmentalism,'" 140.

13. Richardson, *Politics of Conservation,* 108, 119.

14. "Progressive Party Platform of 1912."

15. Socialist Party of America, "The Socialist Party Platform of 1912"; Richardson, *Politics of Conservation,* 147, 152.

16. For descriptions of rural subsistence practices in this period, see Jacoby,

Crimes Against Nature, 23, and Hahn, "Hunting, Fishing, and Foraging"; for Stromberg, see Benjamin Johnson, "Wilderness Parks and Their Discontents," 86.

17. For firewood and Christmas trees, see Benjamin Johnson, "Wilderness Parks and Their Discontents," 86; for pigeons, see Price, *Flight Maps,* 52, 35.

18. Spence, *Dispossessing the Wilderness,* 93.

19. Jacoby, *Crimes Against Nature,* 137.

20. Benjamin Johnson, "Wilderness Parks and Their Discontents," 90, 92.

21. Quoted in Jacoby, *Crimes Against Nature,* 184.

22. Thompson quoted in Spence, *Dispossessing the Wilderness,* 122–23.

23. Ibid., 122, 131.

24. DeBuys, *Enchantment and Exploitation,* 257; Gordon-McCutchan, *Taos Indians and Blue Lake.*

25. Benjamin Johnson, "Wilderness Parks and Their Discontents," 89; Warren, *Hunter's Game,* 28–29.

26. Kinney, *Forest and Water,* 76; Spence, *Dispossessing the Wilderness,* 94; Jacoby, *Crimes Against Nature,* 42–43; deBuys, *Enchantment and Exploitation,* 241.

27. Jacoby, *Crimes Against Nature,* 100; Richardson, *Politics of Conservation,* 91–93; Graybill, "'Strong on the Merits,'" 128–29, 146; Spence, *Dispossessing the Wilderness,* 98.

28. Johnson, "Subsistence, Class, and Conservation," 92.

29. Spence, *Dispossessing the Wilderness,* 73.

30. DeBuys, *Enchantment and Exploitation,* 26; Jacoby, *Crimes Against Nature,* 186.

31. For an extended discussion of Native Americans and the environment, see Krech, *Ecological Indian.*

32. Jacoby, *Crimes Against Nature,* 3, 24.

33. Vennum, *Wild Rice and the Ojibway,* 175–85; Jacoby, *Crimes Against Nature,* 139.

34. Kinney, *Forest and Water,* 57; Hough quoted in Jacoby, *Crimes Against Nature,* 168.

35. Tyrrell, *Crisis of the Wasteful Nation,* 34, 63; Pinchot, *Breaking New Ground,* 225–32.

36. Kinney, *Forest and Water,* 67; Charles Askins in Hornaday, *Our Vanishing Wild Life,* 109.

37. Minnesota Forestry Board, *First Annual Report,* 60–61.

38. Jacoby, *Crimes Against Nature,* 175; Muir, *The Mountains of California,* 107; Jacoby, "Before the 'Ecological Indian.'"

39. Peters quoted in Kosek, *Understories,* 14; Warren, *Hunter's Game,* 26; Hornaday, *Our Vanishing Wild Life,* 102.

40. Benjamin Johnson, "Wilderness Parks and Their Discontents," 91–92.

41. Cronon, "Trouble with Wilderness," 80; Guha, "Radical American Environmentalism"; Kosek, *Understories,* 155.

42. Jacoby, *Crimes Against Nature,* 196, 71; Judd, *Common Lands, Common People,* 197–98.

43. Oberholtzer, *Lakes of Verendrye,* 1; Harvard College Class of 1907, *Secretary's Fifth Report,* 401; Oberholtzer, "Portage Philosophy," 2, 4.

44. *Rainy Lake Chronicle,* "The Quiet Return of Charlie Friday"; Erdrich, *Books and Islands,* 103, 125.

45. Pinchot, *Fight for Conservation*, 45.

46. Pyne, *Year of the Fires*, 22; Marsh, *Man and Nature*, 27; Jacoby, *Crimes Against Nature*, 14–15.

47. Fernow quoted in Pyne, *Year of the Fires*, 7; Kinney, *Forest and Water*, 41; Muir, "American Forests," 154.

48. Pinchot, *Fight for Conservation*, 45; Muir, *My First Summer in the Sierra*, 350–51.

49. McGee quoted in Hays, *Conservation and Efficiency*, 124; Steinberg, *Down to Earth*, 143–44.

50. Fiege, *Irrigated Eden*, 17; Smythe, *Conquest of Arid America*, 3.

51. Langston, *Forest Dreams, Forest Nightmares*, 26, 97, 99.

52. Pyne, *Year of the Fires*, 22; Pyne, *Fire in America*, 194.

53. Pyne, *Fire in America*, 248–49, 168–69; Boy Scouts of America, *Official Handbook for Boys* (1913 ed.), 158–59.

54. Pyne, *Year of the Fires*, 107, 158.

55. Ibid., 196–98, 259–60.

56. *Chicago Tribune*, "Stewart White, Adventurer and Novelist," 20; S. White, "Woodsmen, Spare Those Trees!," 23.

57. S. White, "Woodsmen, Spare Those Trees!," 25, 110.

58. Ibid., 24.

59. Ibid., 116.

60. Pyne, *Fire in America*, 112–13; Graves, "Torch in the Timber," 37, 39.

61. Pyne, *Fire in America*, 107; Pyne, *Year of the Fires*, 168, 78.

62. Langston, *Forest Dreams, Forest Nightmares*, 243; Steinberg, *Down to Earth*, 144, 151–52.

63. Fiege, *Irrigated Eden*, 29–30.

64. Taylor, *Making Salmon*, 69, 82.

65. Ibid., 104, 201.

66. Langston, *Forest Dreams, Forest Nightmares*, 36; Pyne, *Fire in America*, 528.

67. Rome, "What Really Matters in History"; Sutter, "The World with Us," 100–104.

68. For the war's impact on the home front, see Capozolla, *Uncle Sam Wants You*, and Kennedy, *Over Here*.

SEVEN Epilogue

1. *Scientific American*, "Increasing Temperature of the World"; Van Hise, *Conservation of Natural Resources*, 33.

2. *Scientific American*, "Increasing Temperature of the World."

3. IPCC Working Group 2, "Climate Change 2014"; Thompson, "IPCC Says Climate Change"; CO2Earth.org, "Atmospheric CO_2 Growth Rates."

4. Van Hise, *Conservation of Natural Resources*, 33. For a discussion of how scientists came to understand global warming, and the ways in which that process structured and limited responses to it, see Howe, *Behind the Curve*.

5. Fogelson, *Bourgeois Nightmares*, 11–16; for discussions of the ways in which environmental dissents from corporate capitalism were turned into commodities and

stripped of much of their political content, see Shi, *Simple Life*, 213; Tyrrell, *True Gardens of the Gods*, 227; and, more broadly about antimodernism, Lears, *No Place of Grace*.

6. Sutter, *Driven Wild*, 30; Chiles, "Working-Class Conservationism," 158, 161, 163.

7. Hise and Deverell, *Eden by Design;* Minteer, "Regional Planning as Pragmatic Conservation," 100–102; Sutter, *Driven Wild*, 155–58; Mittlefehldt, *Tangled Roots*, 13–18.

8. Phillips, *This Land, This Nation;* Maher, *Nature's New Deal*, 80.

9. Leopold, *Sand County Almanac*, 138–39.

10. Muir, *My First Summer in the Sierra*, 211; Leopold, *Sand Country Almanac*, 243–44, 251; McGee, "Conservation of Natural Resources," 376.

11. Carson, *Silent Spring*, 1–2, 13; Sellers, *Crabgrass Crucible*, 80, 127.

12. Carson, *Silent Spring*, 13.

13. For a recent depiction of conservation and environmentalism as very different movements, see Sellers, *Crabgrass Crucible*, 7, and J. Turner, *Promise of Wilderness*, 395; for postwar environmentalism more generally, see Sellers, *Crabgrass Crucible*, especially 100, 124, 132–36; Rome, *Genius of Earth Day;* Jundt, *Greening the Red, White, and Blue.*

14. Jundt, *Greening the Red, White, and Blue*, 11–15; Sellers, *Crabgrass Crucible*, 127.

15. Sellers, *Crabgrass Crucible*, 245–46.

16. Dowie, *Losing Ground.*

17. Benjamin Johnson, "Wilderness Parks and Their Discontents," 126–27; Executive Order 12898, "Federal Actions to Address Environmental Justice in Minority Populations and Low-Income Populations," February 16, 1994; Targ, "Forward with Environmental Justice," 1; Mock, "Robert Bullard, Pioneer in Environmental Justice."

18. Gottlieb and Azuma, "Re-Envisioning the Los Angeles River," 321–42; Melosi, "Environmental Justice."

19. For discussions of global climate change that stress the need to curtail corporate power and otherwise change capitalism, see Speth, *Bridge at the Edge of the World*, and Klein, *This Changes Everything.*

Bibliography

Archival Collections

Huntington Library, San Marino, California
    Theodore Parker Lukens Papers
Library of Congress, Washington, D.C.
    Gifford Pinchot Papers (GP Papers)
Los Angeles City Archives, Los Angeles, California
    Park Commissioners Record
Oberholtzer Foundation, Mallard Island, Minnesota
    "Indians" clipping file
Pennsylvania State Archives, Harrisburg, Pennsylvania
    Horace J. McFarland Papers

Newspapers and Magazines

The American Federationist
Atlanta Constitution
California Outlook
Chicago Daily Tribune
Chicago Defender
Chicago Tribune
Congressional Record
Forest and Stream
Forestry and Irrigation
Friends' Intelligencer
Ladies' Home Journal
Nature-Study Review

New York Times
North American Review
The Playground
Science
Sierra Club Bulletin
Western Comrade

Books, Articles, and Online Sources

Adams-Williams, Lydia. "Conservation—Woman's Work." *Forestry and Irrigation* 14 (June 1908): 350–51.

Allen, James A. "The Present Wholesale Destruction of Bird-Life in the United States." *Science* 7 (February 26, 1886): 191–95.

American Child Hygiene Association. *Transactions of the Tenth Annual Meeting*. Albany, N.Y.: J. B. Lyon, 1920. Available from the Internet Archive, https://archive.org/details/americanchildhyg010272mbp.

American Forestry. "The Women's Clubs and the Forests." Vol. 16 (June 1910): 363.

Armitage, Kevin. "'The Child Is Born a Naturalist': Nature Study, Woodcraft Indians, and the Theory of Recapitulation." *Journal of the Gilded Age and Progressive Era* 6, no. 1 (2007): 43–70.

———. *The Nature Study Movement: The Forgotten Popularizer of America's Conservation Ethic*. Lawrence: University Press of Kansas, 2010.

Atlanta Constitution. "Plan the Preservation of Appalachian Forests," January 16, 1908.

Audubon, John James. *Ornithological Biography*. Philadelphia: Carey and Hart, 1832.

Babson, Roger W. "Recoveries from the Famous Panics of America." *New York Times*, December 25, 1910.

Bailey, Liberty Hyde. *The Holy Earth*. New York: Scribner's, 1915.

Balogh, Brian. *Government Out of Sight: The Mystery of National Authority in Nineteenth-Century America*. New York: Cambridge University Press, 2009.

Banham, Reyner. *Los Angeles: The Architecture of Four Ecologies*. Berkeley: University of California Press, 1971.

Barrow, Mark. *Nature's Ghosts: Confronting Extinctions from the Age of Jefferson to the Age of Ecology*. Chicago: University of Chicago Press, 2009.

Bartlett, Dana. *The Better City: A Sociological Study of a Modern City*. Los Angeles: Neuner, 1907.

———. *The Better Country*. Boston: Clark, 1911.

———. *The Bush Aflame*. Los Angeles: Grafton, 1923.

Bates, J. Leonard. "Fulfilling American Democracy: The Conservation Movement, 1907 to 1921." *Mississippi Valley Historical Review* 44, no. 1 (1957): 29–57.

Bederman, Gail. *Manliness and Civilization: A Cultural History of Gender and Race in the United States, 1880–1917*. Chicago: University of Chicago Press, 1995.

Binkley, Cameron. "'No Better Heritage than Living Trees': Women's Clubs and Early Conservation in Humboldt County." *Western Historical Quarterly* 33, no. 2 (Summer 2002): 179–203.

Blum, Elizabeth. "Women, Environmental Rationale, and Activism During the Progressive Era." In Glave and Stoll, eds., *To Love the Wind and the Rain,* 77–92.

Boris, Eileen. *Art and Labor: Ruskin, Morris, and the Craftsman Ideal in America.* Philadelphia: Temple University Press, 1986.

Boy Scouts of America. *The Official Handbook for Boys.* New York: Doubleday, 1914.

———. *The Official Handbook for Boys.* New York: Boy Scouts of America, 1919.

Brechin, Gray. "Conserving the Race: Natural Aristocracies, Eugenics, and the Conservation Movement," *Antipode* 28, no. 3 (1996): 229–45.

Brinkley, Douglas. *The Wilderness Warrior: Theodore Roosevelt and the Crusade for America.* New York: HarperCollins, 2009.

Bryson, Phillip J. *The Economics of Henry George: History's Rehabilitation of America's Greatest Early Economist.* New York: Palgrave Macmillan, 2011.

Buchanan, Joseph Rodes. "The Coming Cataclysm of American and Europe." *Arena,* August 1890, 292–313.

California Outlook. "Forward to the Land." Vol. 14, no. 20 (May 17, 1913): 5.

Canby, Henry. "Back to Nature." *Yale Review* 6, no. 4 (July 1917): 755–67.

Capozzola, Christopher. *Uncle Sam Wants You: World War I and the Making of the Modern American Citizen.* New York: Oxford University Press, 2008.

Carr, Ethan. *Wilderness by Design: Landscape Architecture and the National Park Service.* Lincoln: University of Nebraska Press, 1998.

Carson, Rachel. *Silent Spring.* Greenwich, Conn.: Fawcett, 1962.

Chicago Daily Tribune. "Will Discuss Outdoor Art." June 4, 1900.

Chicago Tribune. "Stewart White, Adventurer and Novelist, Dies." September 19, 1946.

Chiles, Robert. "Working-Class Conservationism in New York: Governor Alfred E. Smith and the 'Property of the People of the State.'" *Environmental History* 18, no. 1 (2013): 157–83.

Clar, Raymond. *California Government and Forestry.* Sacramento: Division of Forestry, California Department of Natural Resources, 1959.

Clements, Kendrick. "Engineers and Conservationists in the Progressive Era." *California History* 58, no. 4 (Winter 1979–80): 282–303.

Cohen, Michael P. *The Pathless Way: John Muir and American Wilderness.* Madison: University of Wisconsin Press, 1984.

Collier, John. "Leisure Time: The Last Problem of Conservation." *Playground* 6, no. 3 (1912): 93–106.

Commercial Club of Minneapolis and St. Paul. *Memorial and Appeal in the Matter of Minnesota Forestry and Park Reservations.* 1905.

Comstock, Anna Botsford. "Conservation and Nature-Study." *Nature-Study Review* 18, no. 7 (October 1922): 299–300.

———. *Handbook of Nature-Study.* Ithaca, N.Y.: Comstock, 1911.

Comstock, William. *Bungalows, Camps, and Mountain Houses.* New York: Comstock, 1915.

Conrad, Rebecca. *Places of Quiet Beauty: Parks, Preserves, and Environmentalism.* Iowa City: University of Iowa Press, 1997.

Cooke, Marjorie Benton. *The Girl Who Lived in the Woods.* Chicago: McLurg, 1910.

CO2Earth.org. "Atmospheric CO$_2$ Growth Rates." https://www.co2.earth/co2-accelera tion; accessed June 9, 2016.

Cranz, Galen. *Politics of Park Design: A History of Urban Parks in Americ*a. Boston: MIT Press, 1982.

Cronon, William. *Nature's Metropolis: Chicago and the Great West.* New York: Norton, 1991.

———. "The Trouble with Wilderness; or, Getting Back to the Wrong Nature." In *Uncommon Ground: Toward Reinventing Nature,* edited by William Cronon, 69–90. New York: Norton, 1995.

———, ed. *Uncommon Ground: Toward Reinventing Nature.* New York: Norton, 1995.

Culver, Lawrence. *The Frontier of Leisure: Southern California and the Shaping of Modern America.* New York: Oxford University Press, 2010.

The Daily Show with Jon Stewart. "Rage Within the Machine–Progressivism." February 22, 2010. http://thedailyshow.cc.com/videos/wnbh96/rage-within-the-machine -progressivism; accessed July 9, 2015.

Danbom, David. *The Resisted Revolution: Urban America and the Industrialization of Agriculture, 1900–1930.* Ames: Iowa State University Press, 1979.

Dawley, Alan. *Changing the World: American Progressives in War and Revolution.* Princeton, N.J.: Princeton University Press, 2003.

Dear, Michael. "In the City, Time Becomes Visible: Intentionality and Urbanism in Los Angeles, 1781–1991." In *The City: Los Angeles and Urban Theory at the End of the Twentieth Century,* edited by Allen Scott and Edward Soja, 76–104. Berkeley: University of California Press, 1996.

deBuys, William. *Enchantment and Exploitation: The Life and Hard Times of a New Mexico Mountain Range.* Albuquerque: University of New Mexico Press, 1985

De Long, David G. *Frank Lloyd Wright and the Living City.* Milan: Skira, 1998.

DeLuca, Kevin, and Anne Demo. "Imagining Nature and Erasing Class and Race." *Environmental History* 6, no. 4 (October 2001): 541–61.

Des Jardins, Julie. *The Madame Curie Complex: The Hidden History of Women in Science.* New York: City University of New York Press, 2010.

de Wit, William. "Apartment Houses and Bungalows: Building the Flat City." *Chicago History* 12 (Winter 1983–84): 18–29.

DeWitt, Benjamin. *The Progressive Movement: A Non-Partisan, Comprehensive Discussion of Current Tendencies in American Politics.* New York: Macmillan, 1915.

Donnelly, Ignatius. *Atlantis: The Antediluvian World.* New York: Harper and Brothers, 1892.

———. *Caesar's Column: A Story of the Twentieth Century.* Chicago: Schulte, 1890.

Dorr, Gregory Michael. "Fighting Fire with Fire: African Americans and Hereditarian Thinking, 1900–1942." Unpublished manuscript. Available at Scribd, www.scribd .com/doc/114365898/Fighting-Fire-with-Fire-African-Americans-and-Heredi tarian-Thinking-1900-1942#scribd; accessed September 1, 2015.

Dowie, Mark. *Losing Ground: American Environmentalism at the Close of the Twentieth Century.* Cambridge: Harvard University Press, 1995.

Driapsa, David. "The Cultural Landscape of Ober's Mallard Island: A Masterwork of Landscape Architecture in the Wilds of Rainy Lake." Unpublished manuscript, 2011. Copy in author's possession.

Drummond, Alexander. *Enos Mills: Citizen of Nature.* Boulder: University of Colorado Press, 1995.

Du Bois, W. E. B. *The Conservation of Races.* Washington, D.C.: American Negro Academy, 1897.

Eddy, J. Arthur. *Conservation Alarms.* Denver: National Public Domain League, 1909.

Ely, Richard., Ralph H. Hess, Charles K. Leith, and Thomas Nixon Carver. *The Foundations of National Prosperity: Studies in the Conservation of Permanent National Resources.* New York: Macmillan, 1917.

Erdrich, Louise. *Books and Islands in Ojibwe Country.* New York: National Geographic, 2003.

Erie, Steven. "How the Urban West Was Won: The Local State and Economic Growth in Los Angeles, 1880–1932." *Urban Affairs Quarterly* 27, no. 4 (1992): 529–54.

Fanning C. E., ed. *Selected Articles on the Conservation of Natural Resources.* Minneapolis: Wilson, 1913.

Farmer, Jared. *On Zion's Mount: Mormons, Indians, and the American Landscape.* Cambridge: Harvard University Press, 2008.

———. *Trees in Paradise: A California History.* New York: Norton, 2013.

Fernow, Bernhard. *The Economics of Forestry: A Reference Book for Students of Political Economy and Professional and Lay Students of Forestry.* New York: Crowell, 1902.

Fiege, Mark. *Irrigated Eden: The Making of an Agricultural Landscape in the American West.* Seattle: University of Washington Press, 1999.

Filene, Peter. "An Obituary for 'The Progressive Movement.'" *American Quarterly* 22, no. 1 (1970): 20–34.

Fisher, Colin. "African Americans, Outdoor Recreation, and the 1919 Chicago Race Riot." In Glave and Stoll, eds., *"To Love the Wind and the Rain,"* 63–75.

Flanagan, Maureen. *America Reformed: Progressives and Progressivism, 1890s–1920s.* New York: Oxford University Press, 2007.

Flores, Dan. "Bison Ecology and Bison Diplomacy: The Southern Plains from 1800 to 1850." *Journal of American History* 78, no. 2 (September 1991): 465–85.

Fogelson, Robert. *Bourgeois Nightmares: Suburbia, 1870–1930.* New Haven: Yale University Press, 2005.

Follett, Mary Parker. *The New State: Group Organization the Solution of Popular Government.* New York: Longman, Greens, 1918.

Foreman, Henry. *Recreation Needs of Chicago: Address by Henry G. Foreman, Delivered on Labor Day, 1904, at Morgan Park, During the Morgan Park Day Exercises.* Chicago: Cook County Board, 1904.

Forest and Stream. "To Save the Passenger Pigeon." January 22, 1910, 2.

Fox, Stephen. *John Muir and His Legacy: The American Conservation Movement.* Boston: Little, Brown, 1981.

Friends' Intelligencer. "The Extinct Wild Pigeon." December 17, 1898, 925.

From Pueblo to City, 1849–1910. Los Angeles: LeBerthon, 1910.

Gardner, Robert. "Constructing a Technological Forest: Nature, Culture, and Tree-Planting in the Nebraska Sand Hills." *Environmental History* 14, no. 2 (April 2009): 275–97.

Garland, Hamlin. *Cavanagh, Forest Ranger: A Romance of the Mountain West.* New York: Harper and Brothers, 1910.

———. *A Son of the Middle Border.* New York: Macmillan, 1917.

Gates, Paul W. *History of Public Land Law Development.* Washington, D.C.: Government Printing Office, 1968.

Gebhardt, David. *Schindler.* New York: Viking, 1971.

George, Henry. *Progress and Poverty: An Inquiry into the Cause of Industrial Depressions, and of Increase in Want With Increase of Wealth.* New York: Appleton, 1886.

———. *Social Problems.* London: Keegan Paul, Trench, 1884.

Gisel, Bonnie Johanna. *Kindred and Related Spirits: The Letters of John Muir and Jeanne C. Carr.* Salt Lake City: University of Utah Press, 2001.

Gladden, Washington. *The New Idolatry, and Other Discussions.* New York: McClure, Phillips, 1905.

Glave, Dianne D., and Mark Stoll, eds. *"To Love the Wind and the Rain": African Americans and Environmental History.* Pittsburgh: University of Pittsburgh Press, 2005.

Gompers, Samuel. "The Conservation of Natural Resources." *American Federationist* 15 (1908): 532–36.

Gordon-McCutchan, R. C. *The Taos Indians and the Battle for Blue Lake.* Santa Fe: Red Crane, 2008.

Goss, Peter. "The Ever-Popular Bungalow." In *The Bungalow Lifestyle and the Arts and Crafts Movement in the Intermountain West,* edited by Peter Goss and Kenneth R. Trapp, 2–15. Salt Lake City: University of Utah Press, 1995.

Gottlieb, Robert. *Forcing the Spring: The Transformation of the American Environmental Movement.* Washington, D.C.: Island, 1999.

Gottlieb, Robert, and Andrea Misako Azuma. "Re-Envisioning the Los Angeles River: An NGO and Academic Institute Influence the Policy Discourse." *Golden Gate University Law Review* 35, no. 3 (Spring 2005): 321–42.

Gramm, Gerald, and Robert D. Putnam. "The Growth of Voluntary Associations in America, 1840–1940." *Journal of Interdisciplinary History* 29, no. 4 (Spring 1999): 511–57.

Grant, Madison. *The Passing of the Great Race; or, The Racial Basis of European History.* New York: Charles Scribner, 1916.

Graves, Henry. "The Torch in the Timber." *Sunset* 44 (April 1920): 37–40, 80–90.

Graybill, Andrew. "'Strong on the Merits and Powerfully Symbolic': The Return of Blue Lake to Taos Pueblo." *New Mexico Historical Review* 76, no. 2 (April 2001): 125–60.

Green, Julie. "'She Touched Fifty Million Lives': Gene Stratton-Porter and Nature Conservation." In *Seeing Nature Through Gender,* edited by Virginia Scharff, 221–40. Lawrence: University Press of Kansas, 2003.

Greenstein, Paul, Nigey Lennon, and Lionel Rolfe. *Bread and Hyacinths: The Rise and Fall of Utopian Los Angeles.* Los Angeles: California Classics, 1992.

Grese, Robert. "Jens Jensen: The Landscape Architect as Conservationist." In *Midwestern Landscape Architecture*, edited by William Tishler, 117–41. Urbana: University of Illinois Press, 2000.

Griffith, Griffith J. *Parks, Boulevards, and Playgrounds*. Los Angeles: Prison Reform League Publishing Company, 1910.

Guha, Ramachandra. "Radical American Environmentalism and Wilderness Preservation: A Third World Critique." *Environmental Ethics* 11 (1989): 71–83.

Gumphrecht, Blake. *The Los Angeles River: Its Life, Death, and Possible Rebirth*. Baltimore: Johns Hopkins University Press, 1999.

Hahn, Steven. "Hunting, Fishing, and Foraging: Common Rights and Class Relations in the Postbellum South." *Radical History Review* 26 (1982): 36–64.

Harriman, Job. "Making Dreams Come True." *Western Comrade* 1, no. 2 (May 1913): 54–56.

Harrison, Laura Soullière. *Architecture in the Parks: National Historic Landmark Theme Study*. Washington, D.C.: Department of the Interior, National Park Service, 1986. Available from the Internet Archive, https://archive.org/details/architecturein paooharr.

Harvard College Class of 1907. *Secretary's Fifth Report*. Cambridge: Harvard University, 1922.

Hays, Samuel P. *Conservation and the Gospel of Efficiency: The Progressive Conservation Movement, 1890–1920*. Cambridge: Harvard University Press, 1959.

Hersey, Mark. "Hints and Suggestions to Farmers: George Washington Carver and Rural Conservation in the South." *Environmental History* 11, no. 2 (2006): 239–68.

———. *My Work Is That of Conservation: An Environmental Biography of George Washington Carver*. Athens: University of Georgia Press, 2011.

Hickman, David. "John Muir's Orchard Home." *Pacific Historical Review* 82, no. 3 (2013): 335–61.

Hill, James J. *Highways of Progress*. New York: Doubleday, 1910.

Hines, Thomas. *Irving Gill and the Architecture of Reform*. New York: Monacelli, 2000.

Hise, Greg, and William Deverell. *Eden by Design: The 1930 Olmsted-Bartholomew Plan for the Los Angeles Region*. Berkeley: University of California Press, 2000.

A History of California and an Extended History of Los Angeles and Environs: Biographical. Vol. 2. Los Angeles: Historic Record Company, 1915.

Hornaday, William Temple. *Our Vanishing Wild Life: Its Extermination and Preservation*. New York: New York Zoological Society, 1913.

———. *Wild Life Conservation in Theory and Practice: Lectures Delivered Before the Forest School of Yale University*. New Haven: Yale University Press, 1914.

Hou, Shen. *The City Natural: "Garden and Forest" Magazine and the Rise of American Environmentalism*. Pittsburgh: University of Pittsburgh Press, 2013.

Howard, Ebenezer. *Garden Cities of To-morrow*. London: Swan Sonnenschein, 1902.

Howe, Joshua. *Behind the Curve: Science and the Politics of Global Warming*. Seattle: University of Washington Press, 2014.

Hubbard, Henry, and Theodora Kimball. *Introduction to the Study of Landscape Design*. New York: Macmillan, 1917.

Hunter, Robert. *Tenement Conditions in Chicago: Report by the Investigating Committee of the City Homes Association*. Chicago: City Homes Association, 1901.

Hyde, Anne. "William Kent: The Puzzle of Progressive Conservationists." In *California Progressivism Revisited*, edited by William Deverell and Tom Sitton, 34–56. Berkeley: University of California Press, 1994.

IPCC Working Group 2. "Climate Change 2014: Impacts, Adaptation, and Vulnerability Summary for Policy-Makers." Intergovernmental Panel on Climate Change, https://ipcc-wg2.gov/AR5/images/uploads/IPCC_WG2AR5_SPM_Approved .pdf; accessed September 4, 2015.

Ise, John. *The United States Forest Policy*. New Haven: Yale University Press, 1920.

Isenberg, Andrew. *The Destruction of the Bison: An Environmental History, 1750–1920*. Cambridge: Cambridge University Press, 2001.

Ishii, Izumi. "'Not a Wigwam Nor Blanket Nor Warwhoop': Cherokees and the Woman's Christian Temperance Movement." *Journal of American and Canadian Studies* 18 (2000): 1–15.

Jacoby, Karl. "Before the 'Ecological Indian': Conservationists and Indians at the Turn-of-the-Century." Unpublished manuscript. Copy in author's possession.

———. *Crimes Against Nature: Squatters, Poachers, Thieves, and the Hidden History of American Conservation*. Berkeley: University of California Press, 2001.

James, George Wharton. *Birthday Book: Prose and Poetical Selections from the Writings of Living California Authors, with a Brief Biographical Sketch of Each*. Los Angeles: Arroyo Guild, 1909.

Jefferson, Thomas. *Notes on the State of Virginia*. London: Stockdale, 1787.

Johnson, Benjamin H. "Environment: Nature, Conservation, and the Progressive State." In *Companion to the Gilded Age and Progressive Era: The Making of Modern America*, edited by Christopher McKnight Nichols and Nancy Unger. New York: Wiley-Blackwell, forthcoming.

———. *Revolution in Texas: How a Forgotten Rebellion and Its Bloody Suppression Turned Mexicans into Americans*. New Haven: Yale University Press, 2003.

———. "Subsistence, Class, and Conservation at the Birth of Superior National Forest." *Environmental History* 4, no. 1 (January 1999): 80–99.

———. "Wilderness Parks and Their Discontents." In *American Wilderness: A New History*, edited by Michael Lewis, 113–30. New York: Oxford University Press, 2007.

Johnson, Burges. "Bungal-Ode." In William Comstock, *Bungalows, Camps, and Mountain Houses*. New York: Comstock, 1915.

Johnston, Robert D. "Re-Democratizing the Progressive Era: The Politics of Progressive Era Political Historiography." *Journal of the Gilded Age and Progressive Era* 1, no. 1 (2002): 68–92.

Jordan, Ben. "'Conservation of Boyhood': Boy Scouting's Modest Manliness and Nature Conservation, 1910–1930." *Environmental History* 15, no. 4 (October 2010): 612–42.

Judd, Richard. *Common Lands, Common People: The Origins of Conservation in Northern New England*. Cambridge: Harvard University Press, 1997.

Jundt, Thomas. *Greening the Red, White, and Blue: The Bomb, Big Business, and Consumer Resistance in Postwar America.* New York: Oxford University Press, 2014.

Kates, James. "Liberty Hyde Bailey, Agricultural Journalism, and the Making of the Moral Landscape." *Journalism History* 36, no. 4 (2011): 207–18.

Keith, Henrietta Jewett. *Pipes o' Pan in a City Park.* Minneapolis: Colwell, 1922.

Kennedy, David. *Over Here: The First World War and American Society.* New York: Oxford University Press, 1980.

King, Anthony. *The Bungalow: The Production of a Global Culture.* New York: Oxford University Press, 1984.

Kinney, Abbot. *The Conquest of Death.* New York, 1893.

———. *Eucalyptus.* Los Angeles: Baumgart, 1895.

———. *Forest and Water.* Los Angeles: Post Publishing, 1900.

Klein, Naomi. *This Changes Everything: Capitalism Versus the Climate.* New York: Simon and Schuster, 2014.

Klingle, Matthew: *Emerald City: An Environmental History of Seattle.* New Haven: Yale University Press, 2007.

Knapp, George L. "The Other Side of Conservation." *North American Review* 191 (April 1910): 465–81.

Kosek, Jake. *Understories: The Political Life of Forests in New Mexico.* Durham, N.C.: Duke University Press, 2006.

Krech, Shepherd, III. *The Ecological Indian.* New York: Norton, 1999.

Langston, Nancy. *Forest Dreams, Forest Nightmares: The Paradox of Old Growth in the Inland West.* Seattle: University of Washington Press, 1995.

Lansing, Michael J. "'Salvaging the Man Power of America': Conservation, Manhood, and Disabled Veterans During World War I." *Environmental History* 14 (January 2009): 32–57.

Lasch, Christopher. *The True and Only Heaven: Progress and Its Critics.* New York: Norton, 1991.

Lears, T. J. Jackson. *No Place of Grace: Antimodernism and the Transformation of American Culture.* New York: Pantheon, 1983.

———. *Rebirth of a Nation: The Making of Modern America, 1877–1920.* New York: HarperPerennial, 2009.

Leopold, Aldo. *A Sand County Almanac.* New York: Oxford University Press, 1968 [1949].

Leuchtenburg, William C. "Progressivism and Imperialism: The Progressive Movement and American Foreign Policy, 1898–1916." *Mississippi Valley Historical Review* 39, no. 3 (1952): 483–504.

Lipin, Lawrence. "Nature, the City, and the Family Circle: Domesticity and the Urban Home in Henry George's Thought." *Journal of the Gilded Age and Progressive Era* 13, no. 3 (July 2014): 305–35.

———. *Workers and the Wild: Conservation, Consumerism, and Labor in Oregon, 1910–1930.* Eugene: University of Oregon Press, 2007.

Lockmann, Ronald. "Forests and Watershed in the Environmental Philosophy of Theodore P. Lukens." *Forest History* 23, no. 2 (1979): 82–91.

London, Jack. *The Works of Jack London: The Iron Heel.* New York: Review of Reviews Press, 1917.

Lovett, Laura C. *Conceiving the Future: Pronatalism, Reproduction, and the Family in the United States, 1890–1938.* Chapel Hill: University of North Carolina Press, 2007.

Lowenthal, David. *George Perkins Marsh: Prophet of Conservation.* Seattle: University of Washington Press, 2000.

Lukens, Theodore Parker. *Forestry in Relation to City Building.* Pasadena, Calif.: Throop College, 1915.

The Lumber Industry and Its Workers. Chicago: Industrial Workers of the World, 1922.

Lytle, Mark Hamilton. *The Gentle Subversive: Rachel Carson, "Silent Spring," and the Rise of the Environmental Movement.* New York: Oxford University Press, 2007).

Maddox, Lucy. *Citizen Indian: Native American Intellectuals, Race, and Reform.* Ithaca, N.Y.: Cornell University Press, 2005.

Maher, Neil. *Nature's New Deal: The Civilian Conservation Corps and the Roots of the American Environmental Movement.* New York: Oxford University Press, 2008.

Marsh, George Perkins. *Address Delivered Before the Agricultural Society of Rutland County, September 30, 1847.* Rutland, Vt.: Herald, 1848.

——. *Man and Nature; or, Physical Geography as Modified by Human Action.* New York: Scribner, 1864.

Mattson, Kevin. *Creating a Democratic Public: The Struggle for Urban Participatory Democracy During the Progressive Era.* College Park: Pennsylvania State University Press, 1998.

McCarthy, John. "Dreaming of a Decentralized Metropolis: City Planning in Socialist Milwaukee." *Michigan Historical Review* 32, no. 1 (Spring 2006): 250–73.

McCarthy, G. Michael. *Hour of Trial: The Conservation Conflict in Colorado and the West, 1891–1907.* Norman: University of Oklahoma Press, 1977.

McFarland, Horace. "Are National Parks Worth While?" *Sierra Club Bulletin* 8, no. 3 (1912): 236–39.

——. "The Value of Natural Scenery." *Sierra Club Bulletin* 7, no. 1 (1909): 64–69.

McGeart, M. Nelson. *Gifford Pinchot: Forester and Politician.* Princeton, N.J.: Princeton University Press, 1960.

McGee, William J. "The Conservation of Natural Resources." *Proceedings of the Mississippi Valley Historical Association* 3 (1911): 361–79.

McGerr, Michael. *A Fierce Discontent: The Rise and Fall of the Progressive Movement in America, 1870–1920.* New York: Free Press, 2003.

McGuinness, Aims. "The Revolution Begins Here: Milwaukee and the History of Socialism." In *Perspectives on Milwaukee's Past,* edited by Margo Anderson and Victor Greene, 77–104. Urbana: University of Illinois Press, 2009.

McNeill, J. R. *Something New Under the Sun: An Environmental History of the Twentieth Century* New York: Norton, 2000.

Melosi, Martin. "Environmental Justice, Political Agenda Setting, and the Myths of History." *Journal of Policy History* 12, no. 1 (2000): 43–71.

——. *The Sanitary City.* Baltimore: Johns Hopkins University Press, 2000.

Merchant, Carolyn. "George Bird Grinnell's Audubon Society: Bridging the Gender Divide in Conservation." *Environmental History* 15, no. 1 (January 2010): 3–30.

———. "Women of the Progressive Conservation Movement." *Environmental Review* 8, no. 1 (Spring 1984): 57–85.

Merriam, Charles Edward. *American Political Ideals: Studies in the Development of American Political Thought, 1865–1917.* New York: Macmillan, 1920.

Merson, W. B. *The Passenger Pigeon.* New York: Outing, 1907.

Miller, Char. *Gifford Pinchot and the Making of Modern Environmentalism.* Washington, D.C.: Island, 2001.

Miller, Ross. *American Apocalypse: The Great Fire and the Myth of Chicago.* Chicago: University of Chicago Press, 1990.

Miller, Wilhelm. *The Prairie Spirit in Landscape Gardening.* Urbana: Illinois Agricultural Experiment Station, 1915.

Minnesota Forestry Board. *First Annual Report.* St. Paul, 1911.

Minnesota State Board of Control. *Proceedings of the First State Conference of Child Welfare Boards with the State Board of Control.* St. Paul: State Board of Control, 1919.

Minteer, Ben A. "Regional Planning as Pragmatic Conservationism." In *Reconstructing Conservation: Finding Common Ground,* edited by Ben A. Minteer and Robert E. Manning, 93–113. Washington, D.C.: Island, 2005.

Mittlefehldt, Sarah. *Tangled Roots: The Appalachian Trail and American Environmental Politics.* Seattle: University of Washington Press, 2013.

Mock, Brentin. "Robert Bullard, Pioneer in Environmental Justice, Is Honored by the Sierra Club." *Washington Post,* September 24, 2013. https://www.washingtonpost.com/lifestyle/style/robert-bullard-pioneer-in-environmental-justice-is-honored-by-the-sierra-club/2013/09/24/88e0e882-251c-11e3-b3e9-d97fb087acd6_story.html; accessed September 4, 2015.

Mock, Harry E. "Human Conservation and Reclamation." *American Journal of Care for Cripples* 6 (March 1918): 5–10.

Morrison, Ernest. *J. Horace McFarland: A Thorn for Beauty.* Harrisburg: Pennsylvania Historical and Museum Commission, 1995.

Muir, John. "The American Forests," *Atlantic Monthly* 80 (August 1897): 145–57.

———. "The Hetch Hetchy Valley." *Sierra Club Bulletin* 6, no. 4 (January 1908): 211–20.

———. *The Mountains of California.* New York: Century, 1894.

———. *My First Summer in the Sierra.* Boston: Houghton Mifflin, 1911.

———. *Our National Parks.* Boston: Houghton Mifflin, 1901.

———. "The San Gabriel Mountains." In Muir, *Writings of John Muir: Steep Trails.* Boston: Houghton Mifflin, 1918 [1877].

Mumford, Lewis. *The Brown Decades: A Study of the Arts in America, 1865–1895.* New York: Dover, 1955 [1931].

Murray, Shannon. "Making a Model Metropolis: Boosterism, Reform, and Urban Design in Minneapolis, 1880–1920." Ph.D. diss., University of Calgary, 2015.

Nash, Roderick. *Wilderness and the American Mind.* New Haven: Yale University Press, 1967.

National Conservation Congress. *Proceedings of the National Conservation Congress.* Washington, D.C., 1911.

——. *Proceedings of the Third National Conservation Congress at Kansas City, Missouri, 1911.* Washington, D.C.: National Conservation Congress, 1912.

"National People's Party Platform." *World Almanac, 1893.* New York: Press Publishing, 1893. Available from History Matters, "The Omaha Platform: Launching the Populist Party," http://historymatters.gmu.edu/d/5361; accessed April 15, 2014.

New York Times. "Future of the State's Forests." January 18, 1891.

——. "Music Heard Yesterday." March 17, 1899.

——. "Western Civilization." July 11, 1894.

Nickerson, Michelle. *Mothers of Conservatism: Women and the Postwar Right.* Princeton, N.J.: Princeton University Press, 2012.

Oberholtzer, Ernest. *The Lakes of Verendrye: A University of the Wilderness.* Minneapolis: Quetico-Superior Council, n.d. [1929?].

——. "Portage Philosophy." *American Forests.* Undated copy in the "Indians" clipping file, Mallard Island, Oberholtzer Foundation.

Olmsted Brothers. *Report upon the Development of Public Grounds for Baltimore.* Baltimore: Lord Baltimore, 1904.

Ore, Janet. *The Seattle Bungalow: People and Houses, 1900–1940.* Seattle: University of Washington Press, 2007.

Orth, Joel. "Directing Nature's Creative Forces: Climate Change, Afforestation, and the Nebraska National Forest." *Western Historical Quarterly* 42, no. 2 (Summer 2011): 197–217.

Osterhammel, Jürgen. *The Transformation of the World: A Global History of the Nineteenth Century.* Princeton, N.J.: Princeton University Press, 2014.

Pacific Outlook. "Judge Silent's Report on Parks." Vol. 8, no. 10 (March 5, 1910): 7.

——. "Parks by Assessment." Vol. 6, no. 24 (June 12, 1909): 3.

——. "Pinchot Warns Us Against Predatory Interests." Vol. 7, no. 11 (November 11, 1909): 6.

Paddock, Joe. *Keeper of the Wild: The Life of Ernest Oberholtzer.* St. Paul: Minnesota Historical Society, 2001.

Pernin, P. "The Finger of God Is There." *Wisconsin Magazine of History* 2, no. 1 (September 1919). Originally published as *The Finger of God Is There,* Montreal: Lovell, 1874.

Peters, Scott, and Paul Morgan. "The Country Life Commission: Reconsidering a Milestone in American Agricultural History." *Agricultural History* 78, no. 3 (2004): 289–316.

Phillips, Sarah. *This Land, This Nation: Conservation, Rural America, and the New Deal.* New York: Cambridge University Press, 2007.

Pinchot, Gifford. *Breaking New Ground.* New York: Harcourt, Brace, 1947.

——. *The Fight for Conservation.* New York: Doubleday, Page, 1910.

Pisani, Donald. *To Reclaim a Divided West: Water, Law, and Public Policy, 1848–1902.* Albuquerque: University of New Mexico Press, 1992.

Platt, Harold. *Shock Cities: The Environmental Transformation and Reform of Manchester and Chicago.* Chicago: University of Chicago Press, 2005.

Platt, Lorne. "Planning Ideology and Geographic Thought in the Early Twentieth Century: Charles Whitnall's Progressive Era Park Designs for Socialist Milwaukee." *Journal of Urban History* 36, no. 6 (2010): 771–91.

Preston, Samuel H., and Michael R. Haines. *Fatal Years: Child Mortality in Late Nineteenth-Century America.* Princeton, N.J.: Princeton University Press, 1991.

Price, Jennifer. *Flight Maps: Adventures with Nature in Modern America.* New York: Basic, 1999.

———. "Thirteen Ways of Seeing Nature in L.A." *Believer,* May 2006. www.believermag .com/issues/200605/?read=article_price; accessed December 18, 2013.

Proceedings of a Conference of Governors. Washington, D.C.: Government Printing Office, 1908.

Proceedings of the Public Land Convention, Held in Denver, Colorado, June 18, 19, 20, 1907, by the States and Territories Containing Public Lands of the United States and Lying West of the Missouri River. Denver: Western Newspaper Union, 1907.

"Progressive Party Platform of 1912." Available from TeachingAmericanHistory.org, http://teachingamericanhistory.org/library/document/progressive-platform-of -1912; accessed June 25, 2013.

Pyne, Stephen J. *Fire in America: A Cultural History of Wildland and Rural Fire.* Seattle: University of Washington Press, 1982.

———. *Year of the Fires.* Missoula, Mont.: Mountain Press, 2008.

Rainy Lake Chronicle. "The Quiet Return of Charlie Friday." May 14, 1979, 5.

Rakestraw, Lawrence. "The West, States' Rights, and Conservation." *Pacific Northwest Quarterly* 48, no. 3 (July 1957): 89–99.

Rawson, Michael. *Eden on the Charles: The Making of Boston.* Cambridge: Harvard University Press, 2010.

Richardson, Elmo. *The Politics of Conservation.* Berkeley: University of California Press, 1962.

Righter, Robert. *The Battle over Hetch Hetchy: America's Most Controversial Dam and the Birth of Modern Environmentalism.* New York: Oxford University Press, 2005.

Rimby, Susan. "'Better Housekeeping Out of Doors': Mira Lloyd Dock, the State Federation of Pennsylvania Women, and Progressive Era Conservation." *Journal of Women's History* 17, no. 3 (Fall 2005): 9–34.

———. *Mira Lloyd Dock and the Progressive Era Conservation Movement.* College Park: Pennsylvania State University Press, 2012.

Rix, Rebecca Ann. "Gender and Reconstitution: The Individual and Family Basis of Republican Government Contested, 1868–1925." Ph.D. diss., Yale University, 2008.

Robbins, Roy M. *Our Landed Heritage: The Public Domain, 1776–1970.* Lincoln: University of Nebraska Press, 1976 [1942].

Rodgers, Daniel. *Atlantic Crossings: Social Politics in a Progressive Age.* Cambridge: Harvard University Press, 1998.

Rome, Adam. *The Genius of Earth Day: How a 1970 Teach-In Unexpectedly Made the First Green Movement.* New York: Basic, 2013.

——. "Nature Wars, Culture Wars: Immigration and Environmental Reform in the Progressive Era." *Environmental History* 13, no. 3 (July 2008): 432–53.

——. "'Political Hermaphrodites': Gender and Environmental Reform in Progressive America." *Environmental History* 11, no. 3 (July 2006): 440–63.

——. "What Really Matters in History: Environmental Perspectives on Modern America." *Environmental History* 7 (April 2002): 303–18.

Rosenzweig, Roy, and Elizabeth Blackmar. *The Park and the People: A History of Central Park.* Ithaca, N.Y.: Cornell University Press, 1992.

Runte, Alfred. *National Parks: The American Experience.* Lincoln: University of Nebraska Press, 1979.

Rybczynski, Witold. *A Clearing in the Distance: Frederick Law Olmsted and America in the Nineteenth Century.* New York: Scribner, 1999.

Sachs, Aaron. *Arcadian America: The Death and Life of an Environmental Tradition.* New Haven: Yale University Press, 2013.

——. *The Humboldt Current: Nineteenth-Century Explorations and the Roots of American Environmentalism.* New York: Viking, 2006.

Sargeant, Shirley. *Theodore Parker Lukens: Father of Forestry.* Los Angeles: Dawson's Book Shop, 1969.

Saunders, Charles Francis. *The Southern Sierras of California.* Boston: Houghton Mifflin, 1923.

——. *The Story of Carmelita, Its Associations, and Its Trees.* Pasadena, Calif.: Vroman, 1928.

——. *Under the Sky in California.* New York: McBride, Nast, 1913.

——. *With the Flowers and Trees in California.* New York: McBride, Nast, 1914.

Saylor, Henry. *Bungalows: Their Design, Construction and Furnishing, with Suggestions Also for Camps, Summer Homes and Cottages of Similar Character.* Philadelphia: Winston, 1911.

Schmitt, Peter. *Back to Nature: The Arcadian Myth in Urban America.* New York: Oxford University Press, 1969.

Schulman, Bruce. "Governing Nature, Nurturing Government: Resource Management and the Development of the American State, 1900–1912." *Journal of Policy History* 17, no. 4 (2005), 375–403.

Scientific American. "The Increasing Temperature of the World." Vol. 107 (1912): 99.

Scott, Charles B. *Nature Study and the Child.* Boston: Heath, 1902.

Scudder, Vida. *A Listener in Babel.* Boston: Houghton Mifflin, 1903.

Searle, R. Newall. *Saving Quetico-Superior: A Land Set Apart.* St. Paul: Minnesota Historical Society Press, 1977.

Sellers, Christopher. *Crabgrass Crucible: Suburban Nature and the Rise of Environmentalism in Twentieth-Century America.* Chapel Hill: University of North Carolina Press, 2012.

Sharp, Dallas Lore. *The Face of the Fields.* New York: Houghton Mifflin, 1911.

——. *The Lay of the Land.* Boston: Houghton Mifflin, 1908.

Shellenberger, Michael, and Ted Nordhaus. "The Death of Environmentalism: Global

Warming Politics in a Post-Environmental World." 2004. www.thebreakthrough.
    org/images/Death_of_Environmentalism.pdf; accessed September 1, 2015.
Shi, David. *The Simple Life: Plain Living and High Thinking in American Culture.* New
    York: Oxford University Press, 1985.
Sierra Club Bulletin. "Memorial." Vol. 7, no. 1 (1909): 63.
Simo, Melanie. *Forest and Garden: Traces of Wildness in a Modernizing Land, 1897–1949.*
    Charlottesville: University of Virginia Press, 2003.
Skocpol, Theda, Marshall Ganz, and Ziad Munson. "A Nation of Organizers: The Insti-
    tutional Origins of Civic Voluntarism in the United States." *American Political
    Science Review* 94, no. 3 (September 2000): 527–46.
Smalley, Andrea. "'Our Lady Sportsmen': Gender, Class, and Conservation in Sport
    Hunting Magazines, 1873–1920." *Journal of the Gilded Age and Progressive Era* 4,
    no. 4 (2005): 355–80.
Smith, Carl. *Urban Disorder and the Shape of Belief: The Great Chicago Fire, the Hay-
    market Bomb, and the Model Town of Pullman.* Chicago: University of Chicago
    Press, 1995.
Smythe, William Ellsworth. *The Conquest of Arid America.* New York: Macmillan, 1905.
Socialist Party of America. "The Socialist Party Platform of 1912." Available at Sage
    American History, http://sageamericanhistory.net/progressive/docs/SocialistPlat
    1912.htm; accessed June 9, 2016.
Southern, David W. *The Progressive Era and Race: Reaction and Reform, 1900–1917.*
    Wheeling, Ill.: Harlan Davidson. 2005.
Spence, Mark David. *Dispossessing the Wilderness: Indian Removal and the Making of the
    National Parks.* New York: Oxford University Press, 1999.
Speth, James G. *The Bridge at the Edge of the World: Capitalism, the Environment, and
    Crossing from Crisis to Sustainability.* New Haven: Yale University Press, 2008.
Spiro, Jonathan Peter. *Defending the Master Race: Conservation, Eugenics, and the Legacy
    of Madison Grant.* Burlington: University of Vermont Press, 2009.
Steele, James. *Ecological Architecture: A Critical History.* London: Thames and Hudson, 2005.
Steinberg, Ted. *Down to Earth: Nature's Role in American History.* New York: Oxford
    University Press, 2002.
Stern, Alexandra. *Eugenic Nation: Faults and Frontiers of Better Breeding in Modern
    America.* Berkeley: University of California Press, 2005.
Stevens, Ruth Lea. "Mother Earth." *Western Comrade* 3, no. 2 (June 1915): 24.
Stickney, A. B. *The Economic Problems Involved in the Presidential Election of 1896.* Chi-
    cago, 1896.
———. *The New Comers: Their Relation to Parks and Boulevards; Respectfully Addressed
    to the Rotary Club.* St. Paul, 1912.
Stilgoe, John R. *Borderland: Origins of the American Suburb, 1820–1939.* New Haven: Yale
    University Press, 1988.
Stradling, David. *The Nature of New York: An Environmental History of the Empire State.*
    Ithaca, N.Y.: Cornell University Press, 2010.
Stratton-Porter, Gene. *Freckles.* New York: Doubleday, 1904.

———. "My Life and My Books." *Ladies' Home Journal* 33 (September 1916): 13.

Strong, Josiah. Introduction to *Modern Cities and Their Religious Problems*, by Samuel Lane Loomis. New York: Baker and Taylor, 1887.

———. *Our Country: Its Possible Future and Its Present Crisis*. New York: Baker and Taylor, 1885.

———. *The Twentieth-Century City*. New York: Baker and Taylor, 1898.

Stroud, Ellen. *Nature Next Door: Cities and Trees in the American Northeast*. Seattle: University of Washington Press, 2012.

Sutter, Paul. *Driven Wild: How the Fight Against Automobiles Launched the Modern Wilderness Movement*. Seattle: University of Washington Press, 2002.

———. "The World with Us: The State of American Environmental History." *Journal of American History* 100, no. 1 (June 2013): 94–119.

Swearingen, William Scott, Jr. *Environmental City: People, Place, Politics, and the Meaning of Modern Austin*. Austin: University of Texas Press, 2010.

Targ, Nicholas. "Forward with Environmental Justice." *Human Rights* 30, no. 4 (2003). www.americanbar.org/publications/human_rights_magazine_home/human_rights_vol30_2003/fall2003/irr_hr_fall03_intro.html; accessed September 5, 2015.

Taylor, Dorcetta E. *The Environment and the People in American Cities, 1600s–1900s: Disorder, Inequality, and Social Change*. Durham, N.C.: Duke University Press, 2009.

Taylor, Joseph E. *Making Salmon: An Environmental History of the Northwest Fisheries Crisis*. Seattle: University of Washington Press, 1999.

Thompson, Andrea. "IPCC Says Climate Change is Here, World Needs to Adapt." Climate Central, March 30, 2014. www.climatecentral.org/news/climate-changes-impacts-are-here-will-worsen-without-adaptation-ipcc-says-1; accessed September 4, 2015.

Tichenor, Daniel, and Richard A. Harris. "Organized Interests and American Political Development." *Political Science Quarterly* 117, no. 4 (Winter 2002–3): 587–612.

Turner, Frederick Jackson. *Rereading Frederick Jackson Turner: The Significance of the Frontier in American History, and Other Essays*. Edited by John Mack Faragher. New York: Holt, 1994.

Turner, James M. *The Promise of Wilderness: American Environmental Politics Since 1964*. Seattle: University of Washington Press, 2012.

———. "'The Specter of Environmentalism': Wilderness, Environmental Politics, and the Evolution of the New Right." *Journal of American History* 96, no. 1 (June 2009): 123–48.

Tyrrell, Ian. *Crisis of the Wasteful Nation: Empire and Conservation in Theodore Roosevelt's America*. Chicago: University of Chicago Press, 2015.

———. *True Gardens of the Gods: Californian-Australian Environmental Reform, 1860–1930*. Berkeley: University of California Press, 1999.

Unger, Nancy. *Beyond Nature's Housekeepers: American Women in Environmental History*. New York: Oxford University Press, 2012.

U.S. Country Life Commission. *Report of the Country Life Commission*. Washington, D.C.: Government Printing Office, 1909.

U.S. Department of Commerce. *Historical Statistics of the United States, 1789–1945.* Washington, D.C.: Bureau of the Census, 1949.

U.S. Department of the Interior, *Reports of the Department of Interior.* Washington, D.C.: Government Printing Office, 1920.

U.S. Forest Service. *Report on Forestry.* Vol. 3. Washington, D.C.: U.S. Government Printing Office, 1882.

———. *A Vacation Land of Lakes and Woods: The Superior National Forest.* 1919.

U.S. House of Representatives. Committee on the Public Lands. *Hearings on HR 434 and HR 8668, Bills to Establish a National Park Service and for Other Purposes.* 64th Cong., 1st sess., April 5–6, 1916.

———. *Hetch Hetchy Dam Site.* 63rd Cong., 1st sess., June 25–28, 1913, and July 7, 1913. Washington, D.C.: Government Printing Office, 1913.

U.S. Reclamation Service. *Nineteenth Annual Report of the Reclamation Service.* Washington, D.C.: Government Printing Office, 1920.

U.S. Statutes at Large. Vol. 39, part 1, chap. 408, 535–36. "An Act to Establish a National Park Service, and For Other Purposes" (HR 15522, Public Act No. 235).

Van Hise, Charles. *The Conservation of Natural Resources in the United States.* New York: Macmillan, 1910.

Vennum, Thomas. *Wild Rice and the Ojibway People.* St. Paul: Minnesota Historical Society, 1988.

Verne, Jules. *Paris in the Twentieth Century.* New York: Del Rey, 1997.

Walker, Richard. *The Country in the City: The Greening of the San Francisco Bay Area.* Seattle: University of Washington Press, 2007.

Warren, Louis. *The Hunter's Game: Poachers and Conservationists in Twentieth-Century America.* New Haven: Yale University Press, 1997.

Waugh, Frank. *The Natural Style in Landscape Gardening.* Boston: Badger, 1917.

Weber, Adna Ferrin. *The Growth of Cities in the Nineteenth Century: A Study in Statistics.* Ithaca, N.Y.: Cornell University Press, 1967 [1899].

Western Comrade. "Nature's Banquet Table." Vol. 1, no. 1 (April 1913): 25.

Weyl, Walter. *The New Democracy: An Essay on Certain Political and Economic Tendencies in the United States.* New York: MacMillan, 1913.

White, Richard. "Environmental History: The Development of a New Field." *Pacific Historical Review* 54 (1985): 297–335.

White, Stewart Edward. "Woodsmen, Spare Those Trees!" *Sunset* 44 (March 1920): 23–26, 110–11.

Wild, Mark. *Street Meeting: Multiethnic Neighborhoods in Early Twentieth-Century Los Angeles.* Berkeley: University of California Press, 2005.

Willcox, Louise Collier. "Outdoor Books." *North American Review* 183, no. 496 (July 1906): 116–24.

Williams, A. Wilberforce. "Keep Healthy." *Chicago Defender,* August 2, 1913, 7.

Williams, Rosalind. *The Triumph of the Human Empire: Verne, Morris, and Stevenson at the End of the World.* Chicago: University of Chicago Press, 2013.

Winks, Robin W. "The National Park Service Act of 1916: 'A Contradictory Mandate'?" *Denver University Law Review* 575 (1997): 575–623.

Wirth, Theodore. *Minneapolis Park System, 1883–1944.* Minneapolis: Minneapolis Park Board, 1945.

Worster, Donald. "John Muir and the Modern Passion for Nature." *Environmental History* 10, no. 1 (2005): 8–19.

———. *A Passion for Nature: The Life of John Muir.* New York: Oxford University Press, 2008.

Wright, Albert Hazen. "Martha the Last Passenger Pigeon Dead." *Forest and Stream,* September 12, 1914, 337.

Wright, Frank Lloyd. "A Home in a Prairie Town." *Ladies' Home Journal* 18 (February 1901): 17.

Wrobel, David. *The End of American Exceptionalism: Frontier Anxiety from the Old West to the New Deal.* Lawrence: University Press of Kansas, 1993.

Yablon, *Untimely Ruins: An Archaeology of American Urban Modernity, 1819–1919.* Chicago: University of Chicago Press, 2009.

Young, Terence. *Building San Francisco's Parks, 1850–1930.* Baltimore: Johns Hopkins University Press, 2004.

Acknowledgments

The process of writing this book began in 2003. That is more than enough time to accrue many debts, and surely long enough to forget about some of them. Jean Thomson Black, my editor at Yale, has suffered me with great patience. Three employers—Southern Methodist University, the University of Wisconsin–Milwaukee, and Loyola University Chicago—provided support in the form of travel money, course releases, and excellent interlibrary loan services. I would still be working on the book, at a snail's pace, if it weren't for the support of outside grants: summer funding from the Huntington Library, a summer stipend from the National Endowment for the Humanities, research funding from the Sam Hayes grant of the United Methodist Church, a Ford Faculty Fellowship at SMU, and, especially, a research fellowship, FA 57060, from the National Endowment for the Humanities, which secured a year free from other obligations. Once I moved to Chicago in 2011, the Newberry Library provided a congenial and productive setting. And since I got a surprising amount of reading and writing done on the Amtrak line to Milwaukee, thanks to the conductors and my erstwhile commuting colleagues Marcus Filipello (who was kind enough to give me many rides from the station to campus), Doug Howland, and Daniel Listoe. Jasmine Alinder and Aims McGuinness, and their children Alice and Eliza Mae, made the commuting life much more bearable.

Early work on what became this book benefited from the engaged feedback of scholars at the Huntington Library and the Autry Western History workshop in Los Angeles, and the Dallas Area Social Historians. Special thanks to Steve Aron, Jared Farmer, Peter Mancall, David Wrobel, Katherine Unterman, Sherry Smith, Bob Righter, Crista Deluzio, Sam Haynes, and Walton Muyumba. Jenny Price likewise provided valuable feedback at these meetings, and her tours of the Los Angeles River when I first lived in Southern California, in 2000–2001, played a key role in shaping my interest in urban environmental history and politics. Karl Jacoby's friendship and scholarship were similarly foundational for me. Portions of chapters 2 and 6 are reworked from chapters that

I wrote for an anthology edited by Michael Lewis (*American Wilderness: A New History*) and *Environmental History*. Thanks to Michael and the late Hal Rothman, editor of *Environmental History,* for their guidance and feedback.

Although some I have met only in passing or not at all, a number of historians helped open my eyes to the history of Progressivism and environmental politics, in ways that are difficult to clarify in standard academic notes. Nonetheless, I want to acknowledge, out of deep gratitude, William Cronon, Mike Davis, Brian Donahue, Samuel P Hays, Richard Judd, Daniel Rodgers, Aaron Sachs, Ian Tyrrell, and Donald Worster.

I owe a great debt to the considerable number of people who read the manuscript. Michael Lansing and Robert Johnston were especially helpful with the early portions and with their gentle and wise insistence on the relevance of history to present politics. The opportunity to present to several of Robert's NEH seminars for teachers helped me, in my own mind at least, to see the value of this project. My brother Andrew Johnson spotted numerous syntax problems and unclear phrases that eluded my other readers. Andrew Graybill, Gerry Cadava, and Timothy Gilfoyle provided detailed and helpful feedback. Shana Bernstein graciously read bumbling and early drafts of a few chapters, pushing me especially to think about the connections between environment and human health. Three anonymous reviewers for the press all did excellent jobs, in different ways. I cannot claim to have satisfied them or adequately responded to their critiques, but I did my best on my own terms and am grateful for the thought and time that they invested in the project.

Since the intellectual is the personal, I want to acknowledge foundational figures for things environmental, people who put me on the path to writing this book, without either them or me knowing it. My late stepfather, Walter Isle, introduced me to environmental history by giving me Donald Worster's *Rivers of Empire* and Patricia Nelson Limerick's *Legacies of Conquest.* I am sorry that Walter isn't here to see this book. Time spent at the Wilderness Field Station outside Ely, Minnesota, deeply formed my interest in landscape changes, wilderness, and environmental politics: thanks to my professors Jim White and Bob Black, bosses Harlo Hadow and Skip Whittler, and coworkers Sandy Turbes and Karla Keyes. I had the pleasure of teaching with Bob a few times while still in graduate school, which secured his place as my North Woods father figure. I was looking forward to reconnecting when I moved back to the Midwest, which made his early death all the more wrenching for me. My trips up north with Matt Norton continue to rejuvenate and inspire me, in spite of his annoying refusal to agree with everything I say about environmental politics.

The field station was also where I first lived in sin with Michelle Nickerson, who was foolish enough to marry me a few years later. I am glad that we are still at it, nearly two decades later. Our son, Tobias, does not seem to care at all about my scholarship, and surely his arrival has delayed this book by years. I wouldn't have it any other way. This one is dedicated to him and Michelle.

Index

170–74, 176–77, 182, 183, 208, 216, 224–26, 229, 231, 252, 253; *My First Summer in the Sierra,* 132–33
municipal water systems, 64–65
Murrieta, Joaquin, 78

naming, of natural features, 76–77
Nathan, Maude, 137–38
National Association for the Advancement of Colored People (NAACP), 155, 256
National Association of Audubon Societies, 149
National Association of Colored Women, 10, 155
National Conference on City Planning, 181
National Conservation Association (NCA), 125, 169, 181, 184, 206
National Conservation Commission, 141, 146
National Conservation Congresses, 80, 85, 131, 137, 139–42, 146, 181, 200
National Fire Prevention Day, 234
national forest system, 53–56, 160, 214–15. *See also* forest reserves
national parks, 68, 159–60, 167–69, 186–88, 212, 249
National Park Service, 95, 167, 173, 186–87, 211, 214, 249
National Park Service Act, 187–88
National Public Domain League, 200, 206, 206–7
nature: attitudes toward, 46–47, 49–51, 73–74, 79–80, 217–18, 230–31; challenges presented by, 229–43; as escape from modern and urban life, 70, 95; as model of social order, 193–94; return to, 102–29; salutary effects of, 35–36, 59–60, 67, 70, 109–10, 155–56, 163–64; subsistence living from, 209–15, 221–23. *See also* environment
nature study, 108–9, 133, 156
Nazism, 92

NCA. *See* National Conservation Association
Nebraska National Forest, 89
Neutra, Richard, 116
New Deal, 250–51
New England, 76–77, 226
Newlands Reclamation Act, 85
New Mexico, 214–16, 224
New York State Forestry Association, 135–36
Niagara Falls, 143
Northern Pacific Railway, 159
novels, 38–42, 109–13

Oberholtzer, Ernest, 118–19, 227–29
Ojibway Indians, 218–20, 227–29
Olmsted, Frederick Law, 72, 94–95
Olmsted, Frederick Law, Jr., 61, 95, 118, 166, 173
Olmsted brothers, 248, 249, 269n44
Olney, Warren, 174
open shops, 192–93
Osborn, Henry Fairfield, 91
Outdoor Life (magazine), 151, 194
outdoor recreation, 104–8. *See also* leisure and recreation

Pacific Gas and Electric, 173
Palos Verdes Estates, California, 248–49
park buildings, 117–18
park rangers. *See* conservation officers, wardens, and park rangers
parks: national, 68, 159–60, 167–69, 186–88, 212, 249; urban, 60–63, 94–96, 160–63, 189–92, 249–50
passenger pigeons, 21–25
Pennsylvania, 215
Pennsylvania Federation of Women's Clubs, 147
Pennsylvania State University, 132
People's Party, 39–40
Pepple, Ruth, 151
Peshtigo, Wisconsin, 17–19, 230, 234